Marketing Strategy

Helens COLLEGE

To Jane

The wind beneath my wings

Marketing Strategy

The Difference Between Marketing and Markets

Third edition

Paul Fifield

AMSTERDAM • BOSTON • HEIDELBERG • LONDON • NEW YORK • OXFORD
PARIS • SAN DIEGO • SAN FRANCISCO • SINGAPORE • SYDNEY • TOKYO

Butterworth-Heinemann is an imprint of Elsevier

Butterworth-Heinemann is an imprint of Elsevier
Linacre House, Jordan Hill, Oxford OX2 8DP, UK
30 Corporate Drive, Suite 400, Burlington, MA 01803, USA

First edition 1992
Paperback edition 1993
Second edition 1998
Third edition 2007

British Library Cataloguing in Publication Data
A catalogue record for this book is available from the British Library

Library of Congress Cataloguing in Publication Data
A catalogue record for this book is available from the Library of Congress

ISBN: 978-0-7506-5675-7

For information on all Butterworth-Heinemann publications
visit our web site at http://books.elsevier.com

Printed and bound in Great Britain

07 08 09 10 11   10 9 8 7 6 5 4 3 2 1

Working together to grow
libraries in developing countries

www.elsevier.com | www.bookaid.org | www.sabre.org

ELSEVIER   BOOK AID
International   Sabre Foundation

Contents

Preface to the third edition

The first method is that of a schemer and leads only to mediocre results; the other method is the path of genius and changes the face of the world.

Napoleon Bonaparte

Writing this preface, the first thing to say is, this third edition has been a long time coming, and it's grown in the six years that it's taken to write. There are many reasons for this, not least the development of the SCORPIO approach, which has grown through use with clients and developing real market strategies. Every time I used it, the better it seemed to work, but it always changed a bit – if I put it into print it would be out of date, wouldn't it? By the time SCORPIO had 'settled down', it was full of really good *stuff* but there was a lot of it – and it would entail a lot of writing and where was the time? But, then publishers and past readers stopped asking where the new book was – and that made me worry, so here it is.

Also, apart from the ego and the new position as Visiting Professor at Southampton University, there is another reason that spurred this edition on, the reason why all the way through the book you will find the term 'market(ing) strategy' being used: the increasing danger of the marketing profession falling into mediocrity. Marketing was always intended to be the co-ordinating activity designed to identify, anticipate and focus the rest of the organization on customer needs. This is a far, far bigger job than producing the advertising and the brochures, but apparently one that some marketers feel hesitant to take on. Marketing is all about the 'market'. If 'marketing' is (still) confused with 'marketing communications and services', then you should remember that market(ing) in this book means so much more.

Like some of my readers, I am getting to that stage in life when I start counting things – like the number of years I have been in market(ing), the number of companies I have met who (still) believe that products make profits, the number of times I have met marketers who complain so bitterly about marketing not being given the status it deserves in their organization. But counting does give perspective.

When I started in market(ing), I believed that it was just a question of timing and that, given the correct data (and encouragement), marketers and companies would see the light and become customer led and much more profitable. Ah, the innocence of youth. Today we see a landscape that has not changed significantly over the years: finance departments still calculate product/service profitability; sales departments still dictate prices and payment terms; operations still dictate product/service availability; R&D functions still create new products and services based on technical features rather than customer benefits.

And too many marketing departments still busy themselves with writing brochures, organizing events and creating leads for the sales force.

On top of that, Philip Kotler turns up in Europe and says that it's terrible that marketing really only seems to consist of one *P*, promotion. At the same time, universities and business schools are re-arranging their programmes so that issues that used to appear on marketing modules (such as segmentation) now appear on business strategy modules.

Meanwhile, in business, new board positions are appearing; Commercial Directors have been around for a while but they are now joined by the Business Development Director. Strange that the universities and business schools haven't developed a 'business development' module for their MBA programmes yet.

And too many marketing departments still busy themselves with writing brochures, organizing events and creating leads for the sales force.

The result is that market(ing) is still *not* on the business agenda. Market(ing) is still *not* properly represented on the board. Customers are still *not* receiving the service they deserve. Organizations are still *not* as profitable as they should be and are still *not* differentiated from lower priced international competition. There really is no way of escaping the responsibility here – the 'marketing profession' really only has itself to blame. As long as too many marketers concentrate on the brochures, events and sales leads, we allow market(ing) to be classified as an *optional* business activity – one that can be cut as soon as the recession comes around again.

But, the job needs to be done, customers are still not receiving their due – genuine customer value. This book is written for any manager who is prepared to take up the market(ing) challenge, 'real marketers' included. But this book, and all the books in the world, can only give you the tools to act. Acting depends on you.

Paul Fifield

Preface to the second edition

The first edition of this book was written in 1990/1991 and was my very first foray into the world of books and writing on such a scale. Over the life of the first edition, the world – and our marketplace – has undergone a number of radical changes, some of which I have tried to capture in this revised edition. Working through the revisions, I have been struck by the nature and scope of the changes that have affected marketing over the past six years. Driven by the fundamental changes in society which we have and continue to witness, marketing as it is practised is changing fast. The buoyant markets of the 1980s have given way to 1990s markets which are much more competitive, focused and unforgiving of failure. Time to plan is a luxury of the past although, paradoxically, the need to plan and think strategically is more important than ever. The simultaneous need to think strategically and act tactically in today's business environment of fewer resources and shortening deadlines is working to separate the marketing 'sheep from the lambs'.

The pace of change in marketing is such that at the moment we are still in the process of working out how to solve today's problems. Knowing that yesterday's solutions no longer work is the first step, finding the answers we need is still a voyage of discovery. I had hoped that this second edition would be more illuminating in terms of answers than it has, in fact, turned out to be. But working with clients on a daily basis, it is apparent that markets are moving at a speed that renders 'new' ideas redundant at a rate that makes them inappropriate for a book of this nature. Consequently, I have tried to concentrate on the mindset and attitudes of the successful and practising marketer required in the late 1990s. When there are no successful case histories to guide us, only a return to the fundamentals of marketing makes sense; from here we will have to create our own case histories.

Also, I stress again that this book is designed primarily for the use and guidance of the *practising marketer*. Since writing the first edition, I have spent a number of years as senior examiner (diploma) at the UK Chartered Institute of Marketing. This role has brought me (and this book) into contact with more academic writers and educators. The response of many to this book's approach to marketing worried me at the time and concerns me more as time goes on. My approach to marketing has remained largely unchanged over more than twenty years and is based on the constantly supported belief that:

(1) Long-term profit is the name of the game and

(2) Only satisfied customers (who come back for more) will produce long-term profits.

This book is based on the belief that marketing is about achieving results, not manipulating theories. This is not always a precise or elegant process – not an approach which some of my academic colleagues find to their taste, believing that technical knowledge and ability to manipulate theory is what should be taught and what should be done. I do not imagine that many academics of this mould will be lovers of this book but I remain unbowed by such criticism. This book was, and is still, written for the practising marketer, not the academic. Marketers not driven to find practical and workable answers and to implement them will probably find other marketing texts more to their taste.

Finally I must thank the primary contributors to this edition. They say a writer must always write about what he knows. Working full time as an independent advisor/consultant with large organizations, I am confronted by today's complex strategic marketing problems on a daily basis. The problems of declining resources, increasing competition and short-term targets are real for all my clients, both market leaders and pretenders. For all of them, the overwhelming challenge has been to find strategic solutions that can be implemented and then to implement the solutions which we have found. Achieving this has often necessitated rewriting the old tenets of marketing. Without the experience gained by working with such clients, this edition could not have been written. It is a great pity they must remain anonymous.

Paul Fifield

Preface to the first edition

This book has been written with one clear goal in mind – to make the whole area of marketing strategy (and strategic marketing) accessible to the widest possible audience. I have tried to strip away all the jargon, the mystique and the confusion that tend to surround one of the most simple and common sense areas of modern business – marketing. Only response from you, the reader, will tell me whether I have succeeded.

Putting the theories, the science and the buzzwords to one side, there is really nothing at all complicated about marketing and marketing strategy. We and our organizations will continue to thrive as long as we make what our customers want. As soon as we deviate from this simple line we will start to founder. Obvious – yes. Common sense – yes. Then why do we all have so many problems? Because we are human beings and not machines.

Human nature is what, I hope, typifies this book. Marketers are people, customers are people, even organizations are simply collections of people. Marketing and strategy are about relationships – not organizations to markets but, in reality, people to people – it is this simple dimension that I have tried to bring into play all through discussions about financial objectives, competition, market segmentation, etc. Not that theories are completely absent; they have their place, but they cannot be used to hide behind.

This book is written, above all, for the practising marketer, whether in marketing, finance, engineering, personnel or sales and at any level in the organization that is affected by the customer. The book follows what is, I hope, a logical framework but the most important lesson must be: *try it*. Try something, see how it works and then grow bolder. As Samuel Johnson said, it matters little which leg you put in the trousers first!

When you try, let me know what happens.

Paul Fifield

Introduction

You must not fight too often with one enemy, or you will teach him all your art of war.

Napoleon Bonaparte

I.1 What is market(ing)?

Consumption is the sole end and purpose of all production; and the interest of the producer ought to be attended to, only as far as it may be necessary for promoting that of the consumer. The maxim is so self-evident that it would be absurd to attempt to prove it. But in the mercantile system, the interest of the consumer is almost constantly sacrificed to that of the producer; and it seems to consider production, and not consumption, as the ultimate end and object of all industry and commerce.

Adam Smith, Wealth of Nations, 1776

Definitions of marketing abound, from the lengthy and all-embracing academic versions to the short and snappy favoured by advertising executives. The concept is not new, it is not difficult to understand, it is not difficult to explain to the troops, and our customers love it. Why then does it seem almost impossible to implement? Why, when we look at the quotation from Smith, do we wonder whether we have made any progress at all over the past 200+ years?

Remember

- *Sales* is about ensuring the customer *buys* what the company *makes*.
- *Marketing* is about ensuring that the company *makes* what the customer wants to *buy*.

I believe there are four distinct but interrelated aspects to the concept of marketing. It is at one and the same time:

(1) An attitude of mind;

(2) A way of organizing the business;

(3) A range of activities;

(4) The producer of profits.

The marketing literature's apparent obsession with marketing as a range of activities has tended to overshadow the first two, much more important, aspects. This is the first, but not the last, time that we will see how Western society's preference for *doing* rather than *thinking* has too often made it more difficult for real businesses to make real profits.

Finally, we must mention recent developments in marketing, brought about by marketers themselves. We have seen that, originally, marketing was devised as an 'integrative' function that would work to understand and anticipate customer needs and wants and then work with other functions within the organization to help them to understand the 'customer imperative' and how it related to their activities. In this way the organization became customer/market oriented and its activities gained greater customer acceptance, customs and profits resulted. As a secondary activity, because of its understanding of the market place, marketing was also to be charged with communicating the special nature of the organization's offer to customers. Over the years, so many marketers have preferred to focus their efforts on the communications rather than the integrative activities that now, 'marketing' is practically synonymous with 'marketing communications', advertising, promotion, direct marketing/mail, events, brochures, sales leads, logos and badges.

This book is concerned with so *much more* than marketing communications (we touch on once or twice maybe) that I have decided to clarify the position for everyone – if 'marketing' has been hijacked by the communicators, we need to find another word. It's not great, but 'market(ing)' will appear all the way through this book to remind you (and me) that there is more to market(ing) than award-winning advertising campaigns.

I.1.1 Market(ing) as an attitude of mind

This is what is known as 'market orientation'. Marketing is a fundamental business philosophy; it is a state of mind, which should permeate the entire organization. It states quite categorically that we recognize that our existence, and future survival and growth, depends on our ability to give our customers what they want. Internal considerations must be subservient to the wider needs of the marketplace. In other words, 'the customer is king'.

These are, of course, very fine words and unlikely to raise any serious objections. Nevertheless it must be apparent to all of us, whether consumers or producers, that this happy state of affairs is quite rare in the real world. Why?

We should all realize (but not necessarily use as an excuse) that looking outward and taking cues from the marketplace and the wider business environment is, well, easier said than done. The larger the organization, the more the customer seems to be excluded from the decision-making process. The organization becomes an entity in its own right with self-sustaining systems that demand constant attention from 'worker bees' in the hive. The customer is out of sight and so, increasingly, out of mind. Employees are recruited and promoted for their skill at tending the system and worshipping at the altar of internal efficiency. Worse still, it is often the most able corporate politicians that gain promotion, so signalling to everyone the skills that the organization *really* values. We:

- Can complain;
- Can say it's all wrong;
- Can even say it won't happen in our company; but
- We should recognize that this is in fact the normal state of affairs in all organizations.

This 'internal orientation' or 'internal focus' is the very antithesis of market/customer orientation and the two find it difficult to co-exist. We can decry internal orientation as blinkered, petty and damaging but we cannot ignore its attraction. While we might know that without satisfied customers we do not have a business, we all spend our days on office and factory floors where customers are forbidden. Our working lives are effectively dominated by internal issues such as regular cost-cutting exercises, selecting the next company car (an SUV (sport utility vehicle) for me, please), who gets a private office and who sits in the open-plan area, who gets fitted carpets and a chair with arms. Human nature being what it is, we shouldn't really be surprised that customer interests are forced down the scale of priorities on a regular basis – there are more important things to do when trying to climb the greasy pole at work – and serving customers is no good, customers don't fill in the appraisal forms every year.

The customer/market philosophy can be driven through any organization, but it will not be easy. We cannot expect the logic of the argument to succeed on its own. The principal problem is not one of introduction but one of regression. Presented in the right way and from the right point (the top), market orientation has an inescapable logic and very few people will fail to espouse the cause. *Getting there is not the problem — staying there is.* Unless accompanied by appropriate changes in the systems and the organizational structure, internal issues will continue to distract attention away from the needs of the customer, and market orientation will be yet another flavour-of-the-month exercise dreamed up by management that has nothing better to do. Regression is a real and constant threat. Maintaining a market attitude of mind will be a full-time job for all senior managers of the organization.

Here is your first management conflict; all this takes time, effort and money – how can we be sure that it is necessary and that it will pay off? Much will depend on the particular competitive position faced by your organization. If you are in a cosy market with no real head-to-head competition and no danger of easy substitution, then you probably don't have to change – yet.

If you are in a more exposed and competitive environment and making enough money, you have probably had to change already. Now comes the real test: can you keep on changing to retain the market position you have attained? This is not the time to rest on your laurels and watch the competition leapfrog you in their turn (see Chapter 6).

Finally, are we talking about an 'attitude of mind' or 'a set of policies and procedures'? I had a very heated debate with a famous marketing professor on this very point. I think we were really agreeing but sometimes you just need to let go, so. . .. Thinking about it later, I realized that he may have had a point; talking about an attitude of mind is perhaps just too purist, it assumes that people/managers/marketers have a mind and are keen to use it. Maybe we should be talking about the organizational/institutional policies and processes that are needed to guide the everyday actions of the automatons that we sometimes employ.

I.1.2   *Market(ing) as a way of organizing*

The marketing concept then leads us to make some obvious (but difficult to swallow) conclusions:

- Market(ing) is about customers.
- All the money the organization makes (revenue) comes from customers.
- If we have happy customers, they might come to us more often and spend more money with us.
- If we have unhappy customers, they take their business elsewhere.
- We could have the 'best' product or service on offer and still the customer takes their business elsewhere.
- If enough customers take their business elsewhere, we go bust.

Sit down and take two aspirins.

If we accept that the organization exists and will continue to exist only as long as it continues to satisfy the needs of its customers, we must ensure that the organization has a structure that will enable it to deliver. How many times have you, as a customer, tried to phone a large company to get some information or to register a complaint? If you get past the *press one if you have an order query, press two if you have a technical query. . .*, and are then passed from one person to another, from one department to another, like an unwelcome guest, you might get the impression that the organization had been designed for its own convenience rather than for you, the customer. You might be right.

Organizational structure and design are critically important to marketplace success. No purpose is served by instilling and nurturing the market philosophy if the structure of the organization makes it impossible for the people to deliver on their promises. The traditional structure of larger organizations, the functional pyramid, is designed for internal efficiency but is relatively rigid in the face of a constantly changing marketplace. The temptation for this type of organization is to attempt to mould the market to its own needs rather than adapting itself to the needs of its customers. Organizations of this type are typically long established and may have emerged from a protected or regulated environment. Often laden with older managers who lament the passing of the good old days when customers took what *they were damn well offered — and were grateful for it*, these organizations do not always achieve a graceful transition to the new order. Many of the large and powerful organizations that were created after the Second World War (1950s–1970s) found the internal friction too great to bear and have since been absorbed by more adaptive organizations or have disappeared altogether.

If an organization is to survive in today's ever faster changing environment, it must make itself more responsive to its customers. Typically this will mean:

- Shorter chains of communication and command (fewer 'levels' or 'grades');
- Fewer people employed in 'staff', 'headquarters' and other non-customer-related functions;
- An overall structure and business design that reflects the different needs of the people who buy from the organization rather than technical specializations of the people who work inside it.

The UK's British Telecom (BT) was one of the first of the great 'institutions' to face customer challenge when it was privatized in the 1980s. 'Operation Sovereign', at the end of that decade, attempted to reduce numbers as well as levels/grades in the organization so that no employee was more than six steps distant from the chairman – no mean feat for an organization of (then) 240 000 people. Today, BT describes itself as a UK-wide communications solutions provider with a global reach in the business market and has closer to the 100 000 employees needed to compete in today's communications markets.

As any good industrial psychologist will tell us, structure gives behaviour. The appropriate organizational structure can play a major part in reinforcing the marketing attitude of mind over the longer term.

I.1.3 *Market(ing) as a range of activities*

Market(ing) is also a range of specific activities used by the market(ing) department to meet market(ing) and business objectives. Centred mainly on the concept of the marketing mix (traditionally accepted as including product, price, place and promotion), this is the technical 'how to' of the discipline.

There are thousands of books on this part of the marketing picture, so I will not spend much time here apart from saying that some people think that buying a book on marketing makes them a marketer – unfortunately, no more than watching Star Wars makes you a Jedi Knight.

I.1.4   Market(ing) as the producer of profits

I have been consulting now for more years than I care to count and, in most companies that I meet, it is still not generally accepted that marketing is responsible for producing profits. Sales, operations, distribution and even finance (how do they arrive at that one I wonder) might produce profits but not market(ing).

Peter Drucker on marketing

Only marketing and innovation produced profits for an organization, and all other areas should be regarded as costs.

Profits are generated by markets. Profits are not generated by products, efficiency, management or even diligent workforces. It is only the customer's willingness to pay the right (premium) price for the right product or service which keeps us in business. Marketing, as the primary interface between the organization and the markets that it serves, is then the primary producer of the organization's profit stream (Figure I.1).

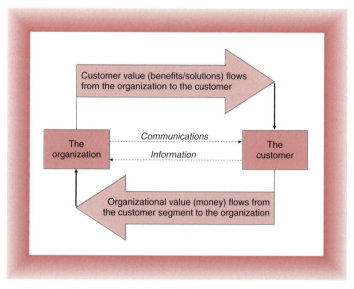

Figure I.1   The market(ing) process

But it is in the area of profit that we meet what is probably the most critical role of market(ing). In almost every organization, there is likely to be a stark conflict between the customer's need for value and the organization's need for profit and efficiency.

It is the role of market(ing) to search for and strike the elusive balance between these two demands. We also need to ask ourselves:

(1) Given that there is more than one way of satisfying customer demand, which route is the most efficient from the organization's cost point of view?

(2) How can we best balance customer need for value against the organization's need for profits?

Profit is a function of (1) the price that the customer is willing to pay and (2) the cost of production and sale. Successful and effective market(ing) (if measured in profit terms) must pay attention to both these areas. Market(ing) is definitely *not* about satisfying customers at any price. Market(ing) is about satisfying customers at a profit.

I.1.5 *Non-market(ing) orientations*

So far we have looked at the holy grail of business in the twenty-first century, the market-oriented organization. There are other forms of business philosophy or orientation; these are not only alive and well but are still in the majority, although this fact should surprise nobody given the problems associated with achieving and retaining a market orientation. The next three styles of business are the most common:

(1) *Production orientation*: The production-oriented organization's primary concern is to maintain a constant and uninterrupted flow of materials and product through the production process. This organization is in the business of finding any market it can for what it happens to make. *It is much more concerned with what it makes than what the market wants.* On a day-to-day basis, its primary concerns are with production efficiency and cost control. This organization relies heavily on sales orders to feed the production system but has little interest in where the product goes. Consequently there is a heavy emphasis on sales volume but little interest in sales direction. 'Marketing' (if it exists at all here) is to supply the salesforce with leads so that customers can continue to play their central role – that of the sponge that soaks up what the factories decide to make.

(2) *Product orientation*: The product-oriented organization's primary concern is to produce 'the best product'. It works to create an ever-better mousetrap and then waits for the world to beat a path to its door. This organization firmly believes that the best product will sell itself (and always quotes Rolls-Royce as

its model). Unfortunately, this organization is so wrapped up in the technical possibilities emerging from research and development that it is disconnected from customers and their needs. It does not know what constitutes 'the best product' – from the customer's point of view – so continually improves and enhances the product with its own opinion of the needed features and wonders (honestly) why sales do not double overnight. This organization still relies heavily on sales volume to feed the production process but knows too little about marketplace demand to offer any useful direction to the sales effort.

(3) *Sales orientation*: The sales-oriented organization, unlike the product-oriented organization, believes that fundamentally all products and/or services are really the same. In what it sees as a commodity market, it follows that *success will come to the company that sells the hardest*. This organization has little allegiance to the product or the production process and may even buy in product from outside suppliers. It believes that sales volume is the only measure of success and it is prepared to support the sales activity fully in terms of heavy promotional activity and price competition – anything to maintain sales revenue levels and volume. Once again the sales activity is given little direction but revenue (rather than profit) targets are an integral part of the corporate culture.

Does your organization fall into one of these three categories, or are you in the special position of being part of a market-oriented organization?

I.1.6   *Market orientation*

The market-oriented organization does not start the whole process with the product. *The most important factor for this organization is the customer*. It understands that it is not, in fact, selling products but is providing solutions to match identified customer needs or problems. This organization realizes that it can be dangerous to become too closely associated with the product or service it produces because customer demand may change, forcing the organization into new or different technologies to retain its markets. It realizes that it will still have to produce and deliver efficiently, but that long-term success will ultimately depend on its ability to listen to its customers and prospects.

When discussing the concepts of market(ing) and market orientation, the most common question I am asked is, *why should we bother to take all this on?* Being practical, it is not an easy question to answer. As we have seen, the road to marketing orientation is not easy; even worse, once you have arrived you have to fight to stay there. As long as you are making enough money to keep your owners satisfied and to allow reinvestment in the fabric of the business, why bother? Why not continue just as we are? The answer to these and similar questions lies in the competitive nature of any particular business (see Chapter 2). If you have identified your organization as production-, product- or sales-oriented and you still command a sizeable market share and are making reasonable profits, then the odds are that your competition is in a similar position. As long as competition stays that way, you will not have a problem. Unfortunately, as (among others) the UK and US motor car producers discovered, competition doesn't always stay that way.

The future as always is unclear but forecasters appear united on a few important aspects. There is general agreement that competition is becoming, and will continue to be, more international in the future. Protected markets will be eroded and more organizations will be exposed to stronger and determined competition. Much competition will come from the developing and the developed worlds and is likely to be based on price (see Chapter 6).

1.2 What is strategy?

> It is therefore essential, when one has fourteen armies, that each wages
> a kind of war relative to the overall plan for the war (strategy), and to
> the strength and circumstances — whether topographical or political —
> of the opposing state.
>
> *Napoleon Bonaparte*

The word *strategy* has become one of the most commonly (and badly) used words in business writing. Everywhere we look we see terms such as business strategy, corporate strategy, marketing strategy, strategic marketing, product strategy, pricing strategy, advertising strategy, Internet/online strategy and even discount strategy. We are not helped by the original, flexible use of the Greek word 'strategos' from which our word strategy derives. In its original form, it meant the art of the General or Commander of the armies. The first time the word 'strategy' was used in a business context was by William Newman, in a book published as recently as 1951. Now the word 'strategy' is almost synonymous with 'important'.

Overworking the word in this way helps nobody. It simply serves to confuse. Strategy in its strictest sense refers to means and not ends. Strategy is all about how an organization will achieve its objectives. Best described as 'business strategy', the original meaning concentrated on how the key decision-making unit of the organization or the board was going to marshal its resources in order to achieve its stated 'business objective'. The use of the word strategy in the business literature arose when it became apparent to management researchers that, in sharp contrast to economic models of perfect competition, companies engaged in the same activity and using the same technology often performed differently. Closer inspection suggested that firms in the same industry adopted different approaches to products, distribution and organizational structures. These differences, within similar market environments, came to be known as 'strategies'. The concept was readily absorbed into Harvard Business School's Business Policy curriculum in the 1950s and 1960s. This concept will be explored in slightly more detail in Part One.

At this point, however, we need to highlight the most significant aspects of strategy. This should help to dispel some of the major misconceptions that have sometimes been encouraged by sections of the marketing literature.

I.2.1 First, some clarification

There will be ample opportunity for you to complicate the issues later on, but for the moment I offer you a simple (but accurate) definition of these important terms:

Objective	Strategy	Tactics
The goal, aim to which all the resources of the business are directed	*The means of achieving the objective*	*Manoeuvres on the field of battle*
This means that objectives are about things we want to achieve – *not* about how we should achieve them	This means that strategies are concerned with *how* we achieve the objectives and action	Tactics are driven by (in order): (1) the strategy and (2) the realities of the battleground/marketplace
Objectives should always start with the word *To*. . .	Strategies should always start with the word *By*. . .	A big, important tactic does *not* become a strategy

Next, some simple 'rules' about strategy, so that we all understand what the term means:

(1) *Strategy is longer term*: As strategy is about marshalling the gross resources of the organization to match the needs of the marketplace and achieve the business objective, this cannot be a short-term activity. Every organization is complex and any change takes time to accomplish. Strategic decisions, like the General choosing his battleground, will have long-term implications. Strategic decisions, such as which business areas to enter, cannot be reversed at a moment's notice – momentum has to be built over a planned period.

(2) *Strategy is not changed every Friday*: Constant change produces uncertainty, confusion, misdirection and wastage – not results. Tactics are designed to change on a weekly or even a daily basis in response to changes in the marketplace caused by customer needs or competitive response. Tactical change causes no problems of uncertainty because the strategy, the broad overall direction of the organization, remains constant.

(3) *Strategy is not another word for important tactics*: Tactics can be likened to manoeuvres on the field of battle and can be changed as often as required in response to the changing situation faced by the organization in its markets. But, no matter how important or critical the tactic under review, this does not make it a strategy. For want of a nail the horseshoe, the horse, the knight, the battle and the war were lost – I agree, but once 1000 soldiers have found a nail each they should all know that the reason why they are there is to win the war, not to search for nails.

(4) *Strategy is not top management's secret*: Strategy is undoubtedly top management's responsibility to define and agree but not to keep as one of the organization's most closely guarded secrets. Top management can decide the strategy on their own (it is normally safer by far that they involve others in the process too) but they cannot implement it alone. Strategy is most effective when those that have to implement it not only understand it but also believe it and can see their own role in carrying it out. As Mintzberg (*The Rise and Fall of Strategic Planning*, Prentice Hall, Englewood Cliff, 1996) states, *Every failure of implementation is, by definition, also a failure of formulation.* The only reason for formulating strategy is to create some profitable activity in the marketplace. If people are to implement, they must know what, how and why. Despite management's traditional reluctance, communication and active involvement will often be the key to success.

(5) *Strategy is not just a public relations exercise*: One of the first rules of strategy formulation, as we shall see in Part Two, is that it must be capable of implementation. Hence the British military strategy in the first years of the Second World War was, despite the fine words and propaganda, not aimed at beating the German armies – Britain simply did not have the resource to do so. Rather the strategy was one of containment of Hitler's ambitions while trying to assemble the resources needed to defeat the enemy. Strategy is about action, not words. It is about implementation, not just planning.

(6) *Strategy is based on analysis and understanding, not straws in the wind*: While tactics are properly based on short-term market developments, they can be either active or re-active in nature. Effective tactics often depend on a rapid summing up of the market situation followed by fast implementation. Strategy, on the other hand, is about the long term. Rapid 'summings up' and reaction are unlikely, of themselves, to be sufficient to build a robust strategy. To build a sound strategy for the future, we will need a deeper degree of analysis – at least beginning to understand why things are happening as well as just knowing what is happening. An analysis of the macro and

market environments is essential even for the more 'emergent' strategic routes that the organization may favour.

(7) *Strategy is essential to an organization's survival*: If you don't know where you are going, then any road will take you there. A well thought–out strategy will allow managers to test actions and propose tactics against that strategy and the overall business objective to ensure the consistency which is essential to continued success. Without a clear guiding strategy, managers will continue to spend time and money agonizing over decisions that could be made in minutes if only they knew what their organization was trying to do. Worse, managers will take decisions that look reasonable given the tactical information available but which will have to be undone at a later stage because of conflict either with other tactical decisions made elsewhere in the organization or with top management's privately held view of the future direction. A well-communicated and understood strategy brings the organization together and provides a common purpose. It, like market orientation, involves everyone in the organization and challenges them to relate what they do to what the whole organization is trying to achieve. If people and departments are not all looking in the same direction, they cannot help but be working against each other. In the more competitive days ahead, it is less and less reasonable to expect customers to pay for our inefficiency.

Of course, some commentators state that organizations should not continually seek to survive. That a regular flow of business failure is necessary to unlock human and physical resources to 'refresh the gene pool from which new business may spring' – but that's another story.

I.3   What is market(ing) strategy?

> If we obtain great success, we must never make a change in policy by plunging into Italy, as long as Germany offers a formidable front and will not be weakened. If national pride and revenge lure us to Rome in the next campaign, politics and self-interest must always direct us against Vienna.
>
> *Napoleon Bonaparte*

Anyone brave enough (or reckless enough) to have consulted more than one of the wide range of books or articles on the subject of market(ing) strategy will have discovered that every author seems to start from his or her own premise and lays down a new set of parameters and definitions before starting to write. It is worthwhile reproducing here a selection of some of the better-known definitions of market(ing) strategy, in addition to those in the second edition, for example:

'Marketing strategy indicates the specific markets towards which activities are to be targeted and the types of competitive advantage to be exploited.'	Dibb and Simkin
'A strategy can be defined as a set of decisions taken by management on how the business will allocate its resources and achieve sustainable competitive advantage in its chosen markets.'	Doyle
'Marketing strategy is the marketing logic by which the business unit expects to achieve its marketing objectives.'	Kotler
'Choosing market targets and a strong market position based on differentiating capabilities to create a robust and sustainable value proposition to customers and networks of critical relationships.'	Piercy
'A good marketing strategy should integrate an organization's marketing goals, policies, and action sequences (tactics) into a cohesive whole. The objective of a marketing strategy is to provide a foundation from which a tactical plan is developed. This allows the organization to carry out its mission effectively and efficiently.'	Wikipedia
'A marketing strategy identifies customer groups which a particular business can better serve than its target competitors, and tailors product offerings, prices, distribution, promotional efforts, and services toward those market segments. Ideally, the strategy should address unmet customer needs that offer adequate potential profitability. A good strategy helps a business focus on the target markets it can serve best.'	US Small Business Administration
'A marketing strategy is an integrated set of choices about how we will create and capture value, over long periods of time.'	MIT

These definitions are by no means exhaustive. There are many, many more for the interested reader to discover. But, a measure of how complicated this area really is can be seen by the number of books that actually carry the words 'Market' or 'Marketing Strategy' in the title – and then fail to define the term at any point in the book. No names, no pack drills.

The major problem for the practitioner, who would actually like to do something about the organization's market(ing) strategy, is where to start. The one thing the many definitions do is to confuse. We are left with burning questions: What is market(ing) strategy? What is included in market(ing) strategy? Where does market(ing) strategy start and finish?

The main reason for this apparent confusion is the writers' attempts to try and force every possible situation into a generalized blueprint concept. Management and marketing are littered with attempts to force theories out of observed 'good practice' and thus make the teacher's and the consultant's job that much easier. We should once and for all accept that this scientific approach just doesn't work in areas like this. Market success depends on customer acceptance and this is just not predictable in any scientific sense or within scientific limits of accuracy.

> Ultimately, market success is about winning customer *preference.*

Also, within the different definitions, we see a whole range of market(ing) strategies that seem to be designed for a specific purpose. Terms such as these abound to describe particular 'brands' of market strategy:

- Market dominance:
  - Leader
  - Challenger
  - Follower
  - Nicher

- Porter's generic strategies:
  - Cost leadership
  - Product differentiation
  - Market segmentation

- Treacy and Wiersema's excellence strategies:
  - Product leadership
  - Management efficiency
  - Customer intimacy

- Innovation strategies:
  - Pioneers
  - Close followers
  - Late followers

- Growth strategies:
  - Horizontal integration
  - Vertical integration
  - Diversification (or conglomeration)
  - Intensification

- Aggressiveness strategies (1):
  - Building
  - Holding
  - Harvesting

- Aggressiveness strategies (2):
  - Prospector
  - Analyser
  - Defender
  - Reactor

- Warfare-based strategies:
  - Offensive marketing warfare strategies
  - Defensive marketing warfare strategies
  - Flanking marketing warfare strategies
  - Guerrilla marketing warfare strategies

Given enough time, we should all be able to understand what these concepts mean in practice – or even in theory. Unfortunately, and here we really must be fair to many of the writers, it is not easy to give prescriptive help that is applicable to every organization. Each situation is different and each organization will have to respond according to its own particular organizational and market circumstances.

Market(ing) strategy will mean different things to different organizations. It will fulfil different needs both within the organization and in the marketplace.

Organizations differ in a number of important respects:

- The variety and nature of markets served;

- The variety and complexity of products and/or services offered;

- The diverse nature of technology and operating processes used;

- The 'sophistication' of existing planning and forecasting procedures;

- The characteristics and capabilities of the individuals involved in the strategy formulation and implementation processes;

- The 'norms and values' of the business environment within which the organization must operate;

- The nature of competitors;

- The *thirst* in the organization for growth and advancement;

- The nature and demands of the stakeholders, and so on.

Having now looked at what other writers have done and criticized everything, I feel duty bound to present you, the frustrated reader, with some sort of answer. This must come in two parts: What constitutes market(ing) strategy? And, what does market(ing) strategy do? We shall leave the first question until later in the book when we delve into the *SCORPIO* model. The second question we should answer now because it is only through practical application that market strategies have any meaning for, or effect on, the business:

> Market strategy is the process by which the organization *aligns* itself with the market it has decided to serve.

Thus market(ing) strategy in fact translates the business objective and strategy into market terms and market(ing) activity.

This critical link between business strategy and market(ing) strategy is invariably lost in the literature, as business or corporate strategy is deemed a different discipline from marketing. While this split is reinforced by the business schools and the management gurus who may have different skills and who certainly come from different business backgrounds, the artificial split between these two areas is absurd and potentially dangerous for two reasons:

(1) *First*, the marketing director, vice-president, managing director, commercial director, business development director or the person in charge of the market(ing) function in an organization is simply incapable of developing a clear market objective and practical market(ing) strategy without a deep and thorough understanding of the organization's long-term business objective and strategy. If we do not have a clear idea of what the organization is doing, where it is going and precisely where it wants to be in three, five or ten years' time, then our market(ing) can be nothing more than a reactive day-to-day function in the organization. In effect, there will not be a market strategy – or worse, it will exist in name alone.

(2) *Second*, the practical success of the organization's business objective and strategy will depend on the quality of the market(ing) input right at the top. In too many organizations, strategy and planning are seen as top management sitting down and transferring to paper their ambitions or wishes of where they would like the organization to be or how they would like the organization to behave. While satisfying and even productive, in terms of producing a written document of some sort, this is unlikely (of itself) to produce success. Documents such as this (and I have seen plenty) tend to be inward looking and often fail to take proper account of external competitive and market factors. As we have seen, profits are produced only by customers and an organization's success will depend on its ability to continue to satisfy customer needs and wants over the longer term. Setting the business objective and developing the business strategy then will depend on a good understanding of the organization's competitive position and the present and most likely future trends in customer demand. In other words, there is a critical

market(ing) input right at the very beginning of the business or corporate planning stage.

To put it bluntly, a business plan that is not securely rooted in the market-place will be irrelevant. Any plan is only as good as its implementation. The 1970s and 1980s saw a proliferation of strategic planning departments – in organizations that are no longer with us today. The reason for this is simple – the growing availability of computer power and statistical modelling techniques blinded managers to one important fact. If the business objective and strategy are not based on a realistic assessment of the organization's present position and likely *market* opportunities, then the plan is not worth the paper it is written on.

As the two areas of business planning and market planning are so intricately intertwined, the next section of this book will look (briefly) at the whole area of business planning with a special emphasis on the market input to the business objective and business strategy before looking in more depth at the whole, presently enormously confused, area of market strategy – both what it is and what it does.

I.3.1   A word on timing and other practical issues

Experience with many clients has proven to me that building strategic market scenarios is a methodology that will provide an organization with real compet-itive advantage. However, there are a small number of annoying but important barriers to this obvious and simple process:

(1) *Understanding the preoccupations of managers*: Any project such as developing plans, strategies or scenarios needs to be much more than a plan. It needs to be *implemented* if it is going to show a return on the investment in the time and money that it cost to develop the plan. Implementation ultimately depends on the manager in the organization wanting to apply it. Whether the manager wants to apply the strategy and implement the plans depends on what's in it for him or her. This is not intended as a criticism of the state of management in the early twenty-first century, but rather a lesson in pragmatic leadership. Getting anything done is a case of understanding that:
    (a) Strategy is the responsibility of *most* managers, *some* of the time – but who and when?
    (b) Most managers, who are driven by the future, are not typically respon-sible for doing things (implementation) today.
    (c) Most day-to-day managers (who do things) are not worried about the future.
    (d) Managers responsible for using/implementing the scenarios are (mostly) motivated, measured and rewarded according to what happens in the short term.

(e) Managers today are doing more work than in the past.

(f) They are working with less administration support.

(g) They tend to be less loyal to their employer than they used to be (there are many reasons for this) and more loyal to themselves and their networks.

(h) They are just as ambitious.

(i) They do not tend to stay in the same job (or sometimes company) for very long.

(j) They have a *day job* which, for most, involves achieving business outputs that can be measured in the current financial year.

(k) If they are to implement longer-term actions, they need to be sure that they will achieve some credit for the risk that they take.

(2) *A question of time*: This can make anything that is focused on the future rather problematic. The key time issues are:

(a) Strategy is, by definition, a view (or several views) of the future.

(b) Most managers are driven by and focus on the short term – the next twelve months.

(c) Good managers can be motivated by the medium term, if it covers the period they expect to remain in the job or the organization.

(d) This medium period normally stretches to about three years.

(e) Managers generally believe that their (and any) market becomes unpredictable beyond five years, so it is pointless (academic) looking out any further.

(f) Customers (depending on the nature of the purchase) live in the present but can vision themselves in the future, using products and services that exist and they know of.

(g) Customers cannot envision themselves using a 'new' product or service.

(h) Customers generally 'learn' about new products and services more slowly than organizations would like.

  (i) There is absolutely no point launching a product or service offer:

  (i) Before it is wanted, because the customers will not understand its benefits and will not buy.

  (ii) After it is wanted and they have purchased, 'me-too' offerings tend to be far less profitable.

(3) *The (inevitable) issue of marketing*: Many organizations (in many industries, it is the majority) are determinedly fighting against becoming customer focused. The reasons for the continuing tension between the product-focused and the customer-focused organizational/business culture are many and varied – and will be covered later (see Chapter 6). Organizations which are still focused on products and processes are fighting a competitive battle they can never win. They only know how to 'push' products at markets and, if they could take a moment to stand back from what they are doing, they would see that there is another way.

I.4   The approach of this book

> I attach great importance to this [military education texts] work, and he
> who performs it well will be well rewarded. It must be at one and the
> same time a work of science and of history. The narrative sometimes
> must even be entertaining. It should stimulate interest, contain details,
> and if necessary have plans added to it. But it must not, however, be
> over the heads of... the young men.
>
> *Napoleon Bonaparte*

Having been lulled into a sense of security so far by (I hope) everything seeming
to make some sense, we arrive at a diagram. The good news is that the whole
strategic process can be represented in one flow chart (Figure I.2); the bad news is
that it is more than a little complicated and we will need the whole of the rest of
the book to go through it! A firm believer is in the need to get all the pain out of the
way at the outset so that we can fully enjoy the recuperation, I have laid out the
full plan below.

Assuming that your eyes are still focusing, a few points should be made at this
stage:

- This chart is intended to show the *approximate relationships* between the various
  aspects, analyses and decisions that go to make up the business and market
  strategy formulation process.

- The arrows are intended to show one possible route for logical thought
  through the process. However, as we shall see later, this is one, but not the
  only route.

- As every organization faces different competitive and market conditions, no
  single strategic process can possibly be proposed to suit all needs. This chart
  should *not* be viewed as a blueprint.

- Practitioners should feel perfectly free to adapt and amend the diagram to
  meet their own needs. Certainly some sections might be jumped and others
  emphasized to meet specific requirements.

- Before you skip or downgrade a stage in the process, make sure that you fully
  understand what it is you are leaving out!

In the same way that an ant may eat an elephant (a spoonful at a time), we will
have to break the complete diagram down to bite-size pieces, before we can hope
to put anything into practice. To do this, it is probably easier to see the whole

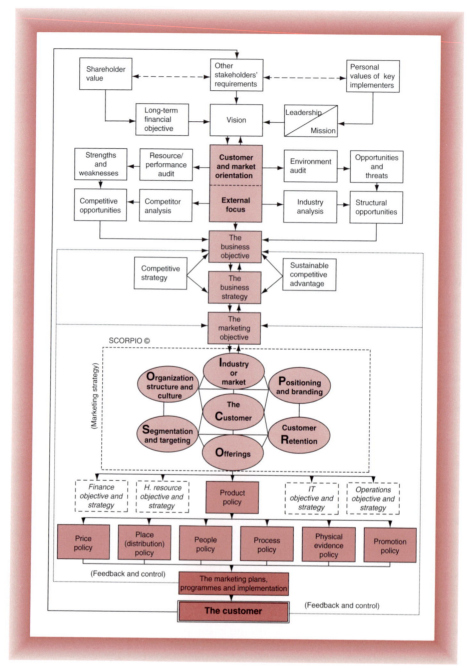

Figure I.2   A flow chart for evolving market strategy

diagram as a composite of the usual steps in strategy development. The three key stages are:

(1) Part One – Preparing for the Market(ing) Strategy;

(2) Part Two – Developing the Market(ing) Strategy (SCORPIO);

(3) Part Three – From Market(ing) Strategy to Tactics.

I.4.1 To start then – at the beginning

This book is aimed, above all, at market(ing) practitioners: people who have to plan and implement customer solutions for a profit.

With such an audience in mind, I have decided to break down the strategy approach according to what seems logical from a practitioner's point of view. Readers approaching the subject from a more academic point of view, perhaps after a course of marketing at a university or business school, may find parts of the process unusual; and to them I make my apologies. I may apologize but I remain unrepentant – implementation not formulation is the key to profitable market(ing) strategy and to get the ideas 'on to the street', sometimes some accepted 'rules' just have to be bent a little.

To make the approach of this book as practical and as accessible as possible for everybody engaged in the market(ing) process, whether from a traditional educational route or completely ignorant of the so-called 'theories' that dominate today's marketing teaching, it will follow the three-step approach to strategy described above.

Part One will look at the detailed analysis that is essential to the development of any robust, practical market(ing) strategy. Part Two looks in more depth at the specific question of how to develop and plan market(ing) strategy. Part Three separates market(ing) strategy from tactics and considers how strategy is implemented.

Part One – Preparing for the Market Strategy

Before the practitioner can hope to develop even the most rudimentary strategic decisions, a degree of analysis is required. Market(ing) may be as much art as science but working on gut feeling is not the same thing as working by the seat of your pants. We should never forget that the quality of gut feeling or intuition improves with the amount of painstaking research that goes before. The groundwork preparation stage can be put into three steps:

(1) *Understand the internal business drivers*: Too many managers try to bluster their way through life with a 'holier-than-thou' attitude towards the organization's customers. Customers are important, more important than they are

treated in most organizations, true – but the customer is not the whole story. There are essential forces alive in every organization that cannot just be ignored. Taking an ostrich-like approach to those forces will not solve the problem. The owners and key managers of the organization are human beings and they have needs, wants and demands that your organization *must* satisfy. You must understand these important forces as many of them can run directly counter to the needs of the customer. It will be your delicate task to manage these often opposing demands so as to satisfy as many people as possible inside the organization while creating unbeatable value for the customer (Figure I.3). Easy!

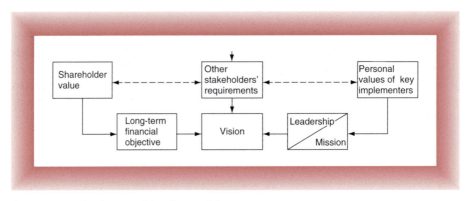

Figure I.3   The internal business drivers

(2) *Understand the external environment*: No man (or organization) is an island – clichéd but true. No twenty-first-century organization, regardless of size and market power, can pursue its goals in disregard of the business environment within which it operates. We will look, in some detail, at this process of analysis, at what can be learned from the environment. More important (when dealing with matters strategic rather than the detailed, tactical aspects of market(ing)) is the way in which this analysis is carried out. Have you ever wondered why, when the same facts exist to be uncovered by all, some organizations are successful in the market-place while others are not? The secret normally lies, not in the quality of the information itself, but rather in the way it is perceived and inter-preted. Customer and market orientation is the key. Investigating and analysing (often for far too long) the external environment from a basic understanding of what the organization needs rather than what the customer needs will only produce (yet another) long series of product/ service-driven answers. The secret, as we shall see, is not what to look for – but how to look (Figure I.4).

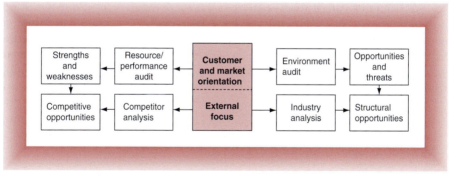

Figure I.4   The external environment

(3) *Understand (or develop) the business strategy*: The whole area of business strategy experienced something of a hype during the 1980s and 1990s, mostly produced by the thoughts and writings of Michael Porter and imitators. While Porter's books adorn countless thousands of influential bookshelves, developing business strategy now seems to be no easier than it ever was (Figure I.5).

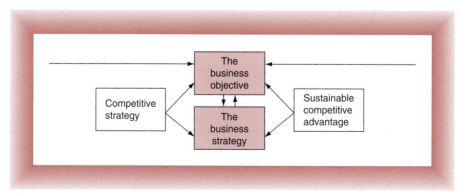

Figure I.5   The business strategy

We shall look at the problems encountered in developing a long-term business strategy as well as the essential (but not developed by Porter) link between the market orientation of the organization, business strategy and market(ing) strategy.

Part Two – Developing the Market(ing) Strategy (SCORPIO)
This, the main part of the book, covers the various elements of market(ing) strategy. I have been careful to separate market(ing) strategy from market(ing) tactics, a common fault in too many writings on the subject, and have concentrated on the critical influence of the market on the organization's activity.

The SCORPIO model of market strategy has been many years in the making, working with real practitioners in real businesses facing real problems. Many of the headings in this part will be familiar to you although how they fit together may not. Nobody wants to play the role of guinea pig when dealing with strategic issues; practitioners want solutions that work, that have worked before, that will produce the results (Figure I.6).

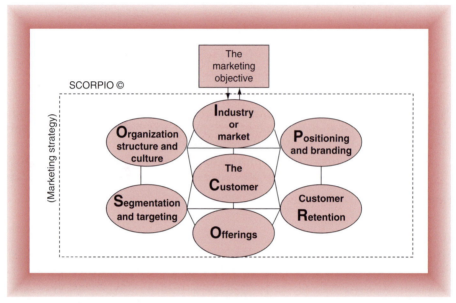

Figure I.6   Developing the market strategy

As a testimonial for the approach, I can quote the case of a recent client who sent the SCORPIO model that we had been working with for six months to an academic friend for his opinion. The blistering e-mail reply was *But is all the stuff we've seen before, there's nothing new here at all.* Exactly, I couldn't have put it better myself.

Part Three – From Market(ing) Strategy to Tactics

The third and final section deals with the subject area that is probably most familiar to readers of marketing textbooks. I shall not deal with the area of market(ing) tactics in any depth – this job has been very successfully accomplished in a number of other publications and you, like me, probably have your favourites.

The main aim of this part is to demonstrate the relationship between market(ing) strategy and tactics. More importantly, we will look at the whole area of strategy implementation, an area far too often ignored by strategic writing.

This section will look at the seemingly endless list of barriers to the implementation of market(ing) strategy and what can be done about them. It will also look at using 'the system' to help support and implement the sometimes radical ideas that market(ing) strategy represents (Figure I.7).

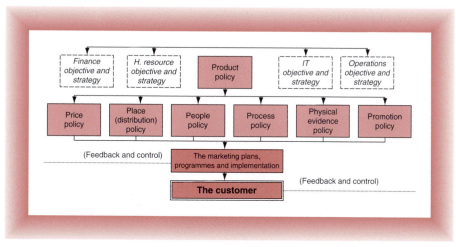

Figure I.7   From market strategy to tactics

Tackling the book

This book is laid out in what I hope is a logical order, although this doesn't mean that you have to start at the beginning and plough straight through to the end. It is meant to be read (sort of) in the order that it is written, unlike the serious textbooks such as Kotler and Gilligan/Wilson which are better 'dipped into' at the relevant sections. On the other hand, I have worked to make each chapter and sub-chapter worth reading as a 'bite-sized chunk'. So, skip around the text as much as you like but if you jump in and out of the book, remember that you might just have missed something useful in the parts you skipped.

Enjoy!

Some (Napoleonic) further reading

Bertaud, J. P., Forrest, A. and Jourdan, A. (2004) *Napoléon, le monde et les Anglais*. Paris: Editions Autrement.

Gallo, M. (2004) *Napoleon; The Song of Departure*. London: PanMacmillan.

Gallo, M. (2004) *Napoleon; The Sun of Austerlitz*. London: PanMacmillan.

Gallo, M. (2004) *Napoleon; The Emperor of Kings*. London: PanMacmillan.

Gallo, M. (2005) *Napoleon; The Immortal of St Helena*. London: PanMacmillan.

Ledru, E. (2001) *Napoleon; The Visionary Conqueror*. Paris: Molieire.

Levitt, T. (1986) *The Marketing Imagination*, 2nd Edition. New York: Free Press.

Luvaas, J. (1999) *Napoleon on the Art of War*. New York: Touchstone.

Part One

Preparing for the Market(ing) Strategy

> The battlefield is a scene of constant chaos. The winner will be the one who controls that chaos, both his own and the enemy's.
>
> *Napoleon Bonaparte*

Any building is only as good as its foundations. The same holds true for any attempt to develop a practical market(ing) strategy. To add a touch of realism, unless you live in an earthquake belt (and most of us don't) there is no reason why you should dig down as far below ground as you are going to build on top. Resources are scarce and should be used judiciously. Analysis is important but 'analysis paralysis' can be deadly and can produce a moribund organization. Balance – as in all things – is essential.

One of the most common questions I am asked is how much research and analysis should we do before we are ready to start taking decisions. This question is almost impossible to answer as it depends on so many different variables. Too little analysis and the organization can end up flying by the seat of its pants, producing products and services it knows nothing about and venturing into markets where it has no right to be. Not that this approach is always disastrous – far from it – there are a number of well-documented success stories of whole business empires based on one person's inspiration. The problem is there are almost as many case histories of the same organizations falling away from a market that has changed because they did not know the reason for that change – or even why they were successful first time round. Disaster comes when an organization is more concerned with its own flair than the needs of its customers and the marketplace (Figure P1.1).

No, the key to information and analysis is knowing, before you start the collection process, exactly what you are going to do with the data. As data collection is a means to an end, not an end in itself, the data collection and analysis process should be driven by strategy and the need to implement it, not the other way around. In this case, the first part of the answer to the question *How much research and analysis should we do?* will be: it depends upon what will convince people inside the organization of the need to do something different for the customer.

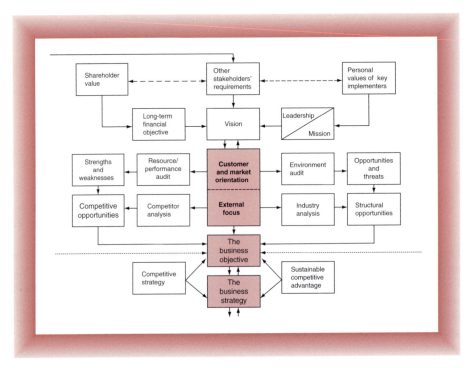

Figure P1.1   Preparing for the market strategy

1 The internal business drivers

Power is my mistress. I have worked too hard at her conquest to allow anyone to take her away from me

Napoleon Bonaparte

How strong are your Generals? What drives them? How good is their vision? Morale might be good for the troops but there comes a time when honesty, certainly among the most senior lieutenants, is the most appropriate policy.

Market(ing) and business strategy, if they are to be practical, must be based on an assessment of reality, not on hopes or wishful thinking. The successful market(ing) practitioner is one whose plans work in the only arena that counts – the market-place. Plans that are based on hopes, inaccurate analysis or, worse, no analysis at all of the factors that drive the business cannot hope to withstand the onslaught of determined competition.

The common thread that binds all these business drivers together is people. Apart from the (all-important) customer, there are other people who also have demands on the business. Like customers, these people expect their needs to be met. Failure to do so may not mean the failure of the business but will certainly mean the failure of the market(ing) strategy.

The 'people/implementers' concerned in this section fall into three categories:

(1) The 'key implementers';

(2) The shareholders;

(3) The other stakeholders in the business.

We will consider these groups in more detail.

1.1 Personal values of the key implementers

[Murat] understood how to conduct a campaign better than Ney and still he was a poor general.

Napoleon Bonaparte

This is a heading that may come as something of a surprise to people who thought they knew what strategy was all about. The main reason for its omission from a number of texts is that, while critically important in any successful business strategy, it is also one of the infamous 'soft' areas of a business organization. Soft business issues such as these that are concerned with what people want, how people think and what motivates people to work are often difficult to quantify and hence to reduce to numbers. Nevertheless, while their inclusion in flowcharts and neat, packaged diagrams is essential, it is also fraught with danger.

The term 'key implementers' refers to that select body in an organization who actually make the decisions and who are central to what the organization does, both in its thinking and in its actions.

The key implementers

They may or may not include the board in its entirety. It may mean the board; it may mean the board plus a number of very senior managers; it may just mean the owner/managing director and a special friend or colleague; or it may mean the chairman and part of the board. In any event, these are the people who really count.

By searching out the key implementers in an organization, often looking behind the titles, we can start to discover which eventual strategic solutions might be acceptable and which patently unacceptable. The key implementers, individually or probably as a group, will have a very clear idea of what type of organization they wish to work for, what type of organization they wish to create, the types of products and services they wish to market, the types of customers they wish to serve and the types of businesses they wish to be in. At the same time, they will also have a very clear idea of what businesses and activities they and their organization will *not* be involved in. It is, if you like, a kind of moral and ethical 'personal ambition blueprint' against which all possible strategic alternatives will be assessed. If a possible strategy contravenes the personal values of this group, it will of course be countered with non-emotional arguments based on good business practice – but it will be countered strongly and then rejected.

The effects of any social system such as a business organization are both strong and often invisible. The key implementers in an organization normally have an important role beyond that of developing strategy – they are the custodians of the corporate culture. They are normally the embodiment of what every manager has to be to progress up the organization. No strategy can be implemented that is 'counter culture' (see Chapter 6). On the other hand, a lot of time and effort can be wasted by pursuing the classical, by-the-numbers approach to strategy formulation just because that is what good business practice calls for.

The lesson is clear – even when the strategy and the strategic approach seem to be 'by the book', you must talk to and understand the key implementers and the social system to which they belong. Implementation is more important than the plans. Implementation has to fit what the organization is. Some organizations (and key implementers) would rather die than change what they are and what they believe in – this is human nature and we should accept it. You always thought it was like that, just you never read it in a book before – oh well. . .

Human nature is just like that (see Chapter 6). And there's no way that we are going to change human nature. The most profitable route for you and the organization is not to beat them but to join them. A strong market influence within the key implementers can do nothing but good.

How? I hear you ask. Well, the first thing to do is to start sharing your experience and insights with others. Show how market(ing) is really just common sense, it's not black magic nor does it have to be a threat to any of the longer established functions in the organization. Most importantly, try to demonstrate that customers are important to the 'vision thing'. If the key implementers hold fast to a vision, that's great. If customers could share that vision, just imagine what we could do together. You will need their help anyway if you are to get your market(ing) strategy on the road – who knows, you might even win a few converts.

1.2   The mission/leadership

> There are certain things in war of which the commander alone comprehends the importance. Nothing but his superior firmness and ability can subdue and surmount all difficulties.
>
> *Napoleon Bonaparte*

What seems to drive the organization? Mission (statements) can give a clue as can the leadership style of the organization.

The mission should bring together the apparently diverse groups that we have discussed earlier and give overall direction. But what is a mission (statement)? At its simplest level, the mission is a statement of the core values of the organization and as such is a framework within which staff and individual business units, divisions or activities prepare their plans. It should be constructed in such a way that it satisfies and can be subscribed to by the most important groups of people who have expectations from the organization. The mission statement is not the same thing as a business objective and it cannot be treated as such; they have been described as long on rhetoric and short on numbers. Missions are, by their nature, non-specific and are difficult to achieve cleanly on their own. A business objective, by contrast, should be both measurable and achievable and is therefore normally expressed in *quantitative* terms. A mission is essentially *qualitative*.

What should the organization think of including in its mission statement? There is no set layout or structure to a mission statement. They tend to be quite personal to the organization and, while some missions can be contained in a handful of words, other mission statements can easily run to one or two closely typed pages. Ideally, the organization's mission statement will be a reflection of the corporate values and ethics that prevail in the organization. It will probably include very broad goals as well as fundamental beliefs about the right ways to behave. It may contain more detailed information and include views about the organization relative to its competition, its technology, its product quality, its role in society or the particular style of ownership of the organization. This is quite a long list but every organization will have what it knows and understands as being its few 'guiding principles', which are particularly important to its sense of unity and its individual character. These are, at the very least, the issues that should be included in a mission statement.

A more important question is what does the mission statement actually do? This will influence its content. Above all else, the mission statement should do as its name implies: it should give the organization a clear mission or purpose. It should give all people connected with the organization (see Section 1.5) a clear sense of where the organization is headed. If the mission statement is sufficiently motivating, then everybody should share a sense of direction, opportunities, significance and, ultimately, achievement. A good mission statement will give your organization a greater sense of cohesion – it will improve the morale in the organization. It has been known to improve the speed of response of the organization's staff to external demands. Of course all this does no harm at all to the organization's external reputation.

Leadership is another good pointer to what will be accepted as good strategy. Whole books (and editions of *Harvard Business Review*) are dedicated to the study of leadership. Profitable careers are made in the area for a wide range of 'experts' from successful military commanders, Atlantic yachtsmen, rugby football captains and mountain climbers. I am sure that we can all learn a lot from these people.

However, here we are looking to understand the 'status quo' in the organization as a way of preparing for a market(ing) strategy that is practical and implement-*able* for the organization. I tend to favour the 'ancients' when it comes to simple concepts and my favourite here is Max Weber.

Max Weber (1864–1920) on leadership

Weber concluded that there are three different *bases of authority* for a leader in an organization:

(1) *Traditional leadership*, such as is exercised by the Monarch where authority is assumed because that is the way things are done;
(2) *Charismatic leadership*, which depends on the personal magnetism of the leader;
(3) *Bureaucratic leadership*, which is authority delegated on the basis of rationally defined criteria such as expertise, qualifications and track record.

It may be old, there may be better definitions around but I see examples of all these leaders every day. Most important, understanding the leadership approach gives an excellent view on what strategic processes and outcomes will be acceptable to the organization.

1.3   Shareholder value

> The crowd which follows me with admiration, would run with the same eagerness were I marching to the Guillotine.
>
> *Napoleon Bonaparte*

In *theory*, the relationship here is very simple. The investors in the organization invest in anticipation of a return on their capital; they are *in fact* the owners of the business. As owners, the investors employ the board to manage the business on their behalf and, should the returns not meet their expectations, the investors (as owners) have the power to remove part or all of the board and replace it with other directors.

In *practice*, the relationship is far more complicated; there are investors and investors. For example, in a publicly quoted company the stockholders may be institutions such as insurance companies or pension funds; there may be private individuals and there may also be other publicly quoted companies holding stock. Also, stockholders may be primarily national or international in character. It also follows that different investors may have different needs. Some may be investing for the long term, some for the short term. Some may require no income – seeking a long-term increase in the capital value of their stockholding; others may be far less interested in capital growth but more concerned to secure a regular income stream from the investment, normally in the form of dividends. Yet others may require a mixture of both capital growth and income.

The organization might also be a smaller part of a larger organization – in this instance there is but one owner. In case of private company, the director or directors may also be the owners. Then the returns required may be for a steady or rising income stream over the longer term or for shorter-term capital accumulation.

The past ten years has also shown that (at least some) investors are willing to exercise their legal rights and take directors to task. There have been some lively annual general meetings where small shareholders have taken the 'fat cat' directors to task over salaries and incentive schemes that seem to pay out even when sales and profits are in decline. Large institutional investors are also flexing their muscles more and are becoming important players in underperforming organizations when it comes time to re-elect directors or even deal with potential takeover bids. In each case, it is the board's strategy that is being assessed, not the directors themselves.

The concept of shareholder value can also be applied (differently) to organizations in the public sector. In this case, the government is the single (or possibly majority) 'shareholder' and hence the effective owner of the business. With public sector organizations, it is important to identify the precise needs of this major shareholder (which are likely to be more complex than just financial returns) and to ensure that any resulting business or market(ing) strategy does not run counter to the owner's expectations. Such expectations may include a return on capital invested, employment, global market share and environmental/social return among others and, of course, are likely to change with political climates and changes in government (or government policy) over time.

The important thing for the director trying to direct or the manager trying to manage is to understand the makeup of the ownership structure of the organization and, as precisely as possible, the returns (financial and non-financial) required by those investing the capital. I have not attempted to provide an in-depth analysis of all the underlying issues of the setting of financial objectives; these are quite complex and the interested reader is referred to one of the specialist texts on the subject. For our purposes, it is sufficient to state that the director will only be allowed freedom to direct as long as the investor is getting what he or she wants. So the market(ing) strategy needs to produce the 'right' value for the organization.

We might complain about modern trends towards US-style short-termism, the rise of speculation, the dominance of 'market analysts' or the 'promiscuity' of investors (nice to see that customers don't get all the bad press) and the harm this has on business which needs desperately to invest in the long term. We may also complain bitterly about the effects that this short-term mentality has on international competitiveness, comparing the UK, the USA or Europe, with their increasingly short-term financial requirements, to the traditional Far East longer-term view and wonder how on earth we can hope to compete over the next ten to twenty years. We may even be using this argument as a convenient excuse for our relatively low performance in a number of other areas. This aside – and I have as many firm views on the subject as everybody else – we all have to realize that we either meet our owners' financial (and non-financial) requirements or we will be forced to give way to someone else better able or prepared to do so.

Apart from the share or stock capital, there is also long-term debt financing normally provided by major institutions such as banks and, more recently, venture capital (VC) companies. The various banks are also the products of their own internal organizational culture as well as the national culture from which they operate. The different banks' views will also differ as to what is long term and what is short term. Venture capitalists work on a different basis and exist (unlike the banks) to invest in *risk*. The dot-com escapade showed the power (if not the sagacity) of the VCs and their willingness to take on all types of *risk*. Nowadays, VCs (the ones that survived the dot-com bust) are a little more careful but still often expect only one investment in five to pay off – which explains why they can look for 35 per cent per annum return on all their investments.

1.4   Long-term financial objective

> Riches do not consist in the possession of treasures, but in the use made of them.
>
> *Napoleon Bonaparte*

By long-term financial objective, we do not mean the plethora of annual, quarterly or monthly financial targets that abound in any sizeable organization and act primarily as control systems against planned targets. Long-term financial objective is that requirement placed on the organization, specifically on the board of directors, by the individuals and institutions who have invested in the organization in the expectation of a financial return.

So far the question of financial objectives has been all fairly mechanical and straightforward. We must understand who the investors in the organization are, understand what they want, deliver what they want and (if we are lucky) we are all left a degree of liberty to run the business. In short, the financial objective is a *hurdle* to be overcome. By translating business performance into numbers, we have a convenient means by which the investors/owners, who have little or no day-to-day involvement in the running of the organization, may understand how their appointed managers have performed over the past period. While it also gives us a fairly good indication of what we must achieve in future periods, it provides absolutely *no indication at all* of how to achieve these future results or how to run the business.

Profits are not only important but are vital for survival. But, the pursuit of short-term profits for their own sake can destroy an otherwise successful business.

When talking to directors and managers of medium and large organizations about what they see as their business objective, the most common response is almost always couched in financial terms. *To achieve a fifteen per cent return on capital employed* and *to achieve a twenty per cent increase in sales with a ten per cent increase in net profit* are quite common. Smaller organizations might respond with *to make enough money today to survive into tomorrow*, which probably amounts to the same thing. Expressions like these are financial objectives (more often short than long!) which, when cascaded down the organization in this form, give the managers, who actually have to produce the results, little or no indication of what they should do. How should they organize themselves, their departments or the resources at their disposal to achieve these objectives? Three managers given the same objective of increasing the profit by 10 per cent will find three different ways of doing it. Not all of the ways will be 'good' for the organization in the longer term. The inevitable result, unless controlled in other ways from the top, is an increasingly fragmented organization, lack of synergy and dangerous misallocation of resources. As we will see later (see Chapter 3), the business objective in its proper form is a far more powerful instrument, both for directing the organization and for developing long-term success in the marketplace.

The long-term financial objective acts extremely well – as a financial objective. Being a narrow measure, it cannot be used as a surrogate business objective as it lacks the breadth to be an efficient driver of the business, and the people in it.

It's all very well him saying that, I hear you say, but who's going to convince the finance director? Yes, I know exactly what you mean. Two things may help. First, a quote from Levitt who puts things much better than I possibly can. In 1986 (*The Marketing Imagination*, Free Press, New York), he stated:

Marketing and the corporate purpose

Not so long ago companies said that the purpose of business was to make money. But that proved as vacuous as saying that the purpose of life is to eat. Eating is a requisite, not a purpose of life. Without eating, life stops. Profits are a requisite of business. Without profits, business stops. Like food for the body, profit for the business must be defined as the excess of what comes in over what goes out. In business it's called positive cash flow. It has to be positive, because the process of sustaining life is a process of destroying life. To sustain life, a business must produce goods and services that people in sufficient numbers will want to buy at adequate prices. Since production wears out the machinery that produces and the people who run and manage the machines, to keep the businesses going there's got to be enough left over to replace what's being worn out. That 'enough' is profit, that's why profit is a requisite, not a purpose of business.

> *Besides all that, to say that profit is a purpose of business is, simply, morally shallow. Who with a palpable heartbeat and minimal sensibilities will go to the mat for the right of somebody to earn a profit for its own sake? If no greater purpose can be discovered or justified, business cannot morally justify its existence. It's a repugnant idea, an idea whose time has gone.*
>
> *Finally, it's an empty idea. Profits can be made in lots of devious and transient ways. For people of affairs, a statement of purpose should provide guidance to the management of their affairs. To say that they should attract and hold customers forces facing the necessity of figuring out what people really want and value, and then catering to those wants and values. It provides specific guidance and has moral merit.*
>
> *Theodore Levitt*

Elegant, I think you'll agree.

If this still doesn't cut any ice with the finance-minded leaders, then I suggest you get hold of an excellent piece of research originally carried out by the RSA (Royal Society for the encouragement of Arts, Manufacturers and Commerce, London, http://www.rsa.org.uk) entitled 'Tomorrow's Company', now managed by a separate charity, Tomorrows Company (http://www.tomorrowscompany.com). Based on research carried out in 1993 (and developed subsequently) among key business leaders and opinion formers in the UK, the RSA concluded that this country has a long trail of underperforming companies and that too many companies are not as good as they think they are. The research stated that *Yesterday's companies do not see the need to have a distinctive purpose or values, and often confuse purpose with measures of success.*

There we have the problem in a nutshell – 'Purpose' or 'Measures of Success'? According to Levitt (paraphrased by Drucker and others), the purpose of a business is clear:

The purpose of business

To create, and keep a customer

An (possibly the most) important measure of how well an organization achieves this is profitability. *Financial measures then are a measure of success – not the purpose of the organization.* As far as I am concerned (and we will see more examples of this unhealthy myopic financial focus), if organizations do not shake free from the obsession with bottom-line measures they will progressively fall behind more customer/market-focused competitors – and will inevitably have less revenues and profits to count!

Now I realize that most of my readers went into market(ing) because they hated dealing with numbers but this phobia just can't be allowed to continue unchallenged. Accountants and financiers are just like us, insecure and so forced to protect their turf with jargon and rituals. We have the product life cycle and the Ansoff matrix – they have the EBITDA and DCF.

Someone has to take the first step to bridge the gap between the two areas; it may as well be you – you need to understand the basic mechanics of the financial system that operates in your organization. You are going to be measured against it anyway.

Why not buy a finance book? Even better, talk to a numbers man – he'll appreciate it.

1.5   Other stakeholders' requirements

> A good General, good cadres, good organization, good instruction and good discipline can produce good troops, regardless of the cause they fight for. It is true, however, that fanaticism, love of country and national glory can better inspire young soldiers.
>
> *Napoleon Bonaparte*

So far we have considered the groups influencing an organization's activities and future, namely, the shareholders or the suppliers of long-term equity capital and the key implementers (or however this team is described within your organization).

Apart from the shareholders and the implementers/key management team, there are others who have needs and expectations and who will, rightly, expect a degree of service and satisfaction from the organization (Figure 1.1).

The RSA study (cited earlier) also draws this aspect of the organization's activity into stark relief. The research discovered that UK society generally no longer 'defers' to business activity, and organizations need to actively maintain public confidence in company operations and business contact if they are to continue to enjoy a 'licence to operate'. The RSA concludes that, in the future, successful organizations will *value reciprocal relationships and work actively to build them with customers, suppliers and other key stakeholders through a partnership approach and, by focusing on, and learning from, all those who contribute to the business, will be best able to improve returns to shareholders.*

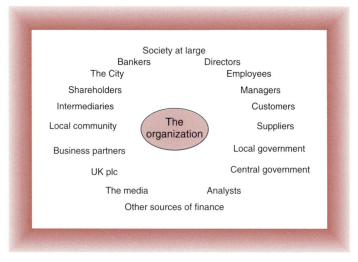

Figure 1.1 A stakeholder map

How unlike many companies today who prefer adversarial relationships with stakeholders! These 'yesterday' organizations still firmly believe that shareholders would have to be the losers if employees, suppliers, customers or the country were made more important.

In short, the 'market argument' runs as follows. Profits come from satisfied customers who come back. Satisfied customers are created by:

● Offering value-added products and services that meet their needs (offer customer value) and

● Service offered by committed and motivated staff.

These offerings are made by companies who:

● Understand their customers and

● Build alliances with their staff, communities and suppliers (to deliver superior customer value).

These companies are created by investors/stakeholders who take a long-term interest in what the organization is trying to achieve – as a way of maximizing long-term financial returns.

The stakeholder concept term is not just a 'good thing'. It is a highly 'profitable thing'. The days of viewing stakeholders as just innocent bystanders are probably gone. For an organization concerned with implementing its strategy rather than simply formulating it, stakeholders may hold one of the keys to success.

1.6   The vision

> Had I possessed 30,000 artillery rounds at Leipzig... today I would be master of the world.
>
> *Napoleon Bonaparte*

A lot has been written about 'the vision thing' in recent years, some good and some laughable. Apart from the evolutionists with their particular brand of commercial Darwinism, all schools of strategy see the vision as central to any form of worthwhile strategy or plan. Again it centres on the key implementers.

The personal values of this central group, once combined, create the vision driving the organization and so what we might call the 'strategic intent' behind the group. This vision, sometimes written, more often than not implicit and mutually understood, needs to be clarified and defined before taking the process any further. The vision is often central to the organization's success. Henry Mintzberg (*Observer*, London, 12 June 1994) has been quoted as saying:

> *Many of the great strategies are simply great visions. Visions can be a lot more inspirational and effective than the most carefully constructed plan. Only when we recognise our fantasies can we begin to appreciate the wonders of reality.*

The vision is not the same as an objective because it is not normally quantified. Rather it is a picture of what the future of the organization looks like. Vision enables the organization to set a broad strategic direction and leaves the details of its implementation to be worked out later. It has been argued (by Mintzberg and others) that the visionary approach is a more flexible way to deal with an uncertain world.

'Strategic intent' was first described as a concept by Hamel and Prahalad (*Harvard Business Review*, May/June 1989) and suggests what vision is to objectives, strategic intent is to strategy. Hamel and Prahalad argue that companies who have risen to global leadership have set ambitious goals such as 'Encircle Caterpillar' (Komatsu), 'Beat Xerox' (Canon) and 'Become a second Ford' (Honda) and then used a dynamic management process that *focuses the organization's attention on the essence of winning*. Importantly, details of implementation are left vague to allow for operational change as market and economic conditions change in time and geography.

While, in my experience, it is quite difficult to identify the personal values of the key implementers and the collective vision/strategic intent which these people hold, the costs of ignoring these often emotional aspects of how an organization is directed and managed may be devastatingly high. No matter how scientific, logical, rational and elegant the eventual plan, if it conflicts with the personal values of the key team, the business objective will not be achieved. The key implementers may ignore the plan; they might sabotage the plan or even leave the organization. Far better a compromise that works to an ideal that doesn't – this has been my approach in all my work with organizations – although 'compromise' doesn't mean capitulation, a strategy that isn't driven by the market is doomed to failure.

In the absence of a clear vision (articulated or not), the organization will probably be in trouble. Without some light to guide it, the organization will flounder aimlessly.

A vision is (categorically) not the same thing as a financial target (see Section 1.4) and everybody needs more than 'to maximize profits' to give them a sense of direction, purpose and worth. Having said this, organizations without a vision are really quite rare. The vision may be unclear, ragged around the edges or even rather too emotional for senior managers to admit to – but it is normally there. It is often better to dig deep to find what makes people come into work in the mornings than to go through the (often pointless) exercise of trying to create a vision from scratch; what people are happy to put down on paper may not be what they are really willing to fight for.

Putting together the vision statement can be quite a lengthy process of discussion within the organization. Indeed, practical experience suggests that visions that emerge like a brand new car model from behind the locked doors of the senior management group tend to be less effective than visions that emerge from discussions that involve staff and the other stakeholders that affect the organization.

So we are faced with the inevitable long discussion period that will produce a multitude of views, feelings and beliefs from all sectors. Unfortunately, this lengthy discussion period is also likely to generate a mission statement that runs to not one but maybe two or more closely typed pages. A good meaty document may make people feel better but it's not necessarily the most effective way of communicating a message. If we have to keep, preserve and enshrine the full-blown version for official use in the annual report and accounts, then so be it. This needn't necessarily stop us from modifying the basic text into something that is more appropriate for passing down through the organization.

The Declaration of Independence is a beautifully manicured document but the general needs something more 'pithy' for the troops to shout as they go over the top!

2 The external environment

It is very important . . . to have good maps of all the country between the Adige, the Po and the Adda . . . which will probably be the theatre of new wars on the same scale as the large map of Italy. It is necessary to have all reconnaissances made at the Topographical Bureau of War in order that we could, if necessary, send the generals all suitable instructions. Then, from the commencement of war, they would know the defensive campaign fieldworks that will have to be prepared in the various positions in case of unfortunate developments.

Napoleon Bonaparte

In Chapter 1, we tried to uncover the most important internal drivers of the business. If the organization has a mission statement or a clearly articulated vision, this will help us focus our attention on the more important aspects of the external environment (Figure 2.1), which we must assess next.

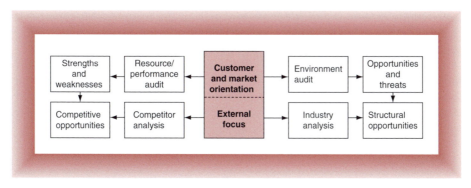

Figure 2.1   The external environment

Attempting to lay any sort of plans for the future without first gathering some (at least enough) information is not only foolish, but also demonstrates dangerous tendencies towards complacency and arrogance. Knowing that information must be gathered is one thing, knowing how much and what to gather is quite another. We will deal with such issues in much more detail in Part Two (see Chapter 6, sections 6.2, 6.3 and 6.6).

2.1   Customer and market orientation – the culture

> A King should sacrifice the best affections of his heart for the good of his country; no sacrifice should be above his determination.
>
> *Napoleon Bonaparte*

We will deal with the whole question of customer orientation and organizational culture in much more detail in Part Two (see Chapter 6). For the moment though, we will consider this question from the data-gathering perspective.

Even the two great best-selling strategy books of the last century, written by Michael Porter (*Competitive Strategy*, Free Press, New York, 1983; *Competitive Advantage*, Free Press, New York, 1990), require (although this is not explicitly stated) that the organization be market/customer oriented for the proposed strategic approach to be beneficial. Porter's whole approach is based on the importance of looking outward to the environment and the competitive marketplace rather than basing our future on purely internal considerations. Unfortunately, Porter doesn't then pay enough attention to the power of markets and their ability to derail the most eloquent of strategic plans.

Mintzberg fares a little better in his respect for customers and markets, stressing, as he does, the need to be more flexible when 'crafting' strategic plans. When it comes to the customer and market orientation of the business, Mintzberg is as myopic as other strategy writers, concentrating for the most part on how strategic planners do, or should do, their job.

A state of mind that is inward looking rather than outward looking not only chooses to uncover the wrong data from the environment, but is also most likely to misinterpret the data which is collected. This emphasis will become clear as we progress through the book.

2.2   The environment audit

> A leader has the right to be beaten, but never the right to be surprised.
>
> *Napoleon Bonaparte*

Auditing the environment in which the organization must operate is arguably the most important and most significant data-gathering activity that any business, firm, service or even government department can undertake. Ten or twenty years ago, managers could turn round, with some degree of justification, and say that they had the market tied up. The very large 'mega' organizations or cartels tended to completely dominate certain market sectors and in the 1960s and the 1970s were able to control competition in the marketplace and determine what customers would buy. When, during this period, chief executives would turn round and say (as one really said to me) *Well, we know exactly what the customers want, it's what we give them*, this remark had some validity. Customers did, indeed, keep buying the company's products or services. They may not have been completely satisfied but more often than not they had no real choice in the matter.

More dangerously, some chief executives are still saying the same thing today. They will probably remain absolutely convinced that they know precisely what their customers want as they watch their organization slide from dominance to obscurity in the more competitive markets which are today's reality. (Who mentioned Marks & Spencer?).

In the UK, the USA and the majority of the western world, the 1960s and 1970s was the era of the large corporation. Size and economies of scale were everything during this time. With size, naturally enough, came power to control. Size gave corporations the ear of government, always concerned with balance of payments, international trade and, of course, employment. It also followed that, compared with these issues, the satisfaction of the individual customer was considered relatively unimportant. The net result was that the larger corporations had a degree of real control over the environment in which they operated – and they used it.

The 1980s saw the beginning of a shift in power away from the producer towards the customer, ignited by the work of Ralph Nader and others. In the 1990s, this trend accelerated. The late 1990s saw a brief displacement as the dot-com era suggested that they had discovered new rules of economics and sales revenue and profits were no longer measures of business success. This stage passed with the dot-com collapse and the early 2000s continued what they 'thought' customers wanted: lower and lower prices at the expense of differentiation, quality and service.

Currently, some astute organizations appear to be veering away as the cliff edge comes into view, but a lot of lemming-like organizations are still heading for the great *let's give it away and have the whole market* graveyard.

Meanwhile, international trade has become more liberal and the barriers to international competition have started to be dismantled as more governments seek actively to promote competition in national marketplaces – well apart from agriculture and steel and where are the political marginal seats at the moment? What the early consumerist movement started has now produced a greater degree of choice for the customer and in many instances a reduction in the absolute market share of the larger corporations. With the wider range of products and services in the market, customers have had to learn how to evaluate and choose among the competing offerings and as a result have become more sophisticated in the exercise of that choice. While there still remain examples of markets where free choice really does not yet operate (British and European banking, fixed line telecommunications and public utilities, among others, still have a long way to go), generally organizations today do not and will not be able to control the environment in which they operate. The environment will control them.

It is only by achieving a much better understanding of its environment that the organization can possibly hope to establish its market position and flourish over the longer term. So what do we mean by the word 'environment'? Another of those words which, of course, means everything and nothing. We must break it down into its most important constituent parts or we will once again get lost in a morass of unnecessary detail. While some commentators seem to take the word 'environment' to mean everything outside the factory gates, this 'catch-all' term is unlikely to be very useful when it comes to laying specific plans for future activity.

Remember, at this stage, we are still concerned with the overall problem of discovering what is going on in the broad business and social environment, within which the organization must operate. We need to understand how we should position the organization relative to its competition and likely future shifts in marketplace demand. The more detailed analysis of specific target markets is not pertinent at this point; this will be considered in more depth later (see Chapter 6). For the moment then we will limit ourselves to the well-known *PEST* analysis (Figure 2.2). It's not particularly clever or advanced but it does the job.

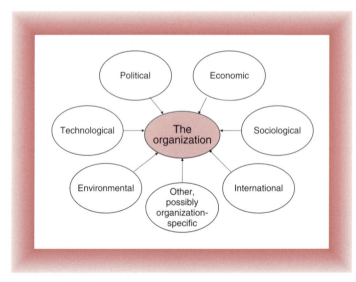

Figure 2.2   The environment audit (PEST)

The traditional 'PEST' analysis includes four headings that create the mnemonic – Political, Economic, Sociological and Technical issues. These are explained in slightly more detail below. Two other more detailed areas are often included under the 'Environment' heading of the PEST. These relate to the question of Competition (and the specific analysis of the industry within which the organization operates) and the Customer. These two sub-headings are important today, so much so that they should have a separate place in the information-gathering phase. We will deal with these two subjects later (see Chapter 6).

To these six headings, you may wish to add a further two – International and Environmental. While twenty years ago, an organization might justifiably have maintained a purely domestic and non-environmental stance, the nature of competition and customer demand have forced us all to look beyond our traditional frontiers. Also, nobody can ignore the environmental issues that governments will make sure we have to face in the future. You might also decide to add a seventh heading that is particular to your business.

We will consider the various elements briefly in turn.

Political	Economic
1	1
2	2
3	3
4	4
5	5
Social/cultural	**Technological**
1	1
2	2
3	3
4	4
5	5
International	Environment
1	1
2	2
3	3
4	4
5	5
Customer/the market	Competition
1	1
2	2
3	3
4	4
5	5

Figure 2.3 *PEST* analysis

2.2.1 *Political factors*

Under the political heading, we are concerned with the motives and the actions of governments and the way, via legislation, regulation and the legal/political system, they impact on business. All too often, especially in the West, managers tend to take the role of government and the influence of political ideology on business as a 'given' situation that we just have to live with. Apart from the regular overreaction of stock markets when national elections are in the air, we don't normally expect or plan for any radical shift in political direction. In some respects this slow, gradual change can be a disadvantage to the organization because gradual change often goes unnoticed. Such gradual, cumulative change can be treacherous. The organization can easily find itself at a competitive disadvantage without knowing how it got there.

It is important that the organization understands the role of government in the marketplace, as regulator or participator or both. We must understand the true impact that government policy can have on business. We must also understand which of the vast array of legislation impacts on our organization and our market(ing) activities.

Commercial activity is regulated, to a greater or lesser extent, in every country in the world. Government control extends from the way we structure and organize our business, how we deal with our employees, how we remunerate and motivate the people who work for us and even the amount of profits which we can make. We are also regulated, overtly or covertly, in terms of what we can sell, how we sell and who we can sell to. Often we are controlled in terms of the prices we can charge, the distribution channels we can use and the promotion activities that we can employ. Very little business and market(ing) activity is free from the laws and acts of government, no matter where it takes place or where the organization is domiciled.

Our first efforts must be directed at trying to understand exactly what effects these measures have on how we run our business. Try, for example, to imagine what we would be doing differently if these rules and regulations did not exist. Secondly, we need to try and grasp the reasoning behind the legislative and legal regulation. What is the political ideology that forms the basis of the regulation? Does the government wish to control and create an atmosphere in which enterprise can flourish or does it feel obliged to control (curb) business enterprise for the social good? Are its measures aimed at raising tax revenues or are they aimed at maintaining maximum levels of employment? – the list continues. It is only by understanding why governments and regulators act the way they do that we will have any chance of anticipating the most likely future changes in legislation. If we can predict future moves, then we can plan for them.

A 'quick' checklist for your political assessment might include:

- Role of government, regulator or participator
- Political ideology
- Political motivations

- Rate of change of political direction
- Political stability over time
- Political attitudes to:
  - Competition
  - Social responsibility
  - Environmental matters
  - Customer protection
- Legislative effects on:
  - Organizational structure
  - Organizational behaviour
  - Employment
  - Salaries and payment levels
  - Employment conditions (health and safety, etc.)
  - Profits (taxation/repatriation, etc.)
  - Permitted markets
  - Product policy
  - Pricing policy
  - Distribution policy
  - Promotional policy.

2.2.2 Economic factors

Under this heading, we should be considering issues such as the current and likely future rate of inflation and interest rates. We should be looking at the current and future positions of exchange rates; especially if we are deeply involved in international markets, we require high levels of foreign content to our product or service or our competitors are primarily international.

Taxation can appear under the economic heading as well as the political heading. Over the longer term, we should also be concerned with the state of the economy, whether we are in a recession or a boom, whether the economy is largely stable and, importantly, the likely future direction of the economy over the next three to five years.

A new dimension that needs attention in the maturing Western markets is the 'real' rate of inflation facing our particular customers. While inflation rates (as quoted in government statistics) seem to be under greater control than in the past, what these figures sometimes don't take into account are the additional family and individual expenses caused by the gradual withdrawal of the welfare state. Most European governments have now recognized that they cannot continue with the welfare payments of the past forty years, confronted as they are with ageing populations and declining workforces. As citizens now have to pay for what was formally offered by the state (health, schooling, university education, pensions) while still paying full taxes, disposable income is effectively declining. These 'new essentials' can seriously affect how often customers renew their cars or take holidays. Competing for 'share of wallet' has a real meaning in these circumstances.

Probably the most tangible aspect of economic factors is the disposable income of our target customer base. The future prosperity of any organization will depend on its ability to win and keep customers who are both prepared and able to pay the prices that we need. If our customers and prospects can't afford what we provide, then we just don't have a business.

A 'quick' checklist for your economic assessment might include:

- Gross domestic product (GDP):
    - Per head
    - Social/private
    - Distribution
    - Regional disparity

- Government policy:
    - Fiscal
    - Monetary

- Industrial:
    - Structure
    - Growth
    - Labour rates

- Income:
    - Current
    - Growth
    - Distribution
    - Relation with population groups

- Wealth:
    - Distribution
    - Effect on buying power

- Employment:
    - Structure
    - Full time/part time
    - Male/female
    - Regional disparity.

2.2.3   *Sociological factors*

This aspect of the environment is probably the most difficult to understand, quantify and predict, dealing as it does with people and human behaviour. Unfortunately, it can be devastating to our business fortunes if we are unlucky enough to get it wrong.

Basically we are dealing with people's motivations, needs, wants and perceptions and, more broadly, how society or culture is changing over time. The most difficult problem is not in acquiring the basic data – these are reasonably freely available, certainly in Europe, the USA and the more advanced markets of the world where governments pride themselves on collecting and maintaining information on their citizens. The problem comes in the interpretation.

There is normally quite an amount of data on local, regional, national preferences and consumption patterns, on changes in society, marriage rates, size and growth of households and so on. Past trends are fairly evident and any number of combinations is available, projecting forward ten, twenty or even thirty years, to show where society is likely to be. The skill, however, as with any form of market research, is to understand exactly what these trends mean for our organization and our future. But beware, even government projections need to be treated carefully; for example, some European governments are so concerned about their current and future pensions liability that they have selected non-standard assumptions to drive their long-term model and predictions.

The essence of good market(ing) strategy is to anticipate and identify what our customers want and then be in the right place at the right time to be able to offer it to them. Sounds simple but the anticipation is the difficult part. The longer the production lead times required for your product or service, the more interest your organization should be showing in trying to unravel the likely future shape of its markets.

A 'quick' checklist for your sociological assessment might include:

- Cultural/sub-cultural groups:
  - Characteristics
  - Growth/decline

- Demographics:
  - Socioeconomic groupings
  - Home ownership
  - Geography
  - Family structure and influence
  - Family life stages
  - Usage patterns

- Natural segments:
  - Characteristics
  - Differentiators
  - Growth/decline/change

- Psychographics:
  - Preferences

- – Benefits
- – Attitudes and belief systems

● Social trends:
  - – Changes in personal value systems
  - – Changes in the structure of society
  - – Changes in moral and ethical positions
  - – Changes in belief systems
  - – Changes in attitudes (to, for example, NGOs, genetics, etc.).

2.2.4   *Technological factors*

The rate of change of technology has been one of the most visible under-currents of the society of the past twenty years. Under this heading, we might be concerned with factors like information technology in the use of computers and automation and communications, with the effect on the cost base of increased IT and automation as well as the use of the Internet and outsourcing. We might also be concerned with the likely changes this may have on the types of materials and the components that we use and the general resource base available to the organization.

There is an important relationship here with the previous section and that is the reaction of our customers to the increased use of IT, especially the role of the Internet. While many managers welcome the advances made in IT and the increased efficiency and cost savings that IT can produce, too many organizations, especially in the service sector, forget that their customers are often by nature technophobic. This means that while cost savings and increased efficiency may be possible in 'back office' operations, it is often less easy and less acceptable to bring automation through into the 'front office' – in full view of the customer. While automation may be an aid, it is very rarely an alternative for (good) *personal* service. We obviously draw the distinction between 'good' service and the case of customers actually preferring to use ATMs rather than go into bank branches or customers preferring to use the Internet to gather information on electrical products rather than rely on the knowledge and 'advice' of sales assistants in the national retail chains.

When considering the technological perspective and drawing scenarios of tomorrow's world, we should be careful not to create scenarios of the world as we would like it to be, but rather as we think it will be. So many of the pictures of the IT and leisure-dominated world of the twenty-first century have simply failed to happen. Look at the future views from the 1960s and see how far out some predictions can be.

A 'quick' checklist for your technological assessment might include:

● Rate of technological change:
  - – Organization's ability to keep up
  - – Customer acceptance

- Research and development:
  - Cost of investment
  - Matching customer needs
  - Control
- Production technology:
  - Costs versus savings
  - Internal skill base
- Protection of technology:
  - Patents
  - Copyrights
  - Impact on investment
- Universal availability of technology:
  - The rat race to technological edge
  - Product differentiation possibilities.

2.2.5   International factors

As industry and commerce becomes more international in nature, so more and more organizations have to deal with an international environment audit. There are, of course, some organizations that are still purely domestic in nature and even face little or no international competition; these need go no further than considering the environment of their domestic market. However, the number of organizations which have no international markets, no international suppliers for various components or raw materials and no international competition in the domestic market is becoming fewer and fewer every year.

If we wish to broaden the environment audit to an international basis for the organization that has overseas markets, we will have to consider the political, economic, sociological and technological aspects of each different market in which it intends to operate and from which we receive competition.

International outsourcing and manufacture has been receiving a 'mixed press' in recent years but it has been with us since the days of the British Empire and will be with us for years to come. Your audit needs to cover such issues if they are relevant: dealing with the (unique) culture in countries such as China is as important as paying attention to the financials.

Any international audit must pay very special attention to the ever-present social and cultural differences that lie submerged in foreign markets ready to trap the unwary. You should be very, very afraid of these hidden differences.

2.2.6   Environmental factors

Environmental and ecological awareness too has entered the mainstream. All types of organizations are now faced with issues that they could ignore just a decade ago. Serious environmental offerings are still in the minority, but the idea of 'organic' has been successfully moved from food to clothing, so where might it go next? 'Fair trade' is also gaining ground as an environmental 'overlap' with the international part of the audit – once the definitions are clearer, we might expect fair trade to extend throughout many different parts of the economy – as the anti-apartheid movement did in previous years.

Nevertheless, it is clear that those of us who like to bathe our consumption in a 'light green wash' are now the majority.

Global warming is also slowly moving from being a political football to a social and business reality. Environmental licences, regulations, taxes and a new 'carbon exchange' (Chicago Climate Exchange) operating are already part of the landscape and with continued emphasis on 'climate change' these issues are not going away anytime fast.

Finally, be prepared for the future. Nothing remains fixed in time and space, not even the trusty *PEST* analysis. As always, much depends on your organization and your market, but beware of over-simplistic models. What does 'external' mean for your business? While these environmental classifications are 'standards' it is important that each organization decide which of the six classifications given earlier have the most severe impact on its activities and its profits. Obviously this is where the attention needs to be directed.

As change is the order of the day in the business environment, the environment audit is not an exercise that can be completed and then forgotten. Nor is it an exercise that can be safely carried out on an annual basis – there is too much important change. Ideally the organization should create a tracking mechanism that will show up the most important changes as they occur. Time is of the essence in competitive markets.

2.3   Opportunities and threats

> A true master of politics is able to calculate, down to the smallest fraction, the advantages to which he may put his very faults.
>
> *Napoleon Bonaparte*

Having looked (albeit briefly) at the environment audit and done our best to make sense of what is going on in the wider business environment, we need to turn this information into action. Specifically we need to search through the environment for the business opportunities that appear to be open to our organization. It takes time to develop new products and new services and to develop and open new markets. If we are given a hint from the environment audit that new market possibilities are likely to open, then we should plan our time accordingly and be ready when the market appears. Arriving six to nine months late (even consistently) along with all the other late arrivals is hardly the best way to win a positive market reputation.

As well as identifying the opportunities in tomorrow's marketplace, we also need to identify the threats that may appear in the business environment, especially those that might seriously hinder our development and continued prosperity. In my experience, managers have few problems in identifying threats in the future environment; normally the list of threats is twice or three times longer than that of opportunities. I must admit I am never quite sure whether this is because the environment really is tough out there or because a pessimistic nature is a prerequisite for the modern manager. Be this as it may, the important thing is not just to identify the threats, but to be able to do something about them. As long as they are spotted early enough, most threats can either be neutralized or avoided by the organization – or even, if you are very good, turned into opportunities. Unfortunately, for every example of an organization which has successfully lobbied government to avoid particular regulations being brought into force or has diversified out of its original core industry into other newer, more secure market sectors, there are three or four examples of organizations that have seen the abyss – and then promptly walked into it.

It's not just tomorrow's threats and opportunities that can be unearthed by a solid environment audit. If your organization is about to start an audit for the first time you are likely to discover an interesting collection of threats and opportunities sitting right underneath you now – you just didn't know they were there!

Foregoing opportunities is one thing, not knowing about a threat until a few years of declining profits makes it too late to do anything about it is quite another.

This may sound like an overly pessimistic note but I know many firms in this situation. By the time the pain gets bad enough to make management do something about the problems, it might just be too late.

2.3.1 *Industry analysis*

We have looked at the broad macro elements of the environment (see Section 2.2) that will impact the organization. These macro elements could be considered the standard factors, which will be analysed by all organizations regardless of the type of business they are in. Now, dropping down a level from the general to the more specific, the organization will need to analyse and understand thoroughly its position within its industry to be able to set out its objective and strategy for the future.

There are a number of (usually quite complicated) analyses used to assess your organization's position. I think these are interesting but too complicated to explain to others in the organization – so can alienate the market(ing) strategy (*too academic*) rather than help involve people in the future. I prefer to use a simpler (less complicated but less accurate) but more easily recognized model, the product life cycle (Figure 2.4). Trust me, in this business, simpler is better.

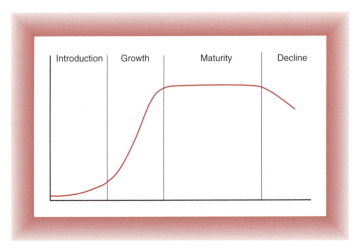

Figure 2.4   The product/service life cycle (1)

I am sure you know that the life cycle can be applied to a product, service, product category, or brand. On the other hand, while it can be a useful 'concept' it is less useful as a 'model' because it is not always easy to tell exactly where you are on the curve – until you have passed the point. But it is still useful for explaining what the future *might* look like (Figure 2.5).

There are four recognized stages to the life cycle as the product or service or category proceeds from introduction through growth into maturity and eventually into decline and death. How long the cycle lasts depends on the market and the organizations. Again, the stages are well documented in most marketing texts (Figure 2.6).

However, we know more about the PLC than is usually explained in the introductory texts. There are two points at which the market consolidates or suffers a 'shakeout' of firms. Naturally consolidation occurs when the entire market starts to decline but an earlier (and more widespread) shakeout occurs before this.

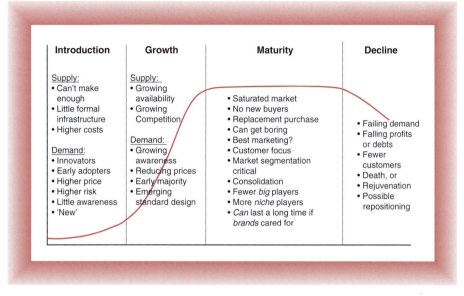

Figure 2.5   The product/service life cycle (2)

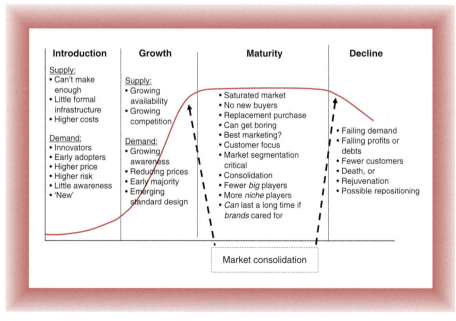

Figure 2.6   The product/service life cycle (3)

At the point between the rapid growth stage and the maturity stage is the most dangerous *for the majority* of organizations. Let's think why.

Growing markets are a special environment and they can support a wide range of organizations, all trying to carve out market share at the same time. Because the whole market is growing, many companies can prosper as they offer very different product/service solutions and do so at very different levels of efficiency and profitability. At this stage, sales is definitely the name of the game and the game is reasonably simple – develop or buy a product or service (that works) and scale the sales operation so that you call on more buyers, more often than the competition. Margins always seem to be under pressure but nobody really suffers very badly; there is always enough margin for sizeable sales commissions and recruitment of new sales people. All in all it is a fun time, it is about new ideas and new technology and new markets and new stars in the business world whether we are talking about mobile telephones, IT, Internet or business outsourcing today or whether we are talking about the telephone, the motor car or airline travel years ago – at the time, everybody is a pioneer and sales is king.

Then comes the 'downfall' – the market becomes saturated. The market stops growing. Sales stop growing. Customers only buy to replace existing product or service. All of a sudden, the business is not growing at the heady 25 or 30 per cent per year – it might even be contracting (Figure 2.7).

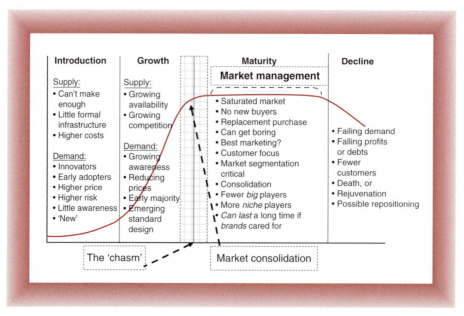

Figure 2.7   The product/service life cycle (4)

Market maturity is not so much a difficult time – it is a different time from the stage that went before it. In the rapid growth period, the successful organization will focus on:

● Managing the product or service;

● Managing the sales operation;

● Managing the business growth.

In the mature stage, the entire emphasis shifts from internal to external – the successful organization will focus on:

● Managing the insight and knowledge of customer needs;

● Managing the focus on the most appropriate market segments;

● Managing the product or service differentiation;

● Managing and caring for the brands;

● Managing the realignment of the organization and its activities to the constantly migrating needs of the customers.

The fact is the skills required by the organization to succeed in maturity are so different from the skills required to succeed in the growth stage that very few organizations manage the change. Here are some salutary figures from Markides and Geroski (Creating new radical markets – The myth of first mover advantage, *Market Leader*, Spring 2004):

> *More than 70 firms rushed to enter the car business in the first 15 years of existence. In fact more than 1000 firms populated the industry at one time or another yet there were only 7 left by the late 1950s. Similarly there were more than 274 competitors in the market for tyres in the early 1920s, 50 years later no more than 23 survived. And from a peak of 89 competitors in the TV market in the 1950s, only a small handful of US owned producers survived at the end of the 1980s and none after 1995.*
>
> *Markides and Geroski*

The European car business is currently dominated by just five organizations and it is commonly believed that there is one too many. If you are currently working in industries such as telecoms, IT, financial services, satellite TV or grocery retailing (there may be others), you might want to start adding up the number of companies you currently compete with – and wonder if your organization will be one of the 'final five'.

Over the years, the *consolidation* is already happening in those industries that are approaching the end of their growth phase. A quick search of many websites will show the number and variety of firms that have been 'taken over' or 'merged' but certainly are already part of the failures to switch to market and customer focus.

Hewlett Packard =

- F.L. Moseley Company
- Sanborn Company
- F&M Scientific Corporation
- Tandem Computer
- Cupertino
- Digital Equipment Corporation
- Compaq
- Indigo.

The above list comes from http://www.HP.com, but the situation is by no means unique.

Table 2.1 shows what typical types of business and market activity will be associated with the different stages of the life cycle. This analysis is not new although I have updated it for this book. You can see how the necessary skills simply scale up between introduction and growth stages and between maturity and decline stages. At the same time, there is an unavoidable 'chasm' between the skills needed in growth and maturity. It is no wonder that so few organizations manage the transition.

Just to show that I too am willing to go out on a limb, Figure 2.8 contains the industries that I believe are in different stages of the PLC at the moment (UK 2006). Feel free to add your own. (I really am going to have to update this book more often than every ten years!)

Whether or not the exact positions are right, the trauma in store for those in the 'chasm' stage cannot be argued. We can already see the impact on these industries as a succession of new CEO/MDs struggle with how to deal with new problems by using the old tools. For a lot of organizations, by the time they realize that they need new (customer and market) solutions to solve the problems, it is just too late.

Table 2.1 The PLC and marketing activity

	Introduction	Growth	Maturity	Decline
Characteristics				
Sales	Low sales	Rapidly rising	Peak/static sales	Declining sales
Costs (per customer)	High cost	Average cost	Lower cost	Low cost
Profits	Negative	Rising am always consciousn am always conscious	High	Declining
Competitors	Few	Growing number	Declining rapidly	Declining to final few
Market objectives				
	Create awareness and trial	Maximize market share and hold	Maximize profits while defending selected market segments	Reduce expenditure, milk the brand or rejuvenate
Market(ing) strategy				
Segmentation/ targeting	Anyone who will listen	'Mass' market	Key to success, identify and differentiate	Focus on final segments
Customer	Innovators	Early adopters	Middle majority	Laggards
Offerings	New and basic	Better product, standard emerging	Differentiation of product and support services	Focused offering to remaining customers
Retention	Less important than initial sales	Sales growth key in growing business	Key activity by targeted segment	Decide when to abandon

(Continued)

Table 2.1 (*Continued*)

	Introduction	Growth	Maturity	Decline
Position/brand	Establish awareness	Establish position as key player	Establish brand as *unique* within smaller field	Focus brand on final specialization or rejuvenate
Industry or market?	New offer may not have industry definition	Industry definition for growth phase	Market definition essential for survival	Focused application definition
Organization	Small, entrepreneurial, start-up	Structured sales organization	Structured market and customer-focused organization	Smaller focused specialist organization
Market(ing) tactics				
Product	Basic product that early adopters will help perfect	Finished offer range with service and warranty	Differentiate, brand and focus on targeted segments only	Phase out weak items and focus on final versions
Price	Cost plus large margin	Reduce price to penetrate market	Increase price to differentiate offer from competitors	Cut price or increase price further to specialize
Place/distribution	Build selective distribution	Build intensive distribution	Build intensive and segment-focused distribution	Go selective: phase out unprofitable outlets
Promotion	Build product/service awareness and promote trial	Build awareness and interest in the mass market	Stress brand differences and benefits to targeted segments	Reduce to level needed to retain hard-core loyalists

Suppliers ←		Control		→ Customers	
Intro	**Growth**	**The 'chasm'**		**Maturity**	**Decline**
• WiFi • VoIP • Digital TV • Gene services • GPS • Space tourism • Functional food	• General practitioners (doctors) • Alternative medicine • Further education • Broadband internet • Call centres • Farmers' markets • Organic food • Home services	• Dentists • Lawyers • Veterinaries • IT hardware • IT software • Mobile telephony • Satellite TV • Financial services • Air travel • Grocery retailing		• Accountancy services • Retailing • Hotels • Consulting • Fixed line telephony • Banking • Pharmacists • Package holidays • Fast-moving consumer goods • Consumer durables	• Domestic laundry services • Home milk delivery • Manufacturing • Mass production • Local pubs

Figure 2.8 A rite of passage?

The questions for you and your organization then are quite straightforward:

● Where do you think you (and your industry) are on the product life cycle?

● If you are in the growth stage, how long (this is the difficult one) do you think you have before the market moves to maturity?

● Do you have the skills to succeed in maturity?

● Can you learn or acquire the skills you need?

● How much resistance will you face from senior management in the organization?

● Do the answers above suggest that you are working for one of the (few) survivors or one of the (many) impending casualties?

2.3.2 *Competition*

In order to survive (and flourish), an organization will not only have to learn to live with and profit from the constraints placed on it by its political, economic, sociological or technological environment, it will also have to learn how to deal with the specific rules, regulations and constraints placed on its activity by its membership of a specific industry. Porter in his book *Competitive Strategy* considers that competitors' strategy must grow out of a sophisticated understanding of the rules and competition that determine an industry's attractiveness. He goes on to describe five distinct competitive forces that will collectively determine the profitability of any industry – industry competitors, potential entrants, suppliers, buyers and substitutes. He suggests that together they influence, at the same time, the prices that the organization can charge, the costs that the organization is likely to incur as well as the required investments of the organization if it wishes to remain in that industry (Figure 2.9).

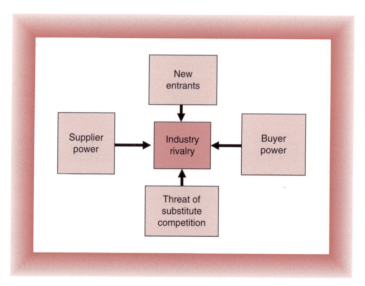

Figure 2.9   Porter's five forces of competition
Source: Adapted from Porter, M. (1980) *Competitive Strategy*. New York: Free Press.

While this view is, to my mind, too dominated by theoretical economics thinking (there are good examples of companies breaking away from industry-driven pricing by offering genuinely unique value to customers), Porter's description of competitive forces is a good one. We can use this classification as a convenient guide to understand how to analyse the industry background of an organization.

Industry competition

Before we consider industry analysis, a point should be made. How does the organization determine what industry (or business) that it is in – not as easy as it sounds? This point will be covered in more depth as part of the important SCORPIO model of market strategy (see Chapter 6).

An assessment of the actual competitors within a given industry is often as far as many, superficial analyses would take an organization. While it is important to understand who the organization's direct competitors in an industry are, it is not the only component to an industry and its long-term profitability. Specifically, as far as industry competitors are concerned, we should be especially concerned with the degree of rivalry that exists between them. Factors such as:

- The rate of growth of the industry;
- The amount of capacity that is considered 'spare' within the industry;
- Its general maturity in terms of image;
- Brand identity and differentiation among competitors; and importantly,
- The exit barriers (the costs needed to exit an industry can often be very, very high).

These factors, among others, will determine how much rivalry exists in the industry, the degree of competition and so the amount of time, money and effort that have to be invested by the organization in competing with its direct industry rivals.

Competition is expensive and can only be financed through profit. The degree of rivalry in an industry will determine the profits that can be extracted from the industry. The organization must decide for itself whether there is sufficient profit potential in the existing industry to meet the current and future needs of its shareholders.

New entrants
While we need to understand the capacities and the abilities of our direct competitors, this, on its own, is not enough. We need to look into the future and to try and see who might possibly want to (or try to) enter the industry as a new competitor. The key to understanding the new entrant threat to an industry will ultimately depend on our ability to assess (realistically) the barriers to entry that exist. For example, have existing players established significant economies of scale in production, marketing, advertising, etc. that would form an effective barrier to a new entrant? Are there specific strengths in brand awareness and brand loyalty in the marketplace? Do we have control over access to distribution? Do we, because of our existing position as an organization in the industry, have real cost advantages over new entrants?

In any discussion about entry barriers, the emphasis must always be on the words 'realistic assessment'. An effective barrier to entry does not exist purely and simply because we wish it to exist. Secondly, entry barriers are not always effective over the very long term. For example, UK banks used to think that an extensive (and expensive) branch network was a barrier to competitive entry – the advent of telephone banking soon changed that idea.

Too often new entrants can cause damage to an existing player simply because of the surprise factor. A history of operating in one sector can make managers believe that there is only one way of doing things and that only they can do it – bad mistake!

Substitutes

This is a *big problem* for many organizations. The whole question of substitute threat is often a very difficult one for the organization to grasp if it is not truly market oriented. There are really two areas in which substitutes can become a threat:

(1) *Product substitutes*: They are often driven by changes in cost structures or technological advance whereby the product or service itself is improved but not essentially changed in nature. Examples of these substitutes may be the progress from real ground coffee to instant coffee, the development of the electric carving knife or the move from black and white to colour TVs. The potential threat of these substitute products is normally quite easy to plot and depends largely on the relative price and performance of substitutes compared to the existing products and services offered as well as the buyers' willingness to change to the substitute offer. Easy to say, but iPod's arrival surprised Sony.

(2) *Benefit/solution substitutes*: The more difficult category of substitute to see, unless the organization (or at the very least the marketing director/vice-president) is in very close contact with the marketplace, is based on the concept that the market does not buy product or service *features*. What it buys is a package of *benefits* or specific *solutions* to a problem that it has. Naturally enough, there is more than one way of solving any problem. So we can see that from a customer perspective, shifting, say, from the department photocopier to individual printers alongside the personal computer is a simple movement to improve productivity. From the perspective of the maker of photocopiers, however, it looks like the world has come to an end – neither he nor any of his direct competitors are selling anything any more. And exactly the same thing has happened to carbon paper manufacturers, photographic film developers and electronic pager makers. On the positive side, companies such as Rolex (watches) and Waterman (pens) have successfully re-positioned themselves and now operate in different markets.

Suppliers

Another important competitive aspect of an industry, which will determine its attractiveness to the organization, is the bargaining power of suppliers to that industry. Here we need to know, who are the key suppliers? How concentrated is supply? Are there hundreds of organizations supplying to the industry or are there just two? How important are the volumes of the supplies to the industry, both in volume and in intrinsic value to the eventual output of the industry itself? How much of the total cost structure in the industry is represented by suppliers' margins?

These sorts of question should enable us to understand the strength of the suppliers and the bargaining power that they hold over the industry as a whole. Naturally, the stronger the power of the suppliers, the greater will be the threat of forward integration. In other words, the greater the threat of the suppliers entering the industry as an additional competitor, possibly with significant competitive advantage, if they have direct access to limited raw material supplies. An additional threat is that the more concentrated the supply aspect of the industry, the greater the risk that one or more of the competitive organizations in the industry might decide to involve itself in backward integration, in other words, buying back into the supply source which feeds the industry. This could place an organization at a competitive disadvantage and might influence its view on the long-term attractiveness of the industry itself.

Buyers

There are two separate aspects that can determine the degree of buyer power in any industry. They are:

(1) *The direct power of the buyers*: It is typified by situations where there are either relatively few buyers or where a fairly small number of the buyers tend to purchase a very large volume of the industry's output. This is typical in many industrial situations. But the situation is more evident in the distribution of packaged consumer goods; grocery distribution in the UK is highly concentrated into a small number of very large organizations. (By 2005, Tesco had reached the point where it accounted for £1 in every £8 spent in the UK – this brings a degree of purchasing power. As the supermarkets move from food to non-foods they spread their buyer power into different industries.) In such circumstances, the industry is at a disadvantage from concentrated buyer power. However, although the eventual exercising of that power will depend on a number of factors such as how important the industry's output (products or services) is to the actual buying unit, how easy it would be to switch from buying products from one industry to buying from another industry or indeed the availability and cost of substitute products and services. Of course, intermediary buyer power has its limitations especially if it is not considered by the end consumer as delivering the benefits required. A number of successful businesses have been started by dissatisfied consumers who, unable to find what they wanted, started their own business in competition. Such is (at least the stated) reason for the beginnings of The Gap, The Body Shop and Virgin Financial Services (Table 2.2).

(2) *The degree of price sensitivity which exists in the marketplace*: This is what economists call elasticity of demand. In other words, the freedom which the industry has to increase its prices and the effect any price increase will have on demand, and ultimately, sales. The economist's concept of a straightforward price/quantity/demand relationship is, although effectively correct, much too simplistic for today's modern market(ing) environment. The relationship between price and quantity demanded can easily be distorted by elements such as brand loyalty, product differences and differentiation and

Table 2.2   Market share (%) of
the top five supermarkets (2005)

France	65
Switzerland	62
UK	59
Belgium	54
Portugal	49
Netherlands	47
Spain	47
Germany	46

customers' perception of quality versus performance and price. However, although elements such as brand loyalty and product differentiation can increase potential profits for the industry, these require significant investment to establish in the marketplace.

Conclusions

As Porter points out, the strength of the 'five forces' can vary from industry to industry and they can change as an industry evolves over time. The net result is that all industries are not alike as far as profitability (and so attractiveness) is concerned. There will be some industries where all of the forces could be considered favourable. In these conditions, all or most of the organizations within the industry will be flourishing and will be attracting average or above-average returns on their investment (and new entrants will be attracted). At the same time, there will be other industries where all or most of the forces will be unfavourable and in these instances, despite the best endeavours of management, profitability will be less attractive (and existing players may be looking to exit the industry).

Most importantly, managers must realize that even if all the forces are favourable at the moment, the future is not guaranteed and the direction and influence of these forces can (and will) change over time.

2.3.3   Structural opportunities

Industries will vary from one to another as the strengths of the five competitive forces differ. The reason for this is largely because of the different market(ing)–economic and production–technical characteristics which underlie each different industry. These important characteristics are known as the industry structure.

The organization has the power, through the business strategies that it chooses, to influence the structure of the industry within which it operates. As every industry is different, the relative importance of the five forces will also be different from industry to industry. So an organization need not necessarily worry about influencing each and every force but may decide to concentrate its effort on one or two to maximize its effect in the organization's favour. It would be difficult here to explore in depth all of the possible structural opportunities open to the organization but a few examples may serve to illustrate the point:

(1) *Industry competition*: There are instances where competing organizations have grouped together to mount collaborative generic advertising and promotional campaigns with the aim of expanding the total market size. Increased market size obviously reduces the intensity of direct competition as there is a larger market to fight over. On the down side, there is the question of a larger market acting as a magnet for outside organizations unless entry barriers are high. Collaboration such as this has been used in Europe in industries such as insurance, shock absorbers and beef.

(2) *New entrants*: Can be combated by building significant (and durable) entry barriers. Market(ing) barriers in terms of brand loyalty and product differentiation can be very effective but tend to take time to construct and are also quite investment hungry. Other methods include lobbying government for protection of the industry or, perhaps through increased specialization, driving down the unit cost of production to a level which inhibits new entrants. But beware; technical barriers are often at the mercy of quantum technical leaps – which overnight can make a very expensive barrier obsolete. (Just imagine how the lowest cost producer of radio valves must have felt when the transistor came along. And the transistor producer when the chip came along. And next ... ?)

(3) *Substitution*: Here it pays (*big*) dividends to keep in very close contact with your customers. Change may not be possible if too many people in your organization would rather die than change – a surprisingly popular competitive response I have found! Substitutes need not necessarily be a threat to the industry or our position – especially if we are the organization marketing the substitute.

(4) *Supplier power*: There are two ways of dealing with the problem: attempt to negate the power of certain suppliers by locating alternative sources of supply and take advantage of the possibly concentrated supply situation by integrating backwards into the supply end of the industry.

(5) *Buyer power*: This falls into two broad categories. The first is concentrated power that comes from either a small number of buyers or a smaller number of very large volume buyers – either further concentrate the purchase activity of the industry to create equal strength to the buyers or the product or service scope could be broadened to encourage new buyers into the industry and thereby reduce the power of the primary buyers. The second category of buyer power is price sensitivity, and the most obvious solution is to build

strength on brand awareness, product differentiation and loyalty in the marketplace. This is a high-cost, long-term solution but should deliver better prices, margins and so, profits. Major packaged goods producers such as Heinz and Kellogg use this approach successfully. As do B2B organizations such as JCB, Accenture and Rolls-Royce engines.

If the organization is able to change and mould the structure of the industry in which it operates, this can then change the fundamental attractiveness of the industry for better – and for worse. What is happening here is that the rules of competition within the industry are being changed. Unfortunately, organizations have been known to make strategic choices of this kind without due consideration of the long-term consequences for the industry structure. Any action, as the law of physics tells us, will elicit a reaction. An organization which makes a strategic choice and approaches what it sees to be a structural opportunity considering only its own potential gain in the short to medium term may generate competitive reaction of such a nature that the whole structure of the industry is altered over the longer term to make competition even harsher and profits even more scarce. In fact, this chain of action–reaction may even produce an industry where everybody is worse off at the end of the day. Nothing causes quite as much devastation as a misguided organization starting a price war without thinking of the consequences. Competitive reaction is an immensely potent force.

2.3.4   *The resource/performance audit*

A resource audit (Figure 2.10) is another of those grand titles, which serves to disguise the existence of a very simple question – what are the capabilities of the organization?

A practical strategy is one that is achievable.

While an organization may wish to achieve certain goals, wishing (on its own) is unlikely to be enough. The organization must have the resources and the capability to achieve those objectives. For example, the Principality of Monaco may wish to be a leader in satellite communications technology; it may even do their economy some good, but it is patently clear that with the resources currently at their disposal this is likely to remain a wish and is not a realistic objective.

When we are considering the resource audit, the simplest approach is for the organization to break down its resources under the four traditional headings – land, labour, capital and enterprise.

Land (physical resource)
Under this heading, the organization should consider its resources such as production facilities and capacity (factories, locations, output capacities, flexibility of production lines, methodologies, age of the plant, recent levels of investment) if it is

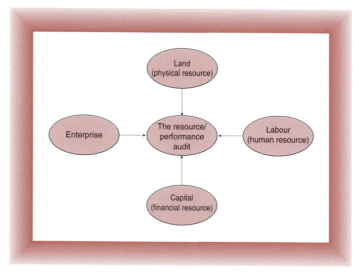

Figure 2.10   The resource audit

a manufacturing business; and space (office space, flexibility of use, the number of retail or other outlets, access points for customers, delivery trucks, rolling stock, mechanized plant and equipment) if it is in the service business. We should have a clear understanding of exactly what the organization can deliver to the marketplace and precisely what delivery levels would be impractical, at least in the short to medium term. In the medium to longer term, constraints may be overcome by building up resources or by buying in additional resource. Strategic alliances to support key strengths might also be considered.

Labour (human resource)

Labour is another simplified term that we use to cover all forms of human resource open to the organization. We are concerned with both manual and mental labour (if such a distinction is still valid today). The organization needs to know how flexible its human resource is to meet the new challenges that the strategy may place on it. We would need to consider aspects such as industrial relations, training and management development, skills base, internal communications as well as organization culture and morale.

There are also specific questions that the organization should be asking about its top and middle management capabilities. How good are they? How responsive is management to change? How competitive in nature? How independent and how needing of guidance/control? The more competitive nature of international and domestic business environments since the 1980s (you would think that after twenty-five years we would have got the hang of this, wouldn't you) continues to expose certain deficiencies in top management, both in Europe and in North America.

- When the small and medium-sized organizations from the industrial revolution started to expand and take advantage of the economies of scale, in the 1940s and 1950s, the 'large', structured systems seemed to be the order of the day.

- These big industrial combines were organized along military lines and, size being the competitive advantage, 'command and control' middle management mushroomed.

- With ever-growing international competition, technology and the demise of the 'mass market' both working to remove the advantage of scale and rapidly reducing life cycles, the traditionally conservative and change-resistant middle management have outlived their usefulness.

- Multiple layers of middle management have, however, been surprisingly difficult to remove in the UK, Europe and the USA.

- Managers who have risen due to their ability to manage organizations in a stable environment have very little expertise or experience running organizations in more turbulent periods.

- If the top and senior middle management structure is made up of people who have 'come up through the ranks', these may not be the best people to see you into even more turbulent times.

- Managers in positions of power today probably rose to their positions by being good at what the organization needed and valued in the past. These skills may not be as valued today. These managers may not see the value in today's skills.

Today, most organizations need managers who can act as well as manage and who are able to work with a degree of initiative when facing unfamiliar market situations. It is simply not true that no decision is better than a bad decision. The markets of the twenty-first century will demand managers to make quicker decisions under ever-increasing pressure, with fewer staff. The organization that does not have, or cannot groom, managers such as these may soon be at a severe competitive disadvantage.

Although we will be dealing with the subject in much more depth later on (see Chapter 6), the whole vexed question of organization structure falls into this category too. At this stage, it is probably sufficient to note that an organization's structure (including its reward mechanisms and administrative processes) will have a major effect on what actions it *can* take in the marketplace. In too many cases, organizations are unable to survive simply because the structure is too rigid and change resistant to allow managers and staff to deliver on its customers' needs. Commercial Darwinism at its most brutal!

Capital (financial resource)
This category refers to the financial muscle called for in a market(ing) strategy. Whether the strategy eventually calls for consolidation, redirection, head-to-head

competition or the erection of barriers to entry to your marketplace, the costs are already high and are getting higher. Financial strength is no guarantee of long-term survival, but it helps. Naturally, the eventual strategy for the organization must be formulated within the confines of the finances that the organization either has or is able to access.

Strategic decisions call for strategic capital. It is as important that the organization attracts the right kind of finance – not just enough. Banks and capital markets always have enough money but it comes with strings attached; financial support from promiscuous investors can put the wrong kinds of pressure on an organization. Short-term returns can always be provided by an organization but one of the other stakeholders will have to bear the cost. If the costs are not equally shared over the long term, strategy cannot be implemented.

Enterprise
This last category covers the whole area of creativity and business acumen needed to survive in competitive marketplaces. Although market(ing) ought to typify the enterprise concept, it has no monopoly over the area. In simple terms, enterprise is the collection of ideas, new thoughts and drive required by an organization if it is going to continue to grow, change and flourish in the years ahead.

We will be looking at this question in more detail when we consider the implementation of market(ing) strategy in Part Three, but at this point it is worth noting that the behaviour of individuals inside an organization is very largely dictated by the organization structure and culture. The structure of the organization, its processes, reporting systems, reward systems, implicit and explicit culture and its communications all serve to spell out to people what behaviours are valued and will guarantee progress within the system. These structures and systems have often evolved, over time, to meet the needs of the organization itself rather than its customers (I'm sorry, it must be said!). In many markets, customer needs tend to evolve faster than organizations' ability to keep up and, over time, an organization may find itself unable to serve its customers as well as it did in the past. Creating the degree of internal change necessary to continue to meet customer needs is extremely difficult – the organization will actively resist it, preferring the life it knows and a falling order book to an unknown future (see Chapter 6). The capacity of the system to *not see* what is going on outside its walls can be astounding.

Once the organization has considered these four areas individually, it is important that the four views be put together and a suitable balance found across all four aspects of the resource audit. *All four* elements are required if the organization is to have a future. We can all think of good examples of organizations that have been perhaps flush with money but have had no good ideas into which to invest (GEC–UK would be a good (pre dot-com) example of this and of course the heady years of the dot-com boom provided us with just too many examples to quote). There are also the young thrusting organizations full of new ideas and revolutionary thoughts but with little or no capital to back them up. These are regularly snapped up by the larger organizations, who find it easier to buy in ideas than invest in their own research and development. More worryingly, there are scores of examples where the creative West has generated ideas, which in the absence of sufficient *patient* capital have gone to the Far East where they have been successfully modified and marketed.

2.4   Strengths and weaknesses

> Nothing is more arrogant than the weakness which feels itself supported by power.
>
> *Napoleon Bonaparte*

Falling straight out of the resource audit, the organization should now be in a situation to identify its particular strengths and its potential weaknesses. The idea is, of course, that the eventual strategy will be one that exploits the organization's strengths and protects its weaknesses. I know it seems obvious to play it this way round but I have met and worked with companies who:

- Didn't like the strengths that the market said they had;

- Believed they had strengths – that the market did not see or believe;

- Insisted that they had no weaknesses at all;

- Would only produce plans for doing what they had always done/what they had told the parent company they would do;

- Incentivized the sales force to sell more of what customers wanted least and lost them most money.Ah, the joys of 'rational' management theory (Figure 2.11).

It is, of course, inevitable that an organization will start looking at its strengths and weaknesses through internally focused eyes; that is essentially what the resource audit is all about. Nevertheless, it is important to realize that *a strength is really only a strength if the target customers perceive it to be so.* This is not always an easy idea to grasp, shut away as most managers are from paying customers.

First, the basics, just so we have the data in the book:

(1) Strengths and weaknesses are 'internal' issues and are therefore 'controllable' by the organization – you are supposed to be able to do something about these.

(2) Opportunities and threats are 'external' to the organization and therefore 'beyond the control' of the organization – you have to work with these two.

(Internal/controllable)	(External/uncontrollable)
Strengths 1 2 3 4 5 6	Opportunities 1 2 3 4 5 6
Weaknesses 1 2 3 4 5 6	Threats 1 2 3 4 5 6

Figure 2.11 *SWOT* analysis (1)

(3) Strengths are strengths that your target customers believe you have.

(4) Weaknesses are weaknesses that your target customers believe you have.

(5) You should not attempt to list every single issue under each heading, just the (six?) most important ones.

(6) Every time I do this, the weaknesses list is at least twice as long as the strengths list – customers are more forgiving than this and of course don't see all that you get wrong!

(7) The objective is *not* to list all the most important issues under each heading and then put the analysis away in a desk drawer. This is *not* an annual event that has no value. The SWOT analysis will *not* affect anyone in the organization, by osmosis, from the desk drawer or the 'word' file.

(8) The objective is *to do something* with the results of the analysis.

Let's look at a few examples. Budget providers of services such as car insurance (Direct Line, Churchill, etc.) and air travel (Easyjet, Ryanair, Flybe, etc.) package their offers carefully so that they 'look' cheaper than the traditional providers. It should be clear to anyone though that it just isn't possible to offer these services at prices that are so different. If you wish to travel to Brussels with Ryanair – and you really believe that Charlroi is a suburb of Brussels rather than sixty miles away in a bus – then it looks very cheap. Scheduled carriers also have some plans for customer care and, in the event of cancelled flights, have some budget to look after their stranded customers; Easyjet customers are told to go home and come back tomorrow. If there are circumstances that make your planned flight impossible, scheduled carriers will try and change bookings or make partial refunds; Flybe customers are told that 'we have a no refund policy' and the customer loses all the money – no discussions. You only have to hit one of these problems every five years (what are the chances of that?) to negate all the 'savings' you have made in the meantime. Luckily for the 'low-cost' operators, their customers tend not to look too deeply at the offer or what might happen and *act* as if the offer is cheaper. The traditional providers have found it difficult to appeal to reason, so have had to copy some of the techniques employed by the 'low-cost' operators; their target customers simply did not believe that customer service was a strength to justify the additional price – BA's cutting too many service staff at the busiest times didn't help this perception either. BA's control of its London hub (Heathrow) is seen as a strength, however, as is KLM's control of its Amsterdam hub (Schiphol).

I have no problem with the organization identifying what it believes (wants, hopes) to be its strengths, but this is not information, it is 'data'. If the organization does not check its hopes and beliefs with the people who pay (customers), it runs the risk of squandering enormous amounts of money and time developing offers that make no sense (to customers), investing in differentiation that makes no sense (to customers) supported by communications that make no sense (to customers), so making no profits. The organization's beliefs must be tested in the marketplace to find out, clearly, whether the customers agree. If they do not agree, all is not lost – at least for the adaptive and flexible company. The choice now is to build on the strengths that the customers believe we have (even if we don't believe it) or doggedly attempt to change the customers' beliefs about the strengths and convince them that we have different strengths from what they understand. Much depends obviously on what the beliefs are but you should remember that:

- Customers believe what they believe.
- Customers' beliefs and attitudes are not formed or changed overnight.
- Customers will not change what they believe just because you say so; they may want to experience the difference for themselves.
- Customers may not be attracted to what you want them to believe about your offering.
- This is starting to sound expensive.

When you help to put together the strengths and weaknesses analysis for your organization you should remember one thing: it pays to be honest – no matter whose feelings you might hurt. The organization may not be able to deal with an honest assessment of its strengths and weaknesses but a simple re-statement of conventional wisdom does no good at all. Restrict circulation of the analysis to preserve morale if you must – but be honest with yourselves. A practical strategy demands it.

Finally, what should you be doing with the analysis?

A *quick* test here is to use the so-called 'convergence arrows'. This is a way of assessing the final strategy/market(ing) plans to see if the environmental (SWOT) analysis has been used or whether it is no more than a planning ritual. The three traditional arrows inserted into Figure 2.12 show the three (really powerful but

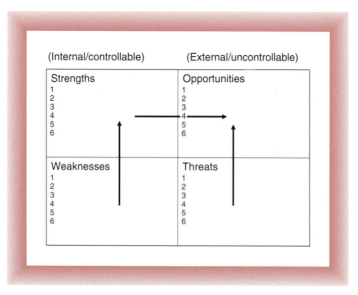

Figure 2.12　*SWOT* analysis (2)

annoying) questions you should ask of the final plans. So bear these in mind when you are doing the analysis:

(1) *Weaknesses → strengths*: How can you (plan to) turn weaknesses into strengths? The traditional skill here is to turn a 'limited' offer into a 'specialist' one. One of the oldest examples must be Avis car rental, who could (at the time) not challenge the power of the market leader (Hertz), so made a strength out of the fact that being 'Number Two' meant that they had to try harder so would give better service. More recently, in the UK we have seen building societies that are too small to turn into banks making a case out of *not* changing and appearing to offer more customer value as a result.

(2) *Threats → opportunities*: How can you turn a threat into an opportunity? Recent EU legislation on recycling has shown how the fastest movers can make their

offerings different from slower competitors. Also, external 'threats' such as legislation, de-regulation, Internet and technology and fashion have helped many organizations change by presenting *big* shifts in market conditions that they can respond to. Often it is the small but relentless changes that provide the most danger because the managers just don't see them until it's too late.

(3) *Strengths* → *opportunities*: How can we focus our strengths on to the opportunities? You thought that this would happen automatically, well ... Once you have agreed them focus the strengths where they will do most good. There is no point directing weaknesses at opportunities or even strengths at threats. But you would be amazed.

2.5   Competitor analysis

> If I always appear prepared, it is because before entering an undertaking, I have meditated long and have foreseen what might occur. It is not genius which reveals to me suddenly and secretly what I should do in circumstances unexpected by others; it is thought and preparation.
>
> *Napoleon Bonaparte*

It is a truism to say that we all need to understand our competitors better than we do at the moment. But before you nod sagely and add yet another mental note to the pile of things that you really ought to do as soon as you get time, let's try and understand exactly why it is so important to uncover what our competitors are trying to do in the marketplace. We must look at the whole problem from the customer's point of view (revolutionary I know but you said you didn't want to be mediocre).

We have also seen that 'competitor' means much more than just the organizations that we compete with (direct competition) in our own industry. Porter's 'five forces' model (see Section 2.3) puts much store by understanding the four other sources of competition.

Regardless of what your organization produces, as soon as you make an offering to the marketplace what's the first thing the customer is going to do? Compare! As much as we would like to believe that our customer is a rational, decision-making being, potential buyers, industrial as well as consumer, are simply not used to making decisions in a vacuum. In order to judge the benefits of your offering and the claims that you make, their first step is always going to be to compare your offering to an alternative offering made by an organization they *believe* to be a competitor. Although we all know this is what happens, it's surprising the number of organizations that operate as if in a vacuum and as if they were the only possible choice in the market. We also know that nothing galvanizes an organization into action better than something new being marketed by an active competitor. We might wish it otherwise, but the bulk of innovation in industry and commerce is in fact stimulated by competitor activity rather than customer need.

One word of warning before we look in slightly more detail about the best way of getting to understand your competitors and trying to predict how they would like you to react in any given circumstances. We can all agree that competitor analysis is a 'good thing', but you can sometimes have too much of a good thing. Competitor analysis is the main area where many of the comparisons between business and military warfare start to fall down. In the military analogy, the objective of the opposing forces is to overcome the enemy; in business terms, the objective is to capture as many of the customers (perhaps in the military analogy these would be the innocent bystanders), at the expense of the competition. While few organizations really have enough information and understanding of how their competitors operate, it would be difficult to justify additional resources to this area if they were to be at the expense of acquiring a deeper understanding of our target customers.

This said, how could we go about developing an understanding of our competitors and then use this in developing our strategic approach? Most organizations have a database (of sorts) on competitors' capabilities and activities. Although this information is often gathered in an ad hoc manner from meetings, second-hand sources such as customers and intermediaries, or perhaps from the sales force, very few organizations collect competitive data in a systematic manner. It is, of course, the systematic process carried out over a longer period of time that tends to develop a better understanding of our competitors' ambitions and capabilities. The entire competitor analysis process should be designed to build a 'response model' for each competitor that we face. This 'response model' is important in the development of our business and market strategy because it should help to assess any possible change in policy or strategic direction for the likely competitive response it will provoke. So we concentrate on the ultimate effects of our policy or strategic change in the marketplace – where it really matters.

There are two separate aspects to competitor analysis. The first is 'data' that is easier to collect; the second is 'information' that is more useful to developing an understanding of our competitors. The first area of analysis concerns what the competitor is currently doing and what (in our opinion) it is able to do. There are three questions to be answered here (again for each competitor):

(1) What is the competitor's current strategy?

(2) How is the competitor currently competing with our organization?

(3) What are the competitor's capabilities?

The first two questions are necessarily linked, and intelligent observation of the competitor's activity in the marketplace is often enough, especially if linked with published material such as annual reports, press commentaries, etc. to work out the competitor's most likely strategy in its approach to its markets. The last question – that of the competitor's capabilities – is deceptively simple. As you have already seen from looking at your own strengths and weaknesses, the important questions are not what you may believe your competitors' strengths and weaknesses to be but more importantly what the customers believe the competitors' strengths and weaknesses to be. Hence there may be two aspects to this information gathering: one, our observation of the competitors and two, some form of market research among our common customers.

The second important area of competitor analysis is concerned with what drives their organization, in other words, what has motivated it in the past to act the way it has and what do we believe to be the motivations behind the organization which may influence its activities in the future? There are two important questions in this section. Both are equally difficult to answer:

(1) What are the future goals of the competitor and of its management?

(2) What are the assumptions that the competitor and its management hold about themselves and the industry in which they operate?

While these questions are undoubtedly more difficult to answer than the previous ones, it is, of course, the motivational aspects of the competitor that will provide us with a far better key to understanding a competitor's most likely future behaviour.

As I have already said, competitor analysis is not just about rushing off, beavering away for the next three to four months acquiring some information and then leaving it at that. It is a question of developing a systematic approach to the gathering of information over a longer period of time (see Chapter 6). It is unlikely that anything as complex as an organization of individual managers and staff is going to be satisfactorily assessed within a short period. We need a slow, gradual buildup over time to develop a clearer picture – each successive piece of paper joins the rest and builds up more of a workable profile of the competitive organization and its key implementers.

A final note: if you have worked through this section with only your direct competitors in mind, then you have left yourself and your organization open and vulnerable. In the previous section, we considered the nature of competition and the 'five forces' of competition described by Porter. Any competitor information system worth the investment must take into account the full range of competition facing the business. After all, it's no use creating an entire department to tell you what your biggest direct competitor is planning to do next year if your market share can be halved by the entry of a substitute product or service that slipped in unseen.

2.5.1 *Competitive opportunities*

Once we have managed to create and maintain a regular data-gathering system that builds up a fuller and fuller profile of the major competitors, what should we be looking to do with it? More precisely, what competitive opportunities are there for our organization?

So far in this section, we've looked at the resource and performance audit of the organization, the environment audit, the analysis of the industry and structural opportunities which may exist for our organization. Finally we are considering the competitive situation. None of these elements on their own are sufficient to construct a strategy for the organization but taken together a picture slowly should start to appear of the range of strategic opportunities that could be open to us. Now, bearing in mind (1) our own internal capabilities, (2) the broad macro environment in which we operate, (3) the structural opportunities that exist within the five competitive force framework of the industry, we need to look closely at our competition before attempting to decide what is possible and what is not.

Once the database (for the technophobes here I am just as happy to mean a ring binder with assorted price lists, brochures and press clippings for each competitor) has started to build, we should be able to answer a number of questions that are important inputs for our strategic decision-making. For example, it should start to become clear in time whether a given competitor appears to be satisfied with its current position in the industry and marketplace. If the competitor seems satisfied we can expect that it will be looking to maintain its position rather than grow. However, we can also assume that it might mass its resources against any likely threat of activity within the industry to reduce its power. Retaliation could be a major threat.

A better understanding of our competitors will also enable us to understand what likely moves they will make in the industry. What segments they are particularly interested in and where they see their future and the types of market they would like to penetrate?

We would also expect to build up a picture of where a competitor is particularly vulnerable to any attack, not, of course, that this means that we would instantly pile in with a major frontal assault, rather this information would need to be aggregated with our better understanding of the industry and its likely stability and structural makeup. It is a good idea to control any 'action-man' managers at this point because hasty action could result in a net loss of market share and profits – a blood bath might be fun but it is bad for business.

Last, but no less important, the competitor analysis might enable us to identify what action of ours could provoke the greatest reaction from any given competitor. Here I come back to one of my opening statements – the primary aim for any organization must be to win and keep profitable customers. Straightforward, bloody, head-to-head feuds are not the aim of the organization (or rather it shouldn't be). While competition itself *may* bring certain benefits to the customer, for the organization it is an extremely wasteful and expensive exercise. An understanding of any likely retaliation should permit us to sift through different strategic alternatives and to choose those activities that will produce the maximum return. The alternative to proper competitor analysis in this instance may very well be in the design of an elegant strategy aimed to make maximum penetration into a new marketplace, which results only in massive retaliation from one or more competitor. The entire market(ing) thrust can be transformed into a fruitless exercise of organization-to-organization competition with no guarantee of marketplace advance for any player.

2.6   Assessing our current position – a conclusion

> In these days the invention of printing, and the diffusion of knowledge, render historical calumnies a little less dangerous: Truth will always prevail in the long run, but how slow its progress!
>
> *Napoleon Bonaparte*

I am always conscious that quietly gathering data and compiling facts is somehow not as satisfying as actually designing a new product, developing a new advertising campaign or even entering a virgin market. It's like preparing the walls before you slap on a new coat of paint, if you don't get the preparation right, the new paint doesn't stay on the walls for long. Just because it's not as interesting doesn't mean it is any less important to the overall success of your plans. Remember that you have to know where you are as well as where you want to be before you can plot the route between the two (Figure 2.13).

Nothing is quite as simple as this but still it's useful to remember how obvious the task ought to be!

In working through the whole range of data-gathering exercises that the organization should (at least) be considering, I have tried to break down the operation into its main component parts. At the same time, I have tried to explain the reasons why each piece of data is going to be important for the eventual strategy/direction of the organization.

In this data-gathering stage, as with any form of data collection or research, you must bear in mind that data gathering is a *means* – not an *end* in itself. Before embarking on the process, the organization must clearly understand exactly what it needs to know and, more important, exactly what it wants to do with the results of the analysis once they are available. To use some jargon here, the entire

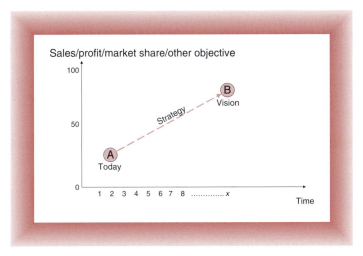

Figure 2.13 Strategy made (too) simple

approach needs to be 'output oriented'. In short, the organization needs to develop a long-term business objective, a business strategy and a robust market strategy that will reduce the threats to its existence over the medium to long term. Whether the strategy is tight, scientific and planned or whether it is loose and flexible depends on the nature of the organization and its marketplace. In any event, there must be, at the very least, a sense of direction.

The nature and complexity of the decisions that we have to make will depend on the nature and complexity of the organization, its markets, its industry and the unique competitive situation that it faces. We need to understand what these factors are, how important they are and how they impinge on the organization if we are to establish our existing position and so have even the vaguest idea of how to set forward from here.

The strategic analyst should be as ruthless in his rejection of unnecessary data as he or she will be in the collection of vital information.

When putting together an outline of the data-gathering process, as I have tried to do above, I have been aware that not all the elements explained will be of equal importance to every organization as every organization is different and every competitive situation is unique. Your organization will need to decide for itself which are the most important factors to consider and which are relatively less important. The route above is only a guide and it is not a blueprint that should be followed slavishly.

Also, a word on 'research'. We talk about research but we don't necessarily mean spending lots of money, getting agencies in or generally *wasting time while we have a business to run.* Depending on the size of the organization, it may mean that someone spends a few hours a week looking at the trade press and the Internet and pasting interesting news into a file, or just 'being' the person everyone knows to send the interesting stuff to when they stumble over it. Just seeing the word 'research' and saying this is only for the big companies is plainly nonsense, and preferring to shoot from the hip is plainly dangerous. We don't want to be mediocre – or dead.

So what about the results? Once the data has been collected it needs to be transformed into information. In other words, it needs to communicate something useful to an audience of people who will have to make decisions based on it. By definition, and specifically in the area of strategy, information is *not* communicated in reports of an inch thick or more. If the entire purpose of the exercise is to facilitate decision-making, then the important aspects should be communicated in the minimum of space. Although it is little more than a rule of thumb, I always suggest that the outputs of this process should be reduced down to approximately one side of the paper for each of the following:

● The resource/performance audit;

● The environment audit;

● The industry analysis;

● One side of the paper for each individual competitor analysis.

At the end of every sheet, there should be a clear section that highlights precise implications for our own organization. This is the 'so what factor'. You might very well find that rendering down a mountain of data into one sheet becomes the most challenging aspect of the whole process. But remember, if you can manage to get the whole complicated problem down to half a dozen or so key bullet points, then you might just have a chance of properly explaining it to others.

There is also a saying that if you can't get it down to one page, you probably don't understand it yourself.

I would make one final point on this important stage in the evolution of the organization's strategy, which is that this project should not be viewed as either a one-off exercise or even an annual ritual. We, and all of our organizations, have to live in a dynamic environment. Nothing stands still and the only constant that we can count on (apart from death and taxes) is change. Also, no model that hopes to predict the future can ever be right. The only thing we attempt to do through the effort spent on predicting is to minimize the error between what we expect and what will actually happen. For these two reasons, the data-gathering activity (and, of course, this is only *one* way of approaching the problem) should really be viewed as the start of a complete 'management information system' (see Chapter 6). In other words, this should be a constant and regular activity to be carried out on behalf of the organization. Someone, at least, should be in charge of constantly monitoring the industry, the environment and our most important competitors and likely future players in the marketplace. Regular data gathering and regular reporting to the decision makers, even if the reports show no change against forecast activity, will itself be an addition to the knowledge held by those managers responsible for plotting the future course of the organization and will add further weight to the plans that they devise.

There is one final warning for the small minority of you who actually found the preceding section exciting. I reiterate my warning about research generally being about ends – not means. There is always the risk, especially in larger organizations, of the research function/activity starting to take on a life of its own. As soon as this happens, extra resources are brought into play and, if we are not careful, research and analysis starts to take place that is not needed for the strategy but rather to justify the continued existence of the research function itself. This situation is extremely dangerous and should be rooted out as soon as possible.

The next stage of the problem is analysis. By its very nature, the type of data gathering with which we have been concerned is subjective in nature. It will be heavily dependent on a relatively small number of 'expert' opinions and views on the structure of the industry, the likely forward progression of various competitors and assessments of strengths and weaknesses (both ours and the competitors). This type of inherently biased subjective information will not really warrant too much quantitative analysis. Qualitative data of this nature will not support quantitative and analytical techniques, so beware the 'spurious accuracy' that such techniques can bring.

3 The business strategy

Strategy is the art of making use of time and space. I am less concerned about the latter than the former. Space we can recover, lost time never.

Napoleon Bonaparte

We have spent some time considering what the organization is able to do, what opportunities exist for the organization in the industry and marketplace and what threats are apparent in the environment. We have also looked at the 'hurdles' the organization must jump in terms of its long-term financial objective. We have also considered the personal ambitions and values of the key implementers or the most senior management team in the organization.

We are still in the 'where are we now' part of the book, which for the market(ing) strategist means that business/corporate strategy is a given that is required for the development of market(ing) strategy. Lest there be any confusion, *business/corporate strategy and market strategy are not the same thing*. Therefore, before we launch straight into a discussion about business strategy, a word about the emphasis of this book. The primary thrust of this work is to strip away some of the misconceptions about market(ing) strategy, that is, after all, why you bought it in the first place – that, and I hope, a strong desire not to cowed by the mediocrity of the business herd.

This is not intended to be a book on business/corporate strategy. To be honest, I start this chapter with a degree of trepidation – business/corporate strategy is a vast and complicated area and everyone in the organization wants to be involved. The debate was started by Ansoff (Strategies for diversification, *Harvard Business Review*, 1957), popularized by Porter (in the 1980s), widened by Mintzberg (in the 1990s) and now you have to beat off the strategy gurus with a large stick. A book on practical market(ing) strategy is not the place to add fuel to these particular fires, so we will try to understand business/corporate strategy as far as it is able to help us in the customer, market(ing) and profit areas.

Assuming you have been following the general flow of the book this far and that you haven't jumped straight to this section in the hope of finding some instant miracle cure to the ills that have been dogging your organization for the past twenty-five years, you might just have enough understanding about your organization to start working on the business objective for the future.

In short, we should now have a fairly clear idea of:

- Where we are now;
- Why we are where we are;
- What we are capable of doing;
- What we face in the outside environment;
- What we are going to do about it.

See strategy checklist in the Appendix.

The next job for the organization is to agree to the business/corporate objective. Again, this is not necessarily a job for the market(ing) specialist but for the managing director/general manager in consultation with the strategic team and the key implementers. Nevertheless, the organization needs a clear objective in order to be able to set its own (market) objective and, if a clear overall objective for the organization is not specifically stated, some sort of hypothesis will have to be made. Although the development and agreement of an overall business objective for the organization is never an easy exercise, it is essential.

Business strategy (Figure 3.1) is important in that it provides the key to the development of the market(ing) strategy. The organization must understand the business strategy concepts and their effects on the market(ing) strategy process; we will look at Porter's ideas and how they influenced business in the 1980s. It goes without saying that anybody seriously interested in strategy has already read Porter, so the following sections will be little more than a reminder of the key points, but from a customer/market point of view.

With the benefit of hindsight we will also look at some more recent ideas of business/corporate strategy and what these might promise for the future.

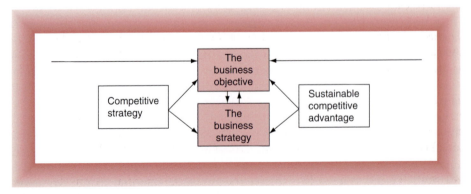

Figure 3.1 The business strategy

Before we can begin to discuss market strategy proper, we need certain minimum data on which to build our plans. To develop the market(ing) strategy, we need:

- A review of the environment within which we must operate;
- A definition of what business the organization is in – and wants/needs to be in (see Chapter 6);
- The financial hurdles that the organization must jump;
- The organization's business/corporate objective;
- The organization's business/corporate strategy.

3.1 The financial hurdles

> Men soon get tired of shedding their blood for the advantage of a few individuals, who think they amply reward the soldiers' perils with the treasures they amass.
>
> *Napoleon Bonaparte*

Every organization has one or more 'financial imperatives' that it must satisfy to remain in business. These are not the same as objectives. These 'hurdles' just need to be seen, measured and *jumped*. They should *not* guide the destiny of the organization (see Section 1.4).

Yes, I know – and the finance director shouts a lot and everybody else does seem to accept that $x\%$ increase in ROI is a normal 'business objective' but that doesn't make it right. Financial targets are just hurdles that we have to jump – but that changes nothing. To make more money, we need to focus, not on money but on the business/customer purpose that makes it possible.

The use of the word 'hurdle' is deliberate (Figure 3.2). You remember the hurdles race at school or at the Olympics? Well, you must also remember that the winner is the one that gets to the finishing line first.

The first one over the line wins. The hurdles are just things in the way that you have to jump over to get to the winning post. There are no prizes for how neatly the hurdles are jumped or how high or how fast or even how many are touched or knocked down. All this is irrelevant. So it is with financial hurdles.

All you have to do is to make sure that the minimum financial returns demanded by the shareholders are achieved. Generally (there are some exceptions such as

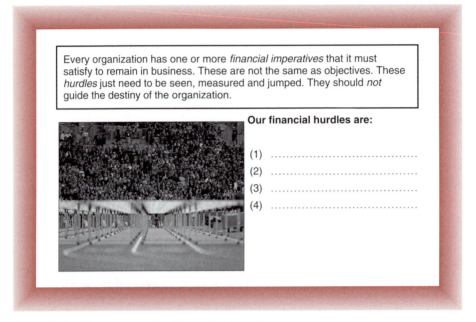

Every organization has one or more *financial imperatives* that it must satisfy to remain in business. These are not the same as objectives. These *hurdles* just need to be seen, measured and jumped. They should *not* guide the destiny of the organization.

Our financial hurdles are:

(1) ....
(2) ....
(3) ....
(4) ....

Figure 3.2   First, agree the financial *hurdles*

environmental or green shareholder requirements) shareholders are not concerned with how you jump over the hurdles, just that you jump them.

Shareholders establish the nature and shape of the hurdles — but customers determine where the winning line is.

In the market(ing) strategy process, it is important that we identify – clearly – the financial hurdles that the organization must jump. We identify them, we list them, we ensure that we do not forget them – but we make sure that we jump them. But we *do not allow the hurdles to dictate our customer/market(ing) actions.*

The business objective will give us the direction that will enable us to jump the hurdles.

3.2   The business objective

There are in Europe many good generals, but they see too many things at once. I see one thing, namely the enemy's main body. I try to crush it, confident that secondary matters will then settle themselves.

Napoleon Bonaparte

There is a surprising amount of confusion in the area, so first, a definition:

Business objective:

The goal or the aim to which all activities of the organization are directed.

An objective should always begin with the word '*To* ...'.

If the organization does not have a single, clear, concise business objective, then it is more than likely that activities will be directed in a number of different (and possibly conflicting) directions with the net result that the organization is seriously wasting resource (money, time and management effort). Assuming the organization's management team has (more or less) followed the process so far outlined in this book (or a similar one), they will be (more or less) agreed on the common direction for the organization and they will have in their minds an (more or less) outline idea of where they feel the organization ought to be in (definitely) three, (probably) five or (maybe) ten years' time. The precise timescale depends on the nature of the organization, its market and the rate of change of its industry base. Following on from this, the business objective ought really to be little more than a formalizing of the common agreement, which should now have already been reached. You wish!

And, we have had one go at this but let's just do it again:

(1) The business objective is not the same as the financial objective (hurdle):
   (a) The business objective is about *codifying the purpose* of the organization.
   (b) The financial hurdle (some call it the financial objective) is about *measuring how successful* the organization has been.

Whichever way the argument goes, we must have a proper business objective to work to when we are creating the market(ing) strategy. We can't work to a financial hurdle; it contains no direction and assumes that everybody, inside and outside the organization, only works for money – a crass and very dangerous assumption. If the senior management is too hidebound to see the reality, we are going to have to come up with a 'hypothesis' of the business objective that meets the needs of all the stakeholders, takes into account the realities of the business environment and, assuming that we achieve the objective, jumps the financial hurdles too.

We can use the business objective as a way of defining, in more quantifiable terms, our view of what our organization is going to become. There is no doubt that an organization requires a sense of shared commitment and common vision for the future. The question remains how will we know when we have got there? This is precisely what the business objective aims to provide. So, now for some basics:

(1) Multiple objectives are easier to agree and everybody can include their 'pet objective' into the grand scheme of strategy. But beware, time saved by not seeking a *single, overriding objective* will soon be lost in the horse-trading and politicking that (inevitably) takes place as soon as more than one objective fights for the same limited resource.

(2) The business objective should be no longer than one sentence: twelve to fifteen words is ideal (if it's more than this it gets confusing and complicated, and people have more problems understanding exactly what the organization is trying to do).

(3) The first word of the objective is 'To …'.

(4) The business objective should be achievable. There is no point in simply codifying wishful thinking. An objective, to be effective, has to be seen by everybody as being achievable and being realistic. Over-ambitious objectives simply do not motivate and are seen as unreal hoaxes emanating from senior management who are obviously either desperate or out of touch with reality.

(5) The objective should be quantifiable in some form. There obviously has to be some time limit on the achievement of the objective and there must also be some form of quantifiable success criteria. This is normally in financial terms but must not be limited to such measures (see debate earlier). It is a sad comment on human business life, but what gets measured gets done. If the organization measures short-term profitability that is what it gets – for a time anyway. It is worth repeating that the *financial measures of success are not, themselves, the objective of the organization* (see Section 1.4). Thinking back to the ideas about competitive advantage, if the secret to longer-term success is creating customer relationships and customer value, shouldn't these be the measures of success? What gets measured gets done – make sure you measure what you want to get done, even if it isn't the easiest thing to measure! (see Chapter 6).

(6) The business objective must be consistent with both the internal capabilities of the organization and the desires of the key implementers and their personal vision of the future. The objective must also be consistent with the external environment and the opportunities and constraints that we have identified.

(7) Finally, and importantly, the business objective must be both understandable and capable of communication throughout the organization. While we are not saying that the business objective must be turned into some form of snappy advertising slogan, it needs to be concise and simple because it needs to be translated down through the entire organization. In terms of communicating the message, lower levels of management will have to understand the objective if they are to be able to convert the objective into sub-objectives in functional areas, such as marketing, operations, finance and so on. They will need

to understand the implications of the objective as they are the ones who will have to implement processes to achieve the objective. The final test here should be: does everybody in the organization understand what the organization stands for and what the organization is out to achieve?

Only if people truly understand the business objective can they start to relate what they do on a day-by-day basis to the needs of the marketplace that the organization serves. The time-honoured example of a business objective comes from NASA in the USA and goes back a few years. In the early days, NASA's objective was very simple – *to put a man on the moon*. To reinforce this sense of understanding, a photograph of the moon was distributed and placed above every desk in the organization. When, at any level, someone was asked what their organization was about it was a simple job of pointing to the picture and saying *to get there*. Unfortunately, the problem became a little bit more complicated once they achieved their primary objective and a second, next stage objective was not developed in the same unambiguous manner as the first.

What makes a good business/corporate objective? It all depends on the organization, its markets, its aspirations and its culture. To start the process, I am happy to offer a short list of suggestions. These have proved useful in the past.

Given all the earlier pointers, you must (specifically, not generally) decide the following:

(1) What business you want to be in (see Section 6.1);

(2) What market(s) or segment(s) you intend to target and do business in (see Section 6.3);

(3) The date by which you will have achieved the objective.

Then you can decide the shape of the objective that will drive the whole organization: 'To be ... by (date)'.

Objectives such as *Be in the top three, Fastest follower* show a serious lack of ambition and start by guaranteeing that you will receive reduced profits than the leader.

Generally, the main problem with setting objectives comes from senior management's apparent unwillingness to spend enough time working through the issues. Most boards and senior managers seem to think that their main job is to manage the functional silo of which they are head – and that directing the future of the business is just a part time job – wrong!

Setting the business/corporate objective is the biggest job of them all. To expect it to be dealt with in a hour in the middle of a busy board agenda is madness.

1. 'The natural choice…	Given that you have agreed the business you are in, this would make you the *no-brainer* (as the Americans say) choice for a selected market or market segment
2. 'The first choice…	Of (specify the) Xxxx customers
3. 'The benchmark provider of…	Specify either (I prefer) benefit or (if you really must) product/service
4. 'The thought leader…	The one that leads the field but isn't necessarily the biggest
5. 'The most…	Links to the specific nature of the differentiation or market position (see Section 6.4) that you have decided to own This might include words such as: most expensive, most common, most recognized, easiest, fastest, quickest, etc.
6. 'The M&S/BMW/BA (add your own benchmark company) of the Xxxx business	Use the values and connotations of the admired brand/company (see Section 6.4) and transfer them into the business in which you operate. Make sure that the customers recognize the same values as you

The message is simple. Take the time you need and get the objective right. The right objective will give the company wings; the wrong one will doom it to being an also-ran in a commodity market.

3.3 Business strategy

> An army ought to only have one line of operation. This should be preserved with care, and never abandoned but in the last extremity.
>
> *Napoleon Bonaparte*

Once the business objective has been set and agreed by all the managers who need to own the process, we are ready to move on to the question of business strategy. Once again we will be looking for a short and concise statement which crystallizes all of the fairly detailed thinking carried out so far and which again is easily understandable and capable of communication throughout the organization.

Our business objective will tell us concisely what we have to do, where we have to be and by when. This must be the 'aim' or 'goal' of the whole organization. If the business objective is the aim or the 'what', the strategy is all about the means or the 'how'.

Business strategy:

The one route which is both necessary and sufficient to achieve the business objective.

A strategy should always begin with the word '*By...*'.

What we are looking for in the business strategy, and you will note that the term is singular not plural, is direction. So, now for some basics:

(1) One strategy is better than lots of different strategies that will conflict and compete.

(2) The strategy must be driven by the objective that it seeks to implement.

(3) The first word of your strategy is '*By...*'.

(4) The best strategy is one that is 'necessary' to achieve the objective. If it's not necessary (to achieve the objective), we shouldn't do it.

(5) The strategy also needs to be 'sufficient', of itself, to achieve the objective.

(6) The strategy needs to be 'different' from the competition if you desire more than average returns from the sector.

For any given objective there is normally a series of alternative strategies, which may be seen as viable ways of achieving the objective.

To take a perhaps over-simplistic example, let us assume that your objective is to get from your home in London to a meeting in Brussels. There are obviously a number of alternative strategies for achieving this objective. You could drive from London to Dover; you could then pick up the ferry or rail tunnel from Dover to Calais and drive through France to Belgium to Brussels. You could take the Dover to Zeebrugge or Ostend ferries and drive down from there. Alternatively, you might decide to get on a train at London, travel through the Channel Tunnel rail link direct to Brussels. You might decide to fly, so you travel from London through to Heathrow, to Zaventem and from there to Brussels which may involve the use of trains or taxis. You might even be one of those élite who has access to a company jet or helicopter.

Whichever route you choose, your preferred strategy will probably be based on other aspects such as the time available, the relative desire for other stops en route, the convenience and timing of the schedules and so on.

Bringing the entire question (inexorably) back into the realm of business strategy, the discussion and decision is an essential part of the process as it clarifies management's views on the environment and the ways in which it wishes its organization to operate. What is clear is that the organization can, and ideally should, only choose one single strategy (that is both necessary and sufficient) to achieve its objective. Moving back to our travelling from London to Brussels as an example, the objective is clear (to arrive in an agreed place at an agreed time for a meeting), but there appear to be strategic options:

- 'By air' is insufficient given that neither airport is in the right place.
- 'By sea' is insufficient for similar reasons.
- 'By rail, sea and air' includes at least one mode that is unnecessary.
- 'By train and taxi' could be both necessary and sufficient if the timetables suit meeting times.

But strategy should be left open to allow for changes in market conditions. To push the example (probably beyond) its reasonable limits, the traveller would set off for Waterloo in good time to allow for last minute changes in travel plans should the rail link be out of action. Finding the tunnel closed, the traveller still has the option of a train to Dover or Heathrow or Gatwick to continue the journey by alternative means. Arriving at Heathrow, options are still open and the traveller can test flights to Zaventem, Antwerp or Paris with connecting trains to Brussels or linking with alternative carriers from Gatwick.

Setting an 'emergent' (described at length by Mintzberg) strategy such as this involves agreeing a general direction that we believe will achieve the objective but then launching testing initiatives and allowing the market environment to show us which way is best.

As we will see later, which strategic route is best much depends on the organization and its marketplace, although it would appear that most organizations would benefit from encouraging more emergent thinking into their strategic approach.

While there are a number of ways of skinning the proverbial cat, there will be more than one way of achieving the business objective. It may not be possible to reduce the list down beyond two or three similar strategies in the short term. Ideally a single common strategy is preferable because it helps bind the entire organization and helps commit resources to one single chosen route, thereby ensuring that the organization makes best use of its inevitably limited resource. Apart from those markets which are controlled by monopoly or legislation, it is extremely difficult to find examples of successful strategies that do not erode over time. Some last for years, some for scant weeks. In any event, it is important that the organization builds flexibility into its approach.

3.4   Competitive strategy

We should always go before our enemies with confidence, otherwise
our apparent uneasiness inspires them with greater boldness.

Napoleon Bonaparte

Before we launch straight into a discussion about the alternative forms of competitive strategy that might be open to the organization, it's worth stopping for a moment (again) to consider the nature of competition itself. Competition, as followers of the capitalist system have been taught, does a lot of very good and worthwhile things in the marketplace it has been known to improve efficiency, reduce absolute cost levels and improve customer choice. Competition is so important that all major capitalist systems (USA, UK, EU) have introduced tough laws to be used against those organizations who conspire to fix prices, limit distribution or otherwise 'restrict competition'. However, as far as the organization is concerned, we should all realize that in a free market, competition works constantly and continually to *erode profits*. As profit is effectively the name of the game, competition is not always a welcome visitor on the commercial and industrial scene

In short, the situation is as follows – the heavier the competition, the higher the cost of fighting that competition, and the lower the profits. What then can an organization do about this? If your organization wants to achieve above-average profits (and even a superior return on investment), you need to take action to control, or at least manage, the level of competition in the marketplace. Management needs to recognize that the competitive force is something that has to be dealt with and contained. The organization must seek and establish what can only be described as a defensible position against competition.

In other words, competition should be avoided if possible – at least the damaging direct, head-to-head, blood-feud, slug-it-out competition between old adversaries, which should be avoided at all costs. The secret then is to build barriers around the organization in its marketplace and reduce the worst (and most costly) competition. This action should reduce costs and improve profits. According to Porter, there are three generic strategic alternatives open to the organization. There is, in fact, a fourth, which, although it is not to be recommended, does seem to be very popular with large sectors of industry. According to Porter, the organization which decides and then consistently follows one of these three prime strategies successfully will achieve good profits and above-average returns on its investment. The three strategies that Porter describes are cost leadership, differentiation and focus (Figure 3.3). Porter has come under some criticism for the apparent simplicity of this approach, but then there is always somebody willing to complicate life. Nevertheless, as long as we recognize that these

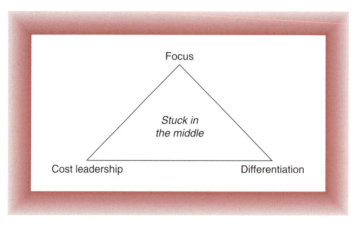

Figure 3.3   Porter's generic strategies
Source: Porter (1983).

alternatives are broad orientations rather than fixed points to be occupied, it is worthwhile here spending a little time looking at these three suggestions.

3.4.1   Differentiation

The organization that wishes to pursue a strategy of differentiation (see Chapter 6), will be operating throughout the complete market rather than addressing one or two specific segments of the marketplace. The organization will probably be marketing a fairly wide range of products but to be successful in this strategic context, the company and its products will have to be differentiated in some way from the competitive offerings. The product must in some way be 'unique' in the customers' perception. In fact, differentiation is all about creating brand identity and loyalty. The power of a well-known and revered brand helps avoid price competition and often offers scope for relatively higher margins than would otherwise be the case.

To be a practical strategy, the difference between the organization's product or service and the competitors' offers must be sustainable and believable over the longer term. Any given marketplace will only be able to support as many clearly differentiated positions as the target customers deem credible. The number is difficult to predict and will depend, among other things, on the sophistication of the market and how much investment has been made by the main players in explaining the different positions. Buyers, both industrial and consumer, are *free spirits* (like cats), and perceptions of what constitutes a credible and differentiated position will differ from person to person and change over time. You must carefully monitor the situation and adjust your market position over time if it is to endure.

Costs (investment) for the differentiating organization are likely to be higher because of the costs of developing and maintaining a 'unique' market position. Much of the cost will be associated with promotion and market(ing) support although products and services may require additional investment too. The potential rewards from a differentiated strategy can be significant but it is not a route to be recommended for those organizations driven only by short-term considerations. Over time, costs will have to be kept close to the industry average – differentiation can't be used to disguise inefficiency.

3.4.2   Cost leadership

To follow a strategy of overall cost leadership means that the organization will do everything in its power to drive its cost base down to the point at which it is able to produce products or services at a lower cost than any of its competitors. Cost leadership is an absolute term. Driving to be *the* lowest cost provider means that there can only be one in any market. In simple terms, this means that, given the unfortunate situation of a price war, the lowest cost provider will be the last survivor in a market. At the point where everybody else is making losses the cost leader will, by definition, be the last organization making (any) profits.

Importantly, *lowest cost does not have to mean lowest price*. There is nothing to stop the lowest cost provider marketing at a price that is similar (or even above) its competitors. As every manager (ought to) knows, cost does not influence price. The market dictates price while cost dictates profit. Marketing at an average or relatively high price level just means that the lowest cost provider will be making larger profit margins than anyone else in the market – as long as their offer meets customer expectations.

The skills (and management attitude/obsession) required to pursue and achieve a strategy of lowest cost are very, *very* different from those that we have looked at for the differentiated position. To achieve overall cost leadership, the organization must dedicate itself to leading-edge (for the market) cost reduction activities. If the lowest cost position is to be achieved (and in this strategy there are no prizes for second place), the organization will have to be ready to invest a considerable amount of time, effort and money. The cost leadership position can be quite capital intensive, especially in information and production technology. It might also require a higher degree of product or service standardization. The position requires a culture of unrelenting commitment to cost control. This attitude must permeate the entire organization and everything it does.

Strategy, as we know, is all about the longer term. Over the longer term, the cost leadership position can have one or two dangers. For example:

(1) Cost inflation can erode the advantage over time.

(2) Organizations that have a significant amount of international business need to locate parts of the world where they are able to maintain and drive down the average cost per unit for their production (e.g. China) and any other operations (e.g. India for IT and call centres).

(3) Technology doesn't progress smoothly but has an unnerving habit of advancing by (leapfrog) jumps. Just imagine the despondency in the organization that had managed to drive its total cost base down to the lowest possible level in the market for cathode ray (CRTV) screens when flat screens are all that people want for Christmas; years of work can be rendered obsolete at a stroke.

(4) Internal focus might be the biggest single danger for the organization pursuing the cost leadership strategy. Improvements in production and technology needed to drive down the cost base may deflect top management's attention away from the all-important customer need. Cheap might be good, but *not* if it doesn't deliver the benefits the customer is looking for. This might be further aggravated by the significant cost savings to be made from a standardized product range. If we manage to achieve the lowest cost position but are producing products or services that the market doesn't value (so doesn't buy), we have gained little more than pyrrhic victory.

If your organization decides to follow this strategic route, the position of the marketing function can be difficult. Without the ability to keep a close contact with the developing and evolving customer needs, the organization can soon become production and finance led; it will lose contact with customer requirements and this will affect market share. The resulting drop in volume will, in turn, affect the organization's ability to keep its unit cost base low – a classic downward spiral.

3.4.3   Focus

The organization that pursues a focused strategy concentrates its effort, not across the entire market as in the case of the differentiation and cost leadership, but on one or more specific segments of the marketplace. As with the differentiated strategy, the organization will need to develop a credible position in the marketplace because customers will have to see even more uniqueness from the focused organization and must understand the reason for its specialization in a segment. We will deal with the specific aspects of market segmentation in Chapter 6. But for the moment let us concentrate on the overall strategic approach of focus compared to the other two generic strategies.

A focus strategy, if successful, is a powerful way of building barriers to competition in a small (but profitable) part of the total marketplace. The management skills required of the focusing organization are similar to those required of a differentiating organization; success will come from the organization's ability to tune its efforts to its customers' needs. The focused organization will need to be more precise than the differentiated organization because the focused organization has, by definition, fewer customers in its target market. It will then need to make its offer that much more attractive to that target segment if it is to achieve a profitable level of penetration.

Customer trends of the past twenty-five years; increased disposable income, higher levels of individualism and self-determination have been apparent in most of the Western world. As a result, much of the recent growth in new businesses has been from new firms emerging to meet market demand currently unsatisfied by larger organizations with their more standardized, global approaches. The truly focused organization should not be forced to operate on prices that are determined by the competition. The whole reason for being focused is that the organization can defy accurate comparison with competitors and is (relatively) free to operate at prices that it sets.

If your organization (like the Financial Times, Porsche, Rolls-Royce Marine Engines and Heidelberg Printers) is to successfully pursue a focus strategy, this will call for the complete and total dedication of the organization to the needs and wants of your specific target customer base (and the exclusion of non-targeted segments). Your product/service range will probably be quite narrow, but at the same time deeper, to offer greater choice to a restricted part of the marketplace. Your whole organization's operations will also have to be seen by your target market as being consistent with the specialized stance which you have taken in the marketplace. Customers are prepared to pay premium prices but need to be convinced of the value of specialization.

The focused organization, like the differentiated, must be seen to be rejecting sales that do not fit the specialist profile. This, in my experience, has always been the single largest problem for organizations who wish to pursue the focused route. This means that it must actively avoid activities and business, which fall outside of the target segment and turning business away if it's not of the right kind. You can imagine how popular this can be, especially with those (sales) working to short-term targets (maybe with bonuses attached).

Finally, the risks. The focused organization, while protecting itself from competition by building barriers around itself and its target segment, is also running certain risks:

(1) Placing all of its eggs into one or two baskets, there is always the risk of a structural shift in the marketplace and the mass emigration of customers to new markets. This is known as the empty segment syndrome.

(2) How do we define the segment into which we are going to focus our attention in the first place (see Chapter 6)? Once we identify the segment, we focus our activities to developing products and services exclusively to that segment and we grow with the segment.

(3) As we grow the segment (and the revenues/profits that flow from it), it might become vulnerable to attack from the larger organizations. These will always compete on price (they have little creativity or imagination), so they are predictable, but still. . .

(4) As the segment grows we could become prey to even more focused organizations who come in and stake a claim to one particular part of our target
segment. In other words, we get carved up from underneath.

The single most important secret to success in a focus strategy tends to be the
organization's market orientation. If you have only a small part of the market to
aim for, the job of getting and keeping extremely close to your customers is made
that much easier. You will have to become an expert on market segmentation
which, although everybody has heard of the term, is an extremely difficult
concept to understand and to implement properly – more of this in Section 6.3.

3.4.4   Stuck in the middle

In case you are confused, this is not a generic competitive strategy (as such) but it
seems to be very popular for lots of organizations. It is, in fact, the result of *not*
following through on any one of the three strategies described earlier. To explain
how this position arises, let us take the example of the following quite 'fictitious'
organization (any resemblance to organizations, living or dead, is purely coinci-
dental). The organization in question is a composite of a number of firms featured
in the business pages of any good business magazine and could easily be in any
market providing any product or service. The sequence of events is so familiar
that probably all of us can imagine a number of companies that act in just this
way. The sad history is:

(1) Our (fictional) organization has been reasonably successful for a number of
years and so has not recognized any need to develop a clear and distinct long-
term strategy.

(2) Competition increased during the late 1980s and early 1990s and at a certain
point it became clear that unless something was done, the business was going
to be in a perilous state.

(3) Top management got together, looked at the situation, wondered what it
ought to do, started looking at which parts of its business were being hit
hardest by competition and saw that the historical core of the business was
still sound.

(4) Senior management start to ask some 'strategic questions'. But then along
come the 'dot-com' era and the 'millennium bug', so all the difficult questions
are put on hold for five years.

(5) In late 2000, someone suggests what we ought to do is to concentrate on what
we are good at: *Let's drive for a specialist position and let's hike the prices.* This seems
like a reasonably good idea and the organization pursues this for almost a year
without seeing any significant return on the bottom line. They have, of course,
kept fighting the competition in the allied areas as well as deepening penetration of the core market but competition is still making inroads.

(6) *OK*, somebody (else) says, *What we ought to do is to spend some money on advertising. Broaden the scope, let's get some more people involved in this market-place and let's get out and push the name, push the products and widen the appeal.* This is agreed and the organization then embarks on a reasonable sized advertising campaign. It puts the pressure on the sales force to extend the distribution channels, extend the coverage of the product range, maybe brings in one or two product variants to move the organization forward. Almost a year later, sales have increased somewhat but profits are largely unchanged.

(7) Worry and concern sets in again and somebody (else) says *It's all become a bit slack around here, what we ought to do is to start planning some cuts to control the costs and improve the profits.* Naturally, one of the first things to go is the advertising campaign and ancillary areas. So the move now in the organization is to develop cost-cutting exercises and improve the margins. After almost a year, the superficial economies are all used up and cost-cutting, to be taken any further, will start to eat into the core of the business.

(8) Rather than do this, people will start looking for alternative ways to beat off competition. Somebody (else) then says *What we should do is focus a bit more on what we do really well and dump all this additional activity, it does nothing but confuse everybody.* The *focus* strategy is on the agenda again.

This 'fictitious' organization is one that is completely dominated by short-term considerations and lacks/sees no value in a long-term strategic view. The problem is not that it doesn't try various strategic approaches but rather that it *perseveres* with none of them. Unless the management of this organization demands and receives control of the future of the enterprise, the organization will continue its circular route trying one strategy after another.

It is stuck in the middle of the process: never managing to break out of what is a vicious circle leading ultimately only to its own demise. Being 'stuck in the middle' means that there is no clear differentiation between the players. Where there is no differentiation, price competition follows.

Worse still, there appears to be safety in numbers. It isn't likely to be the only organization in the market that is stuck in this vicious circle. These are the organizations that are doggedly trying to maintain the 'all-things-to-all-men' approach to the marketplace. They find it difficult to compete against clearly and credibly positioned competition. They find it difficult to maintain a customer and market orientation because the nature of the customers that they think they are serving changes on too regular a basis. As the profit situation steadily deteriorates over time, they inevitably become prey to shorter and shorter time constraints and end up driven by either short-term sales cultures or short-term finance requirements. These are just additional hindrances to their ever breaking out of the circle.

The only solution for organizations that find themselves stuck in this position is to attract particularly strong management capable of forcing the organization through the pain barrier and driving for one or other of the strategic routes. Undertaking a rational analysis of the marketplace and the opportunities and threats that confront the organization must be followed by a decision on the best strategic route for the future. A relentless drive for that position is the only thing that will break the vicious circle.

3.5   Sustainable competitive advantage

> The transition from the defensive to the offensive is one of the most delicate operations in war.
>
> *Napoleon Bonaparte*

The concept of sustainable competitive advantage is not a new idea. It can be found in the early origins of economics, basic marketing – and in everyday common sense. Simply stated, if an organization is able to do something better (customer perception) than its competitors, it will make better profits. If an organization is only as good as everybody else, it will only make standard profits. If an organization is worse than its competitors at what it does, it will make inferior profits – nothing too difficult there!

As the avowed aim of competitive strategy is to find ways of avoiding competition and making superior profits, then, logically, the search must be for ways of achieving some form of 'advantage' over our competitors which will enable us to make better-than-average profits. Also as business and commercial activities need to be directed at the longer term, the advantage itself must be sustainable over the long term to generate reasonable and consistent profit flows.

Identifying (and then selecting the most appropriate) competitive advantage is not as easy a process as it would appear to be at first glance. In the marketing texts of the 1960s and 1970s, we would read a lot about the same thing but then it was called a USP (unique selling proposition), although at the time the concept was applied mainly to product features rather than organizations. Many textbooks still attempt to reproduce lists of areas of sustainable advantage that the organization might wish to consider; these used to cover SWOT, industry analysis, structure, environment and all sorts. Over the years though, the lengths of the lists have all shortened. With the widespread application of knowledge and technology, there are few areas that can now offer any long-term advantage. Having said this, a short-term advantage may still be worth having – but it will have to be replaced eventually. When we look at today's competitive markets, it becomes obvious that long-term sustainability is rare.

Since Porter first proposed his ideas on strategy in the 1980s, there has been a lot of frenzied academic research and scribbling to try and either prove or disprove the ideas, depending on the particular orientation. Some of it even attempted to define what sustainable competitive advantage was – and where it might be found.

3.5.1 Core competencies

We will look at this issue within the SCORPIO approach in Chapter 6. However, for those in a rush, the basic concept of 'core competencies' was suggested by Hamel and Prahalad (*Competing for the Future*, Harvard Business School Press, Boston, 1996) and it fits perfectly with Porter's idea of sustainable competitive advantage – if a core competency yields a long-term advantage to the company, it is said to be a sustainable competitive advantage.

Core competencies are those capabilities that are critical to an organization achieving competitive advantage. The starting point for analysing core competencies is recognizing that competition between businesses is as much a race for what Hamel and Prahalad call 'competence mastery' as it is for market position and market power. Senior management cannot focus on all activities of a business and the competencies required to undertake them. So the goal is for management to focus attention on those competencies that they believe will really affect competitive advantage.

A core competency can take various forms, including:

● Technical/subject matter know how;

● A reliable process;

● Close relationships with customers and suppliers;

● Product/service development;

● Particular culture such as employee dedication.

Many modern business theories suggest that most activities that are not part of a company's core competency should be outsourced.

3.5.2 Achieving competitive advantage

Much of the different work on Porter's original ideas has little or no application value to the practising manager but there are points of light out there, specifically some work by Treacy and Wiersema (*The Disciplines of the Market Leaders*, HarperCollins, London, 1996) which has been built on by Doyle (*Value-Based Marketing: Marketing Strategies for Corporate Growth and Shareholder Value*, Wiley, New York, 2000) that add some useful insights.

Treacy and Wiersema looked at the Porter generic strategies model and came up with some nice, simple ideas. They looked at the problem and concluded that:

(1) Strategy is about resource allocation. In other words, it is about how you decide to spend/invest your money, which is always limited.

(2) You can decide to spend it on:
   (a) *Being the same* as everybody else (Porter's idea of 'stuck-in-the-middle');
   (b) *Being different* from the competition.

(3) If you have decided that you (really) want to be different, you can decide to invest you money on *one* of:
   (a) *Product leadership* (producing better or the best product);
   (b) *Management efficiency* (being slick and/or the most efficient operator);
   (c) *Customer intimacy* (getting closer or closest to your customers).

Working on the earlier options, Treacy and Wiersema then looked at the idea of 'excellence' (Figure 3.4) in relation to spending/investing the money and suggest that, from a customer perspective, only 'Excellent' and 'Adequate' really exist – How true!

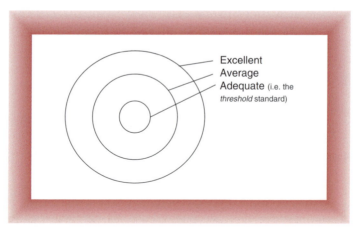

Figure 3.4   Excellence is the key to strategy
Source: Adapted from Treacy and Wiersema (1997).

In other words:

(1) *Customers notice* if an offering is 'excellent' because it stands out from the competing offerings.

(2) *Customers notice* if an offering falls below what is the minimum acceptable standard (the threshold standard) because it falls below what the customer expects it to do (benefits) for them, it is not 'fit for purpose'.

(3) *Customers don't notice* if the offering falls anywhere between these two points, it is just another (undifferentiated) player in the competitive melee.

(4) *'Average' is not a customer concept*; it is produced by the industry and is the 'industry standard' produced through inward-looking benchmarking activities.

This is perhaps easier to see if we overlay the three ways of spending/investing money in the organization (Figure 3.5).

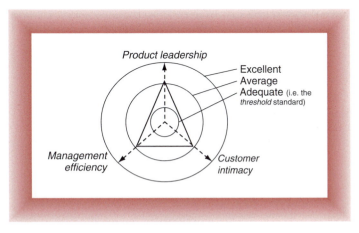

Figure 3.5   Being average is not strategy
Source: Adapted from Treacy and Wiersema (1997).

Treacy and Wiersema suggest that most organizations prefer to work, invest and spend to be 'Average' on all three dimensions, fearing that to fall below the 'industry standard' on any single dimension would be to make the organization vulnerable.

This is of course internally focused nonsense; these managers should get out more. Customers are the key to our business survival and growth and what they say should always take precedence. Treacy and Wiersema recognize that money (and other resources) are always limited and need to be spent carefully, wisely and with a view to creating a customer-based competitive advantage.

As Figures 3.6–3.8 show, the idea is to spend/invest enough to create a competitive advantage by being 'excellent' in one of the three key internal areas, either by creating the best product/service, by being the most efficient organization or by being closest to the customer. They suggest you do this (resources always being limited) by diverting resource away from those two areas that you have decided *not* to compete in. Diverting the resources will make you fall below the

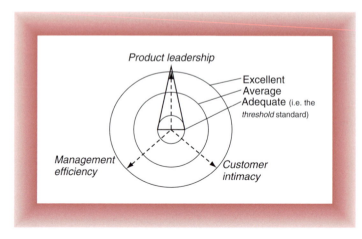

Figure 3.6 Excellence – in product leadership
Source: Adapted from Treacy and Wiersema (1997).

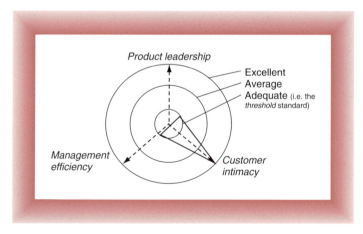

Figure 3.7 Excellence – in customer intimacy
Source: Adapted from Treacy and Wiersema (1997).

industry-defined 'average' but customers won't notice this – as long as you ensure that you don't fall below the 'adequate' level. In this way, you have the choice to 'win' by focusing the search for competitive advantage on:

(1) *Being excellent at product leadership* means producing what the customers see as the best product or service and then making sure that the back up service and support is 'good enough' not to be an issue.

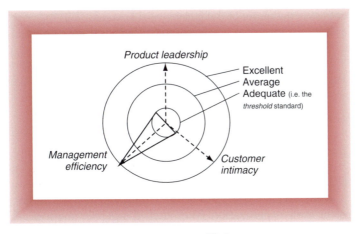

Figure 3.8 Excellence – in management efficiency
Source: Adapted from Treacy and Wiersema (1997).

(2) *Being excellent at customer intimacy* means knowing the customer better than anybody else and delivering solutions that customers really value, all the time ensuring that you don't let anybody down and the product/service works and the service/distribution, etc. all work too. In the B2B situation, this alternative is more popular than many organizations would be prepared to admit – in the world of professional direct sales forces, relationships, repeat business and profits are less due to 'excellent products' than excellent relationships between individuals. The typical response from a purchasing manager who trusts and respects a particular sales executive, *We always buy from Xxxxx because they have the technical expertise if things go wrong and their national accounts manager visits us twice a week and knows our business inside out (he also takes me to the Open)*, is a very effective barrier to competitive entry.

(3) *Being excellent at management efficiency* means being the best at systems, distribution and processes and making sure that the product/service is 'okay' and that you are close enough to customers to meet their needs.

To sum up the conclusions from Treacy and Wiersema, we have to:

(1) *Pick a market to dominate*: Do *not* dabble or aggregate markets.

(2) *Decide a single factor for competition*: Do *not* try to be good at everything.

(3) *Focus resources to that end*: Do *not* allow history and politics to direct resources.

All in all, excellent advice – but beware.

Practical strategy is the name of the game – and I do it for a living. All the logic of the Treacy and Wiersema approach is so sensible, obvious and unavoidable which means that:

- *It won't be argued against* in any sensible strategy meeting or process – which also means that
- *It probably won't be followed.*

No matter the agreement in the groups or the consensus on the away day, when real managers go back to real jobs they will consider it just so much group hysteria. They just won't reduce expenditure back to threshold levels. Somehow it will seem just too difficult and they will feel an all-encompassing need to protect their organization from such dangerous madness. How could anyone allow their business to be exposed in such a way? What would happen if the competition found out?

Believe me, this will definitely be a step too far. And of course, if your managers don't reduce their expenditure in the areas where you (all) have decided you won't seek excellence, then:

(1) *You will not have the resources* available to dedicate to the excellence project.

(2) *You will not be excellent or different*, you will be exactly the same as your competitors, 'average'.

(3) *You will not find additional resources* for the 'madness'.

(4) *You will only have price to compete on* because you will be 'ordinary'.

(5) *You will remember that Paul Fifield said that strategy was fun, he didn't say it was easy.*

The area of sustainable competitive advantage is critical for the overall long-run success of the organization. It's important because it gives the organization the opportunity of imposing its will on the competitive marketplace, of choosing how it is going to compete – and on what grounds. If your organization can get its sustainable competitive advantage right, then you will be taking control of your own destiny. You won't be forced just to react to competition. You won't always be on the defensive, reacting to what other organizations are doing.

Conclusions – Part One

In war you see your own troubles; those of the enemy you cannot see. You must show confidence.

Napoleon Bonaparte

Now as the baton is about to change, it is worth looking back at what we have achieved so far, where has the thinking taken us up to this point? So far we have tried to answer questions such as:

- What is the organization trying to do?

- What are the organization's circumstances?

- What can the organization do?

- What must it do?

- And as we approach the end of the exercise, what will the organization do?

Although we have been following the strategic process flow chart described in the Introduction, we have already said (but it bears repeating) that there is no one way of coming to the all-important strategic decisions that the organization will have to develop. The strategic process is, by its very nature, an iterative process – this is why you will note many of the arrows in the flow chart go in more than one direction.

So far we have taken the organization through its broad macro decision-making process, we have looked at the distinctive competencies, what it's good at and what it's bad at, its competitive position and its sustainable competitive advantage. Because we are about to move on to the more detailed aspects of strategy, developing the market(ing) strategy – the process by which we take the business objective to the market – this does not mean that the subjects and topics that we have looked at so far can now be safely put away into a box somewhere. It is more than likely (as we delve deeper into the situation) that a number of the specific issues will have to be re-visited and analysed in more detail as our information needs become more precise the closer we get to our target marketplace.

It could almost be argued that, up to this point, the investigation process has been as important as the decision-making outputs. Certainly it is important that the organization realizes that nothing so far decided can be considered as set into stone. At the very least, we have become sensitized to the alternatives open to us – the various paths which we could take in our market operations and which paths are most likely to bear fruits in the short, medium and long term. Now as we develop the process and get closer and closer to our customers and the marketplace, we will be able to start getting real feedback on our plans, our vision and our aspirations for the future. As we develop the thinking, the understanding and analysis, and generally get closer to the people who pay us our money, we may have to re-visit some of the decisions made in the process as circumstances and external conditions change.

While in no way wishing to denigrate the decision-making process to this point, it is important that the organization understands just how far there is still to go as well as what it has already achieved. Above all, the business objective and strategy decisions must contain a degree of flexibility within them if they are not to crack under the pressures (always) applied by customers and competition. The market that the organization serves is by its nature a dynamic system, and flexibility and adaptability will mark the winning organizations of the next decade.

A market strategy developed in the absence of a clear guiding business objective and business strategy is likely to be all action and no purpose.

A business strategy with no marketing is likely to be all thinking and no action. It will always be achieving a balance between the two that creates a stable and growing organization.

To check progress then, we should have started asking the most important questions – and getting some answers. Check your progress against the strategy checklist in the Appendix.

Part Two

Developing the Market(ing) Strategy

In war, the general alone can judge of certain arrangements. It depends on him alone to conquer difficulties by his own superior talents and resolution.

Napoleon Bonaparte

4 From business to market(ing) strategy

He that makes war without many mistakes has not made war very long.
Napoleon Bonaparte

So we arrive at the question of market(ing) strategy proper. When I circulated the very first draft of this book for comments, a number of people asked why they had to get so far into a book on market(ing) strategy before coming to the topic itself. The answer was (and still is) that we started looking at market(ing) strategy on page one and have never really left it.

To be fair, the section on SCORPIO wasn't anywhere near complete, so they had no idea how much was still to come.

One of the problems with 'Marketing' is that people tend to confuse what it *ought* to be with what it actually *is* in too many organizations. Nobody I know reads the Preface to a book, but this one has some opinions in it – I thought you might want another opportunity, and to save you skipping back (who reads that stuff anyway?):

Abstract from the Preface to the Third Edition

Like some of my readers, I am getting to that stage in life when I start counting things – like the number of years I have been in market(ing), the number of companies I have met who (still) believe that products make profits, the number of times I have met marketers who complain so bitterly about marketing not being given the status it deserves in their organization. But counting does give perspective.

When I started in market(ing), I believed that it was just a question of timing and that, given the correct data (and encouragement), marketers and companies would see the light and become customer led and much more profitable. Ah, the innocence of youth. Today we see a landscape that has not changed significantly over the years: finance departments still calculate product/service profitability; sales departments still dictate prices and payment terms; operations still dictate product/service availability; R&D

functions still create new products and services based on technical features rather than customer benefits.

And too many marketing departments still busy themselves with writing brochures, organizing events and creating leads for the sales force.

On top of that, Philip Kotler turns up in Europe and says that it's terrible that marketing really only seems to consist of one *P*, promotion. At the same time, universities and business schools are re-arranging their programmes so that issues that used to appear on marketing modules (such as segmentation) now appear on business strategy modules. Meanwhile, in business, new board positions are appearing; Commercial Directors have been around for a while but they are now joined by the Business Development Director. Strange that the universities and business schools haven't developed a *business development* module for their MBA programmes yet.

And too many marketing departments still busy themselves with writing brochures, organizing events and creating leads for the sales force.

The result is that market(ing) is still *not* on the business agenda. Market(ing) is still *not* properly represented on the board. Customers are still *not* receiving the service they deserve. Organizations are still *not* as profitable as they should be and are still *not* differentiated from lower priced international competition. There really is no way of escaping the responsibility here – the 'marketing profession' really only has itself to blame. As long as too many marketers concentrate on the brochures, events and sales leads, we allow market(ing) to be classified as an *optional* business activity – one that can be cut as soon as the recession comes around again.

But, the job needs to be done, customers are still not receiving their due – genuine customer value. This book is written for any manager who is prepared to take up the market(ing) challenge, 'real marketers' included. But this book, and all the books in the world, can only give you the tools to act. Acting depends on you.

Too many marketers and managers seem to content themselves with the mundane *tactical* marketing service issues such as advertising, promotion, direct mail, writing the brochures and producing the sales presenters. These are all valuable activities, don't get me wrong, but while they are certainly *marketing services* activities, they do not constitute the whole market(ing) agenda. These activities are not what market(ing) was originally intended to be, nor can they form the basis of strategy. Marketers and market managers of all sorts need to be involved in the broader strategic issues facing their organizations, if only to make it possible for them to develop a proper market(ing) strategy when the baton passes. In the absence of professional market(ing) involvement in business strategy development, the marketer will be left with the problem of trying to make the best of objectives and a strategy to meet either financial or sales-driven goals.

Market(ing) is first of all an attitude of mind, a philosophy and a way of approaching business. Market(ing) is also, but secondarily, a set of specific techniques. Part One emphasized the first aspect of marketing; Part Two will emphasize the second.

In Part Two, Developing the Market(ing) Strategy, we will be looking at how to set a worthwhile marketing objective and then how to create a market(ing) strategy to achieve it (Figure 4.1).

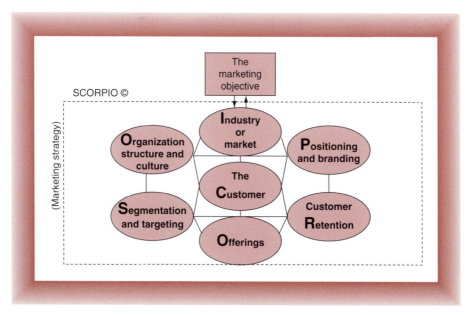

Figure 4.1 Developing the market strategy

Successful market(ing), as we all know, starts with the marketplace. In the same way then, detailed market(ing) strategy must necessarily start with the detailed analysis of the marketplace that we are targeting. In the market(ing) organization, all activity will stem from the marketplace, from an understanding of its needs and its wants, and success ultimately comes from our ability to satisfy those needs by bringing the necessary resources to bear.

I know that the temptation is sometimes irresistible, but we must put aside thoughts of existing organizational strengths and particular product or service advantages until a little later on.

At last, the answer to that age-old conundrum, which came first, the chicken or the egg? – First comes the customer.

5 The market objectives

If the art of war were nothing but the art of avoiding risks, glory would become the prey of mediocre minds. I have made all the calculations, fate will do the rest.

Napoleon Bonaparte

Setting market (or market(ing)) objectives is never an easy business. But it is an important one.

First, we need to draw a distinction between 'corporate' or 'business' objectives and market objectives. We have already seen that corporate or business objectives are (very different from financial hurdles and) defined as *the goal or the aim to which all the resources of the organization are directed.*

Market objectives are different from business/corporate objectives. Market objectives do not focus on the overall 'goal or aim' of the organization.

The market(ing) objectives

Take the business/corporate objective and translate it into terms that can be actioned by the organization.

Normally this means translating the business/corporate objective into terms of products/services and markets (the product–market match).

In this review of market(ing) objectives, we will look at:

(1) *The planning period*: What is a reasonable timescale for a market(ing) objective?

(2) *What makes a good market(ing) objective*: There is a wide choice – and what doesn't work as well?

(3) *Using market(ing) objectives*: What do you do with them once you've got them?

5.1   The planning period

> There is one kind of robber whom the law does not strike at, and who steals what is most precious to men: time.
>
> *Napoleon Bonaparte*

The planning period depends on the organization. Typically I would always suggest a planning period of three to five years for business/corporate objectives and eighteen to twenty-four months for market(ing) objectives. This does not mean that you can't make them longer if you are in a slower changing business with longer lead times. On the other hand, it does mean that you can't make them shorter just because the conventional wisdom in your industry is that speed is everything.

Before you work on quarterly targets for everything (yes, such nonsense does exist), ask yourself whether customers' needs and wants really change that fast. Some argue that fashion markets (such as toy crazes among primary school children and fashion accessories in secondary schools) really do come and go that fast but then the serious organizations in this business manage a series of 'crazes' (tactical events) within an overall (longer-term) market(ing) strategy to achieve a business objective. Market(ing) objectives are driven by the market (customers), not by products or technology.

Also, with the link between market objectives and key performance indicators (KPIs), it doesn't do to change your market objectives on too regular a basis. 'Nudging' or 'fine tuning' is fine; wholesale change is unsettling for the whole organization as well as customers.

5.2   What makes a good market objective?

> Liberty and equality are magical words.
>
> *Napoleon Bonaparte*

There is a range of different measures that may make good market(ing) objectives for your organization. Here is a list of some of the ones that I tend to use, but the list is not exhaustive and others (if they are customer driven) may be added.

The market(ing) objectives need to be chosen carefully. There is no hard-and-fast rule but I tend to work on selecting between four (better) and six (maximum) objectives, which, taken together, *will create behaviours in the organization that we believe will achieve the business/corporate objective.*

Remember, it is not a question of any individual market objectives; it is a question of the combined effect of all the market objectives selected.

For example, selecting apparently conflicting objectives, such as:

- Market/segment position
- Product development
- Profitability
- Innovation

... will promote a market plan (and KPIs, see below) that drives the organization towards a branded position in selected market segments that require innovative solutions – but that also improve profitability.

Not an easy task but it ensures that the organization identifies real customer value in its research and product/service development rather than just producing 'new' offerings for which customers are not prepared to pay premium prices – pointless activity at any time. It also ensures (as long as you insist that *all* the market objectives are of equal value and that all must be achieved) that implementation doesn't simply follow the path of least resistance/persistence.

With apparently 'conflicting' objectives such as these, you can point implementers towards the right, selected market opportunities (that will achieve the organization's unique business objective) rather than just any objective like *grow*. In the example earlier, the implementers will be targeted (and maybe bonused) on achieving a particular market position within certain identified segments, doing that with products/services that are really innovative (offer greater customer value) because that is the only way that the profitability objective will be achieved. As long as rewards are only linked to achieving *all* objectives, not on an objective-by-objective basis, you should be successful.

The rule is, start with the business objective and strategy and then decide what combination of market(ing) objectives will achieve it. Some components for your own original combination might include:

(1) Market/segment position
(2) Market/segment share
(3) Market/segment harvesting
(4) Market/segment entering

(5) Market/segment exiting

(6) Market/segment penetration

(7) Market/segment development

(8) Product development

(9) Diversification

(10) Growth (after Doyle)

(11) Innovation

(12) Productivity

(13) Sales revenue

(14) Profitability and/or margins

(15) Cash flow

(16) Public responsibility

(17) Other measures.

The detail of many of these measures will be covered in the SCORPIO market strategy section, see Chapter 6.

5.3   Using market(ing) objectives

> It should not be believed that a march of three or four days in the wrong direction can be corrected by a counter march. As a rule, this is to make two mistakes instead of one.
>
> *Napoleon Bonaparte*

There is absolutely no point in deciding on market(ing) objectives unless you use them. Apart from using market(ing) objectives to drive the market(ing) strategy and plans (more of that later), there are two other key areas where the hard work in developing objectives must be used with great effect.

5.3.1   Resource allocation

We have already seen that resources are finite; this is not strange, unfair, impossible or in any way unusual; this is how competitive organizations work – by stretching what they have, to go as far as possible. There is no more resource to be had. In my experience though, this really isn't a problem; the real issue in most organizations is not that there is insufficient resource, but that the available resource is being misallocated.

This is a common problem, resources are often allocated to what was important yesterday and what customers used to want rather than what they want and are going to want tomorrow. Managers or all types tend to be much quicker at asking for money to develop new products/services or new markets, but much slower at cutting off support from products/services or markets that are in decline.

Don't blame the finance department; nobody has told them (yet) that they are also responsible for understanding customers, so they won't – and if you don't tell them. . .

But you can use the market(ing) objectives to rectify the position. I use the time-honoured (but still effective) traffic light method (Figure 5.1). In this monochrome version you will have to imagine the colours, but your new-found market(ing) objectives should allow you (through a process of internal consultation and discussion, of course) to agree:

You will be surprised how much this exercise can focus management attention on agreeing what the right market(ing) objectives should be. What might have appeared to some to be an academic exercise suddenly has the potential to reduce the size and importance of internal empires. If you are kind, you might even warn people that the selection of particular objectives has certain effects. You will gain their attention and their involvement.

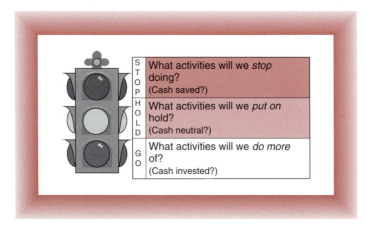

Figure 5.1　Marketing objectives

[Red]	*What activities and projects must stop now* because they do not support the objectives?
[Amber]	*What activities should be put on hold* pending more information that will decide whether they support the objectives or not?
[Green]	*What activities and projects must be supported/accelerated* now because they support the objectives?

5.3.2   *Organizational behaviour (market focus)*

Even more important, if you are to achieve the business objective, the market(ing) objectives must happen. The only way to guarantee this outcome is to ensure that the *market(ing) objectives become the organization's key performance indicators.*

Most organizations have KPIs and many managers wonder where these KPIs come from. Now is not the time to look into that mystery although if the organization doesn't focus everyone on the importance of meeting (external) customer needs, then finance, HR, operations or another internal function can't be blamed for stepping in to fill the vacuum.

This is the way it is meant to work:

(1) *Customers* provide all the money.

(2) *Customers* will continue to pay the organization money as long as it delivers what they want and value.

(3) *Customers'* needs, wants and values change over time.

(4) *Everyone* in the organization needs to work together to satisfy the customer, everything else is an additional overhead/burden on those working for the customer.

(5) *Market(ing)* should be the coordinating function that focuses the resources and effort of the organization on the one thing that will ensure survival and growth – the customer. Marketing services departments are not the same thing.

(6) *Market(ing) objectives* are derived from a detailed assessment of the market/ customer opportunities and threats and encapsulate the very best chance the organization has of commercial success.

(7) *The market* is highly competitive and everyone is fighting for the customers' attention and business. To be successful, our organization has to focus all its resources and efforts (as single mindedly as possible) on achieving the market/customer objectives (and so achieving the business objective).

(8) *We do this* by using the (agreed) market(ing) objectives as the KPIs for the whole organization.

	Marketing objectives	Key performance indicator	detail
1			
2			
3			
4			
5			
6			

Figure 5.2 Marketing objectives become *KPIs*

As Figure 5.2 shows, we take the four (or if you insist, a maximum of six) market(ing) objectives and turn these into KPIs. This process should not involve changing the nature or content of the market(ing) objectives, just modifying the odd word so that it can easily be used and communicated internally.

The KPIs can then be broken down into more detailed sub-objectives for transfer internally – but they must retain the customer focus from the market(ing) objectives that generated them. The more people understand that they work and thrive only at the pleasure of customers, the better the organization will function.

In a detailed process, the KPIs would eventually translate into personal objectives and form the main part of appraisal systems – so focusing the organization on the external market that supplies it with life.

But don't expect to achieve this without a fight (see Chapter 6).

Check your progress against the strategy checklist in the Appendix. Remember, with every addition to the checklist, we should re-visit the previous decisions and ensure that they are still valid in the light of the latest analysis.

6 Developing the market(ing) strategy (SCORPIO)

> There is no man more pusillanimous than I when I am planning a campaign. I purposely exaggerate all the dangers and all the calamities that the circumstances make possible. I am in a thoroughly painful state of agitation. This does not keep me from looking quite serene in front of my entourage; I am like an unmarried girl labouring with child. Once I have made up my mind, everything is forgotten except what leads to success.
>
> *Napoleon Bonaparte*

I have been working in the area of market(ing) and market(ing) strategy for many years now, sometimes teaching, sometimes (as little as possible) setting and marking examinations – but mostly working with organizations and helping them develop their market-based strategies for future growth and prosperity. Every so often over the past years, as some previous readers will know, I have taken time out to write books on the subject of market(ing) and market(ing) strategy; two of these books even carry the title of *Marketing Strategy* and in both of these previous editions I managed to write an entire book without ever exactly defining market(ing) strategy – but as nobody else who wrote about market(ing) strategy ever managed to define it either I always felt I was in good company.

Having worked with another twenty or so large organizations since the previous edition of this book was finished, I have finally worked out what market(ing) strategy is about, what activities and issues it includes and the process and organization it needs to go through to develop its own market strategy.

I have managed to 'package' all these various elements into a model/mnemonic that I have called SCORPIO (Figure 6.1). Every good idea deserves a great package.

SCORPIO is more of a checklist than a model *per se* in that it is designed to help practitioners both remember and coordinate the various activities required to create an enduring and practical market(ing) strategy for their organization. Unlike more academic models, SCORPIO does *not* attempt to introduce any

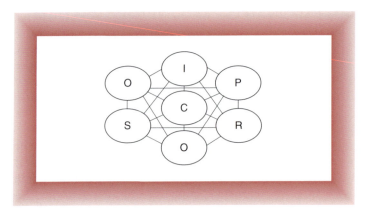

Figure 6.1   The SCORPIO model drives market strategy

'new' thinking (who needs it?), nor does it attempt to theorize about what might be either good or bad market behaviour. Instead, it is based on the practical observations and experiences that I have gained in working for numerous organizations over the years and what I and my clients know needs to be assessed, included, sifted and implemented to create workable market(ing) strategy in today's competitive environments. In my experience, the last thing that hard-pressed managers want is something 'new'. Competition is hard and getting harder; markets are blurring and uncertainty is everywhere. The last thing today's manager or market wants is more new, untried ideas – they haven't used the ideas they have already, why look for new ones?

The other important note on SCORPIO is that it is, and will always remain, work in progress. Markets change, organizations change, priorities change and, of course, some new market(ing) ideas arise (some are new and lots are just old ideas repackaged – did I mention CRM?) and these ideas, concepts and approaches will need to be reflected in the different SCORPIO elements over time. The version which I will describe below has already undergone a number of changes but is, I believe, going to remain stable for a while now. While the key elements of the SCORPIO model will remain largely unchanged, there are likely to be some modifications to the detail under each of the seven sections because, frankly, I learn more about markets and strategy every time I work it through with a different organization. Although books are still an extremely convenient way of packaging and communicating complex ideas, they tend to be fixed in time.

If there are any changes to the SCORPIO model, you will find these on http://www.fifield.co.uk/scorpio.

The origins of SCORPIO

The SCORPIO model wasn't originally developed and designed to work as a theory or a business model or even a clever book, but rather as a personal checklist to enable me to assess the current state of market(ing) strategies (or lack of) in organizations. Anyone who has attempted to check out the academic literature under the heading of marketing strategy will soon find that they have a problem. There is a very large amount written about business strategy with the big hitters such as Michael Porter and Henry Minzberg still taking centre stage. At the other end of the scale, the bookshelves and the reference libraries are full to bursting with books on marketing tactics and day-to-day problems such as writing marketing plans, developing product portfolios, new product development and, of course, marketing communications (Figure 6.2).

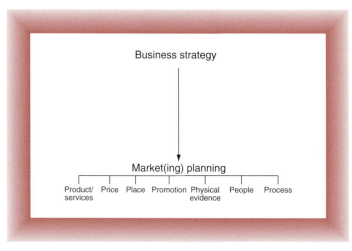

Figure 6.2 Strategy and marketing

The corporate strategist might ponder long and hard (at the very highest levels of the organization) and then pass down a missive to the operating divisions that from now on (or until someone has a better idea) the organization is going to be 'differentiated'. Even when backed up by yards (or metres) of detailed analysis, the seasoned practitioner will still have major problems flexing the inevitable 'marketing mix' into something that might be considered 'differentiated'.

Not only is there an uneasy relationship between these two quite different fields of endeavour, but there is also a very easily identified vacuum between the two. This vacuum can be spotted quite simply by identifying *what is not included* in the two more popular areas of work. Let us take but one example – the brand. Where is the brand in either of these two specialisms? If we look at the marketing tactics first, we will expect to find the brand somewhere but no (it doesn't begin with P, so it's at a disadvantage straight away) it just doesn't seem to figure in the list. If you look at the books you will find elements of brand tucked away under the area of product; you'll find some elements under pricing in the sort of vague hope that brand might generate a premium pricing; you will find something in the area of distribution and people in that the brand needs to guide both of these areas of work to achieve some form of synergy. And, of course, we will find elements of brand under anything to do with promotion – but everything seems to have been hammered into the promotion element at some point by somebody (Figure 6.3).

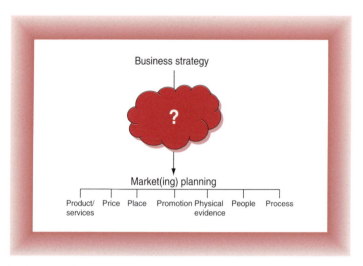

Figure 6.3   Strategy and marketing

If we look for brand in the corporate strategy end, do we find it there? The answer (again) is a resounding *no*. Does brand appear as a primary method of differentiation in Porter's generic strategies? No. Is it picked up under the financials as probably the most successful method of acquiring wealth? No, but then the accountants have been working for over fifteen years to get brand onto the balance sheet – and (you are no doubt relieved to hear) are still working at it. The very best you can say about brand is that you might (if you are very lucky, and very, very good) be able to re-assemble all the various, dismembered components of brand to create something useful for your market(ing) strategy and organization. The problem with this state of affairs is that (outside of the examination room) market(ing) plans and strategies just are not put together with this level of rigour; secondly, elements such as the brand are simply too important to be dealt with at the individual component level. The brand and other elements (as we shall see soon) need to be analysed, assessed, presented and developed as a whole rather than as a component tucked away/hidden/compartmentalized/lost in four or five different elements of the marketing mix and the corporate strategy process (Figure 6.4).

Once you get to the point of realizing that there is something missing in the literature, it is a relatively easy step to identify exactly what it is that is missing.

Figure 6.4 Strategy and marketing

The components of SCORPIO

All the elements of what has to be market(ing) strategy are missing.

So, for about the last ten years I have been trying to put these different elements into a simple structure and in some easy-to-deal-with format that would serve me as a day-to-day guide for assessing and developing real-life market(ing) strategy. We have already looked very briefly at brand but the list of 'missing links' as it stands at the moment (this may be subject to minor change) is as follows:

(1) *Segmentation and targeting*: This is another of the enormously important areas of modern market(ing), which is just missed completely in the skirmishing between the corporate strategy specialists, large organizational marketers and business school academics. In today's complex and rapidly changing markets, it *has* to be evident that the 'mass market' is an idea whose day has (definitely) gone. If the mass market is dead, then the segment must be the key to success. Issues such as:

- What is *the market*?
- What is a market segment?
- Which segment(s) should we approach?
- Which segment(s) must we own?
- Which segment(s) should we avoid?

tend to be completely missing from most operational market(ing) plans. Market segmentation crops up in promotion (doesn't everything?) where it tends to be treated as a promotional tactic that 'might' help the organization determine the most appropriate message or medium for any given product – but it is strangely absent from any strategic consideration. The closest we get is under Porter's generic strategy of 'focus' but apart from hinting that a focus strategy might imply a segment or a *niche* he then leaves the difficult thinking to marketers who, once again, fail to pick up the challenge.

(2) *The customer*: Now this is the really scary bit. The customer doesn't formally appear anywhere in 'takeaway' marketing theory. The corporate strategy people all (sort of) imply a customer-focused organization rather than a product- or production-focused one but then never go very far down the line to explain exactly what this means. They are obviously too concerned about treading on marketing's toes. The marketing mix, on the other hand, merrily proceeds to identify four or seven interacting elements of things that we should be *doing to the customer*. But who is the customer? Where in the marketing mix (or even in the corporate strategy) do we find any worthwhile discussion about who the customer is, what the customer wants, what the customer needs are and how we should be anticipating these needs for products and/or service development? There is rarely any concept of what constitutes 'Customer Value' – so little idea of how the organization should extract value from the market. There can be no compromise here, customers are much too important to deal with in component parts.

(3) *Organization – processes and culture*: Don't say this has no place in market(ing) or corporate strategy discussion but belongs in human resource management, this is exactly my point. Even if we are faced with a superb corporate strategy, brilliantly executed market(ing) tactics and an ingenious and customer-focused market(ing) strategy between the two, *nothing will ever happen unless the people in the organization want to do it*. The people and the organization are the mortar, blood (I never was very good at metaphors) in the system. Different organization processes and different organization cultures will produce different market behaviours. The market (if we listen) will tell us what it wants and how it wants it delivered. It is then up to us to work out the most appropriate processes and culture to enable us to deliver the benefits that our customers require of us.

(4) *Retention (customer)*: In the years since Reichheld's book (Reichheld, F. F. and Teal, T., *The Loyalty Effect: The Hidden Force Behind Growth, Profits, and Lasting Value*, Harvard Business School Press, Boston, 2001) on customer retention, we now all know that it is far more profitable to retain an existing customer than go to all the expense of acquiring a new one (well, mostly, but more of that later). But apart from talking about it at length (with great wailing and gnashing of teeth) on conference platforms, and spending large amounts of money on CRM computer systems (more of this later), we have done very little to improve the level of customer retention in most businesses. This is because retention is a strategic issue rather than a tactical one and it needs to be developed and structured into the very psyche of the organization if it is to succeed. But again, this is another of the great missing links between corporate strategy and market(ing) tactics, it appears in bits all over the place but as a whole nowhere.

(5) *Positioning and branding*: We have already spoken about branding and how it is one of the most important missing links between corporate strategy and marketing tactics but to this needs to be added the concept of positioning which is simply far too important to be left to the promotional element of the marketing mix. Blending positioning and branding together starts to identify routes and processes that enable us to look for unique positions in a market. This will create brands which have real market, customer and financial value.

(6) *Industry or market?*: This question picks up the whole area of what business the organization is in (industry) and contrasts this with what business the organization ought to be in (markets), a question first posed by Theodore Levitt in his famous article 'Marketing Myopia' (*Harvard Business Review*, 1960). This question (and the ensuing debate) is critical if an organization is successfully to break away from its product or production legacy and focus its efforts on supplying customer value. Again the question is over forty years old and the answer (and the debate) is nowhere to be found in either corporate strategy or market(ing) tactics.

(7) *Offerings*: Not to be confused with the product under the 7Ps, the 'offering' forms the critical link between the discussion at corporate strategy level about value chains and the debate about product at the market(ing) tactics stage. The core of the offering is the value proposition and this brings together the knowledge we have about current and future customer needs, the market we are in, the competition we face, brand, differentiation and pricing, in a cohesive way that the marketing mix can never achieve. Ultimately the organization will be as successful as its offering is perceived by its target market – no more.

For a diagrammatic form, see Figure 6.5.

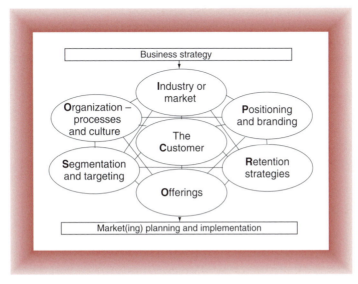

Figure 6.5 SCORPIO market strategy

We will spend the rest of the section of this book looking at these seven key elements of market(ing) strategy that make all of these processes work. In the meantime, there are just one or two rules to the game:

(1) *All of the seven elements are interrelated*: That is to say that you cannot make decisions or progress in one of the seven element areas without affecting decisions in the other. Therefore,

(2) *You will need to work on all of the seven elements at the same time*: Rather than work on one element and attempt to complete it before starting on the others.

(3) *Not all of the seven elements will carry equal importance*: For your business. The nature, structure, size and competitive situation of the organization will determine which of the elements have most importance at any point in time. However,

(4) *None of the elements can be omitted from the strategy*: Every time I work with SCORPIO, I find that the balance between the elements is different. On the two occasions when I thought I'd found a situation where one or more of the elements was not relevant, I actually found that I had missed something important in the analysis.

(5) *There is no preordained order to the process*: I tend to use the sequence that I have used in this book, starting with industry and market and finishing with offerings, but you need not necessarily follow this process order. Feel empowered to move as you feel most comfortable.

(6) *The process is 'iterative'*: You will need to move from one section of the figure to another as you build (or even craft) a market(ing) strategy that makes sense. As you grow your understanding of one area, you will inevitably affect decisions made in another.

(7) *The process grows and develops over time*: Like the famous marketing mix. Don't expect to arrive at a 'SCORPIO moment' where everything falls into place and the 'answer' is revealed. The right answer (if such a thing exists) depends on the market and there, we know, rules change daily.

(8) *Apart from these rules there are no rules*!

In the rest of this section, I intend to look through each of the seven elements of the SCORPIO model in more detail and show how exactly they work and link together (Figure 6.6).

Effectively, SCORPIO becomes the template for your organization's strategic market(ing) plans; ultimately you should be able to plot:

(1) Where you are on each SCORPIO dimension;

(2) Where you need to be;

(3) How to get there by actions on each SCORPIO dimension.

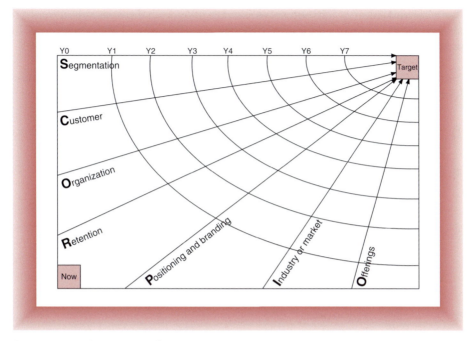

Figure 6.6 Planning with SCORPIO

Every organization and every market and brand position is unique. It follows then that no two organizations will need to approach SCORPIO in exactly the same way. Depending on a number of factors, your own blend of SCORPIO will constitute your market(ing) strategy for the future. Consequently, it will be extremely unlikely that you will need to go into the full depth on all of the seven elements, but on those one or two that you really need to dig quite deeply I hope I will have allowed you the data to carry out your search. For the other areas where you do not need to dig so deeply, you need only skim the information to assess how well you are doing versus the competition.

All clear? Then let's get involved in some of the debates.

6.1 Industry or market?

> How many things apparently impossible have nevertheless been performed by resolute men who had no alternative but death.
>
> *Napoleon Bonaparte*

The whole question of what business you are in and what business you ought to be in or want to be in has been a great debate since Theodore Levitt first raised the issue in his seminal article 'Marketing Myopia' (*Harvard Business Review*, 1960).

Traditionally, there are two ways in which 'the business' might be described and defined by the organization (Figure 6.7):

(1) *The products* and services sold, the technology that it will use to produce products and services or the industry the organization is in.

(2) *The customer* needs that the organization will satisfy.

Figure 6.7   SCORPIO market strategy

We could take, for example, a medium-sized organization operating internationally, which makes fire hose. This company could define the business that it is in differently and it would seek different opportunities, for example:

(1) *Industry or technology thinking*: If the organization defines its business as hose technology this would then naturally send the organization seeking opportunities in a variety of markets where there was a need for this type of technology. This might include garden hoses or using the hose technology to reline gas and oil pipelines as an alternative to pipe replacement.

(2) *Market or customer thinking*: Depending on how the organization defines its customers and their needs, it could define itself as being in the 'fire business' and meeting the needs of people in that group. In this case, if the organization wishes to expand it might start looking at alternative products and services to

deliver to the fire industry as a whole, such as extinguishers and fire blankets. Alternatively the organization could define itself as being in the 'electronic fire detection and safety business' which might lead it to investigate sprinkler systems or escape products. Another alternative could be the 'fluid transfer business'. It would then, should it wish to expand, be seeking opportunities in which perhaps the fire industry would remain a large but just one segment within a market needing to transfer various fluids from one point to another. Examples here might include entering the pipeline business or managing a fleet of tankers for flight refuelling.

Now, the importance that the way we define the business we are in has on how the organization sees itself should be apparent; it will affect the way the organization sees its markets and, most importantly, the way in which the organization sees its future. The *art* in the process should also be evident – there is more than one way that the organization can define its business, even in the market area. For example, we can see the advantage for Kellogg of not being obsessed with 'cereals' because it would lose business to non-cereal competition, but where should it see its future? Business definitions such as 'breakfast', 'cereals', 'breakfast', 'morning goods', 'first meal of the day', 'snacks', 'nutrition', 'children's health' will all offer very different competitors, opportunities and threats to the organization. Which is the best way?

In my experience, the questions of what business we are currently in and what business we want or, maybe better put, we need to be in are separate questions and need to be asked separately.

6.1.1   What business are we in (now)?

The first question, what business are we currently in, needs to be answered with some honesty. If you truly believe that your organization is market oriented and that its primary concerns are with identifying and satisfying customer needs, then you need not worry about answering this first section. If (and I must say that this relates to practically every company I have ever worked with) you feel that you have market aspirations but your organization is primarily dominated by production/technical and industry factors, then you should ask yourself what business you are really in at the moment – this drives the whole culture and thinking in the business.

Before you pile in and make yourself unpopular, take a moment to look at things in a slightly more analytical way. We need to ponder the question of 'Value Migration'. We will look at this phenomenon more than once as we consider market(ing) strategy but here it helps to understand how the organization thinks and sees its world. You can't hope to change things unless you understand why things are as they are.

The value in a market is a function of what customers perceive to be valuable to them (solutions to problems they believe they have) and so, what they will be willing to pay. Unfortunately for organizations (who would like stability), customer value changes over time. To some extent, this change is driven by organizations and product/service improvements and to some degree driven by customer needs, taste and fashion, etc. One easy way to understand this is through an example; let us take the case of the motorcar over the past fifty years. As soon as Henry Ford had managed to bring the car within the reach of the common person, having a car was all that mattered and any colour was fine. The value in the market then shifted away (migrated) from just having a car to get around, towards design, fashion and styling. The 1950s saw an explosion of different designs, styling, colouring and annual developments in fashion. In the 1960s, perceived value migrated again and customers were willing to pay more for reliability and economy with the arrival of the Japanese cars in many world markets. The 1980s and 1990s saw a gradual shift away from reliability *per se* (all cars were now seen as reliable and so this was no longer a differentiator) and the value migrated (back) to style as well as fuel economy and environmental issues. Similar migrations of customer value will have happened in your markets and business as well. Remember, it is likely that the organization was well positioned against customer value in the past; it was successful after all. But things move on and value migrates in a market – if you don't keep up, you lose out.

Louis Vuitton doesn't sell 'luggage', it offers solutions in 'The Art of Travelling'.

A final word of warning: organizations are collections of people – people sometimes act in irrational ways (or, the seemingly irrational person is being totally logical – at least from their perspective; maybe we just don't understand the mindset?). People generally seem to dislike change; not only do people not like change, but they also resist change. Sometimes they are right to resist change and sometimes they will kill the organization by resisting. We need people in organizations to get things done and to deliver customer benefits and so make profits. With change as fundamental as the definition of what business we are in can, if it is carried out effectively, it can change the entire stance of the organization including which parts of the organization are seen as the most valuable for the future. But let us be quite clear: there is in the nature of people such a strong tendency to keep with the past, to keep with what is known (even if that is *proved* to have no future customer value), that some (especially senior) managers would rather see their organization die than make the (necessary) changes. Here I speak from experience; having worked with two organizations (both of which happened to be in the UK financial services sector), we succeeded in researching and identifying new business definitions which were both understood by and welcomed by their respective existing and future customer bases – but which required both organizations to start moving away from their (previous) technological strengths. In both cases, the solution was placed in front of the operating board and although they could see the logic and the value in the change (as well as the inevitable cost of not changing) both boards decided not to proceed along the well-researched and finely mapped change route. Both companies were taken over by larger organizations as their financial situations deteriorated, both boards were replaced and in both instances significant redundancies took place when change was forced on them by their new owners. This is probably rational if the board really wants to retire as soon as possible – misguided maybe but still rational.

Ah well . . .

6.1.2 What business do we want to be in or should we be in?

The second question, what business your organization wants to be in (or needs to be in), is one which is fraught with difficulties and problems. Not only is any move away from the traditional 'industry-based' definition of business seen as 'flaky', 'irrelevant', or even worse 'Californian', it is often seen as just dangerous and misleading especially if the organization is under some pressure from market and competitive activity. In this environment of cynicism and hostility, you are well advised to tread very carefully indeed. The ideal business decision is not something you should come to lightly nor is it something you should do in isolation of the rest of the organization and particularly the senior management team. It is something you should do carefully and slowly, testing the concepts and ideas with the target marketplace as you go. The best way to proceed here (I have always found) is to look at some examples of organizations who have conducted this approach and who appear to have implemented it successfully.

Figure 6.8 is a selection of examples (based on data in the public domain); they are not particularly new but they tend to be both well known and (importantly) quite successful in getting the message across. I have listed these organizations together with what might be viewed as their typical industry or technology/product definition – in other words defining the organizations by the products or services that they produce. So, for example, Harley Davidson obviously makes motorbikes, Swatch makes watches and Black & Decker produces products with electric motors in them.

While most (if not all) of these companies are household names, they have also looked quite carefully at defining the business that they are in and have publicly commented on the effects that this definition has on their day-to-day operations.

Industry definition	Company	Market definition
Motor cycles	Harley Davidson	Big boys' toys
Watches	Swatch	Fashion accessories
Electric motors	Black & Decker	DIY (do-it-yourself)
Railroads	Amtrak	Transport (people and goods)
Electronics	Sony	Entertainment
Cars	Jaguar	Status
Watches	Rolex	Jewellery
Coffee shops	Starbucks	The 3rd place (between home and work)

Figure 6.8   Industry or market?

If we then look at some of the business definitions that these organizations have made for themselves (I make no comment as to whether these are the right business definitions), we can see that some interesting scenarios start to take shape. For example, Harley Davidson was doing quite badly as a classic motorcycle manufacturer in the USA, under threat from the Japanese imports as were other domestic producers at that time. When it was trying to work out how to respond to the Japanese threat, it started (innovatively) by talking to its existing customers and it found a number of interesting pieces of information: the average buyer of a new Harley Davidson was over fifty years old, predominantly male and before the purchase of the new Harley had compared this, not to other motorcycle products, but to quite different categories such as a home swimming pool or a European vacation. This insight caused Harley Davidson to reconsider its position and to start thinking about exactly what were the benefits which were flowing from the purchase of a new Harley Davidson motorbike. Their new business definition has led them into many new market areas with a completely different marketing mix from classic motorcycle producers. For example, they now make the majority of their profit from accessories rather than the motorbikes and the product is to be found on display, not in out-of-town low-rise motorcycle outlets but next to other fashion retailers such as Armani and Versace on the premier fashion streets of most major cities in the world.

The other examples are similar in that they demonstrate how a new (market- and customer-focused) business definition can often lead to both innovative

Google doesn't run a 'search engine', it 'organizes the world's information'.

marketing solutions and powerful and profitable market positions for the organization and the brand. Swatch makes fashion accessories that happen to tell the time rather than watches. Black & Decker is a major player in the DIY (do-it-yourself) business with products such as the Workmate which do not include an electric motor at all. Amtrak (US Railroads) is from Theodore Levitt's original work in 1960 and has already been cited. Sony says it is in the entertainment business rather than electronics and this is the definition that led to the acquisition of film studios and music labels. Jaguar obviously sells status rather than motorcars while Rolex finds it much easier to sell jewellery pieces at prices far above those that would be commanded by simple (or even ornate) watches. Starbucks say that it is the third place between home and work which explains why its coffee shops are full with people making telephone calls having meetings outside of the traditional office and workplaces and increasingly Starbucks offer Internet connection for today's mobile workforce.

Working out your own definition of the business you want to be in is not going to be easy; do not assume you can rattle it off in a few hours.

We all understand the technical/industry definition and have lived with it for years. We may be ready to move to a new definition but most other people in the organization will not, so tread carefully.

For B2B markets, definitions can be more technical or scientific as long as the target market understands clearly what the definition means – what offerings would fall within this definition and which ones would definitely fall outside. For example, 3M may define itself as being in the 'coatings' business, as long as this means something tangible and specific to its target customers and prospects – it is a business definition that focuses activity on customers' (coatings) needs and so moves the company away from the technology definition behind its operations.

Services are relatively new to marketing too and will have similar problems. There is no point in settling for an impossibly wide definition such as 'peace of mind' instead of insurance – it is simply too big to get your arms round and, far from giving the dominant sales force 'room to move' it provides too much room to create a profitable differentiation.

No, we are talking days or even months of work here. A hint. The more people you can involve in the process, the slower the decision-making *but* the easier the internal market(ing) of the new business definition and the change process, and the more likely you are to secure agreement at all levels.

6.1.3   How does this define the market/customer needs we should be satisfying?

Now the process starts to get tricky; we are entering real market(ing) territory.

How we define the particular market that we will be addressing is critical for our organization and our scope as well as our competition. Even more important, the business definition defines exactly the particular customer needs, wants, desires and motivations that we should be satisfying – *and those that we should not*. This distinction becomes apparent when we look at some of the companies in Figure 6.8, it is clear that Rolex's definition of being in the jewellery business starts to define a particular market and a set of customer needs. An obsession with watches and the minutiae of the product is unlikely to reveal the market need for a £10 000 (€15 000) piece of jewellery that also happens to tell the time!

Finally, it is important to note that if the new definition of the business does not clearly define the market/customer needs we should be satisfying, then maybe it is not the right definition.

You can achieve a lot with experience and insight but independent research can sometimes add a previously unimagined dimension to the discussion.

6.1.4   Where/how should we be growing the business?

This is the next question to define whether or not we have discovered the most appropriate new definition for the business; does it give you some idea about how you are going to grow the business in the future? Growth is a big and difficult area and too many books and commentators deal with the concept 'growth' without really defining exactly what they mean – so you need to be careful.

Previously you would have worried about how to hit the numbers. It used to be easy to see where the cuts could be made; you could see the costs clearly. Spotting where extra sales could come from was more difficult; everywhere you looked you were fighting the same competitors every day.

Changing the business definition should change much of this. Depending on how you re-define the business you want to be in, you should see many more business opportunities than you saw before. Previously, you saw product opportunities and sales objectives – but you were never sure if there was a willing market ready to buy. Now you should see the world differently, market opportunities – your concern now should be can you make a product or service that will meet the needs?

Deciding where to grow the business now becomes a strategic question; your job should not be *how do we grow?*, but *where should we be growing?* Take back control.

Successful organizations all tend to start by being strongly customer driven and using a benefits-based definition of the business they are in. In a competitive environment, it is the only way to succeed against entrenched competitors. Over time, focus tends to move away from customers to processes, systems and 'professional management'. Established organizations do have a choice, however; rather than simply succumbing to the new entrants in their turn, they can decide to re-define their business and regain their customer focus. Corporate 'renewal' is never easy although some may prefer it to a steady decline.

6.1.5 What are the strategic opportunities and threats?

If your *new* business definition has held up this far, then it is time to start doing some basic analysis. What we need to do next is identify the key numbers that will eventually feed into the plans and the planning process.

We should start, at the beginning, with an understanding of the external environment – of the business described by the 'new' definition. We know that organizations produce standard *PEST* and *SWOT* analyses as a type of market(ing) and planning 'habit' and then do nothing with them. It's like many activities in modern business: we do them because we have always done them, but we can't remember why.

Our first task then is to brush off and re-focus these two analyses to find out whether they give any more insight into the needs/wants of the target marketplace and what our ultimate market objectives should be.

Starting with the PEST analysis, typically we don't look for too many major changes in the PEST analysis because the newly defined business won't (or shouldn't) be too far away from the one in which the organization is currently working. However, some of the impacts of the external environment can be more or less severe within different business/market definitions.

With the SWOT analysis we will be expecting a greater degree of change. A proper SWOT analysis (although these are still rare) should take strengths and weaknesses (the internal and controllable elements) as they are seen by customers, not as seen by the people inside the organization. Opportunities and threats (the external and uncontrollable elements) will be dictated by the 'new' business in which we want to operate. Here we have more work to do. Strengths and weaknesses will now need to be assessed from the perspective of your 'new' target market; for example, big boys (Harley Davidson), fashion seekers (Swatch), DIY enthusiasts (Black & Decker) and travellers (Amtrak).

6.1.6   What competition are we facing?

Review the new definition of the business that you have chosen.

As you move from an industry to a market-driven definition of the business you are in, it's fairly sure that you will leave a lot of your (former) industry competition behind you. It is equally sure that, as you move, you will encounter new competition from different 'industries'. Again, using examples from the discussion earlier, Harley Davidson loses its direct competition with other motorbike manufacturers but starts to pick up competition from holiday companies, swimming pool makers and (in the UK) producers of conservatories! Equally, Sony loses some direct competitors who just make electronic products but then faces new competition from other forms of entertainment such as live shows, gambling, older technology books and magazines and newer technology iPods.

On the one hand, it might be attractive to move into a position where you're no longer competing with the people and organizations you have historically met (and benchmarked) time and time again. On the other hand, you would be well advised to assess the 'new' competition that you will be facing quite carefully. For example, a manufacturer of small electrical domestic appliances (such as kettles and irons) who redefines the business as being in 'household tasks/ chores' might suddenly come face to face with the cleaning giants such as Unilever and Johnson & Johnson. Moving from a 'small pond' to compete in a 'bigger pond' means that there might be more opportunities for growth but you meet bigger fish.

This may be a good opportunity to dust off the old 'Porter's five forces' figure (see Chapter 2) and apply it with some degree of vigour.

6.1.7   What are the boundaries for effort?

If you have got to this point with only insignificant or cosmetic changes to the new business definition, it could be that you have found the most appropriate route for future development. In which case, you now need to start planning the actual activities that the new business definition implies you should be undertaking.

Any good market organization knows that its activities and plans are driven not by its products or services, but by the markets and customers it wishes to serve. The more you focus on defining your business around the customers who (you hope) will buy your products and services, the better chance you have of understanding what they need from you and what you have to provide in order to grow the business. The more you are able to move to a customer-driven understanding, the more you are able to put the industry requirements into the background.

The other side of the coin says that no matter how fast, nimble and good you are, resources will always be limited – the pot is never bottomless.

In which case, we need to know where to place our limited investments (time money and ingenuity) for maximum return. Again, the customers will tell us if only we can imagine and formulate the right questions.

Enter the trusty traffic lights. The right business definition should be able to tell us:

(1) Where we should devote our time and resources (the GO/green area) and

(2) Where our attention will be wasted (the STOP/red area).

Beware here. Some activities are really wasteful in customer terms and can be stopped, but some of these 'wasteful areas' may be viewed internally as important to the organization – so only stop these carefully. Some areas may be important in providing service to customers but they are not seen in that light (imagine, for example, doctors' receptionists or hospital casualty administration); in these cases, the activities cannot be dropped but they need to be re-packaged, re-presented or reformulated so that they are seen positively by the customers.

6.1.8   Conclusions – industry or market?

In this first part of the market strategy discussion, we have looked at the all-important question of 'what business are we in?'

Levitt attempted to answer the question in 1960, and I have been trying to do the same with organizations for a very long time.

The question is deceptively simple, the logic is unavoidable and the solution is devilishly difficult. Some organizations manage the change and others do not. Of course, not all organizations survive to an old age.

We have looked at some of the issues involved in deciding how to re-define the business and what the best definition might be. As always, there are no hard and fast rules as every organization is just a collection of people – and people need much more than hard logic to persuade them to do something different.

Check your progress against the strategy checklist in the Appendix.

Finally, a few questions that you should now be able to answer:

Industry or market?

1	What business are we in?	
2	What business do we want to be in or should we be in?	
3	How does this define the market/ customer needs we should be satisfying?	
4	Where/how should we be growing the business?	
5	What are the strategic opportunities and threats?	
6	What competition are we facing?	
7	What are the boundaries for effort?	

6.2   The customer

Unhappy the general who comes on the field of battle with a system.
Napoleon Bonaparte

To recap (on the whole book), the customer is the name of the game (Figure 6.9).

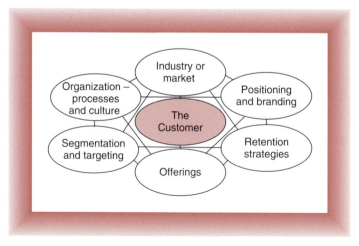

Figure 6.9 SCORPIO market strategy

Customers produce all the organization's revenues and profits and are the only reason for an organization's continued existence. At the very least, the organization intent on survival will need to know who its customers are and what they want. The organization intent on achieving success rather than simple survival will need to know much more if it is to compete successfully in rapidly internationalizing and commoditizing markets.

Although 'knowing' may itself be a tall order – often customers don't really 'know' what they want, they just want – and need. But, before we go any further, it really needs to be said that there is a world of difference between 'knowing' what your customers (and prospects) really want from you and:

● You assuming you know better than they do, what they want.

● You knowing what they 'ought to' want.

● You guessing who they are and what they 'might' want.

● You hoping that they are going to want what you have decided to make.

● You not really caring who they are or what they want because you have sales targets to make and you'll find somewhere to unload the stuff.

Knowing exactly what your customers (and prospects) want is not easy – it's impossible. Many customers don't really know what they want; they might know it when they see it but they can't be sure, so how are they going to tell you? But at least you can reduce a fair share of the risk if you ask them!

I don't want to get too technical, too early but asking customers (rather than guessing) is called market research.

There's no reason to start re-checking your hard-earned budgets – it needn't be either difficult or expensive. It is probably going to be better than guessing whatever you do. So let's deal with the issues of research – right up front.

6.2.1 *Market research*

Before we start we need to deal with one or two definitions:

(1) *Market research or marketing research?* These are *not* the same:
   (a) Market research is research into markets, in other words their size, composition, buyer's needs and wants, and so forth.
   (b) Marketing research is research into the organization's market(ing) activities and its ability to address its markets.

(2) *Data or information?*
   (a) Data can be defined as, *things which are known or granted from which inferences may be drawn*, they are essentially the raw material of market research.
   (b) Information is best defined as *that which reduces uncertainty in the receiver*.

(3) *Product research or market research?*
   (a) Market research implies research into the workings of the market and customers' needs, wants and motivations.
   (b) Product research normally involves batteries of questions asking respondents for their thoughts and attitudes on existing products (or services), new product concepts and possible modifications.

(4) Real market research is not easy. Maybe that's why it isn't common. We need to know how our customers lead their lives, how they run their businesses, how they regard their families, what they do in their leisure time and what problems they believe they have. Interestingly enough, the reasons for *not* conducting this type of market research clearly demonstrate some of the problems facing market(ing) and market(ing) strategy today:
   (a) *We've never done it.*
   (b) *Qualitative research is all a bit touchy-feely.*
   (c) *How do you find out what the customers themselves don't know they want?*
   (d) *This organization works on numbers — not loose concepts or ideas.*
   (e) *The market research agencies we use just don't do that sort of thing.*
   (f) *Sorry, the finance people just wouldn't buy it.*
   (g) *The product managers hold the research budget and they have their product targets to meet this year thank you.*
   (h) *There's no budget for that sort of thing, every pound/dollar we spend has to be set-off against an existing profit centre.*

6.2.2 What can market research do?

Maybe this final section ought to be called, *what can't market research do?* because nowadays market research has become a major tool in the armoury of the market-facing organization. It goes too far when managers will not move a muscle without a market research project to back up any activity.

The first thing that we need to say about market research is that it is definitely *not* an alternative to management decision-making. No market research, no matter how deep, complicated and detailed, can ever be seen as a substitute to creative decision-making by professional managers. At its very best, market research might be able to remove some doubt and clarify some options or alternatives. It may even be seen as a tool which can improve the quality of decisions – but it is not, of itself, a decision-making mechanism.

Market research, in common with a number of scientific and pseudo-scientific management tools, suffers from the widespread complaint of 'spurious accuracy'. Market research results can never be completely accurate as they are dealing with human nature. They are dealing with a small sample of a dynamic marketplace which has been 'grossed up' to give total market results. There will always be a form of inherent bias in market research results. This error should be plainly and clearly understood by everyone reading research results. There is not only a place, but also an ongoing need for creativity and imagination when dealing with market research results – certainly when making any attempt to apply them in the market.

Last, it should always be remembered that market research is not an end in itself. It is simply a means by which some risk can be removed from market(ing) activity. Ultimately, only the market(ing) activity counts, not the market research itself.

Market(ing) strategy doesn't need market research as much as it desperately needs some good answers. Practical market(ing) strategy has to be based on reasonably well-understood customer needs, wants and motivations if it is to provide longer-term solutions that customers will want to buy. The better we understand our customers and their needs the better the quality of the market(ing) strategy will be and the better the bottom line will look. Unfortunately, all that glitters is not gold – and some 'market research' documents are not what they might appear.

6.2.3 Who are our customers?

A wise organization knows its own customers.

A good way to think about your customers is like an *asset*. In fact, your customers are probably the biggest single asset your company owns. Like any asset, the job is:

(1) To identify it;

(2) To maintain it;

(3) To maximize returns from it.

Stage one is to know where your assets are. In market(ing) terms, know your customers. Customers are human beings (even B2B) and are much more than serial numbers or barcodes. In this section, we will look at how we can get to know our customer base and where the invaluable data is held.

The market(ing) information system (MkIS; Figure 6.10) is a good place to start. It may not be called a 'system' or even be overtly concerned with marketing information – but it always exists (in some form) in every organization.

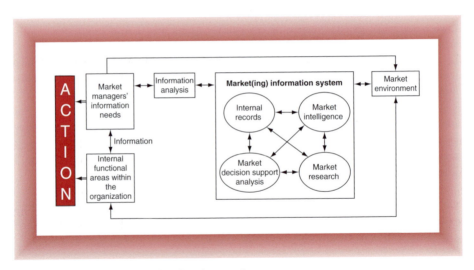

Figure 6.10   The market(ing) information system
Source: Adapted from Fifield and Gilligan (2000).

The MkIS has gained a whole new lease of life recently with the creation of a new area of academic research, 'knowledge management' (KM) (see Section 6.6). It's important to note that while KM is often facilitated by IT, technology itself is not KM.

Call it what you will, information is the lifeblood of any organization in a competitive marketplace. Often the source of true competitive advantage, if an organization is better informed on the needs of its target customers then it has a better chance of developing and offering products and solutions than the competition. Faster too. Unfortunately, there is more to developing an effective market(ing) information system than simply piling miscellaneous data into a computer database – and hoping. One of the most common problems in developing information systems is that they simply become too complex and too data-heavy. To be effective, the system needs to produce information in a form that is really needed – and then delivered to the people who need it most.

From the figure, it can be seen that an MkIS has four principal components:

(1) *The external record system*, which may include data on orders and invoicing, pricing stock levels, sales and payments.

(2) *The market intelligence system*, which may consist of regular data flows on market and product developments in the market and customer environment (often gleaned from trade press, media, conferences, exhibitions) to monitor trends and flag any unexpected changes.

(3) *The market research system* as described earlier.

(4) *The market decision support system* which may include any tools or statistical decision models (including simple ratios) that the organization uses to make sense of the data and turn it into useful information for decision-making managers.

The best test of any information system must be the extent to which it contributes to the decision-making process – that helps managers to make better, faster and more informed decisions. Obviously, to do this it must be updated regularly, be easily accessible – and produce information in a form that managers find usable. Of course none of this is possible unless we have a reasonably good idea of the market(ing) strategy's information needs. Without this it is likely that any system will prove both unfocused and unusable.

Moving from today's data-rich world to an information-rich environment in which market(ing) strategy can be developed and implemented is not as easy as it might sound. The faster that data grows (compounded by the IT department's ability to store more and more of the stuff) the greater the problem becomes of winnowing the wheat from the chaff. Frankly, there is little point in congratulating yourself upon your ability to store six quarters worth of transactional data in your brand new data warehouse if you lack the skills to:

● Analyse the data for trends and changes and the ability to

● Understand the reason behind any movement in customer behaviour and

● The strategic marketing skills to do something about the changes you have identified.

6.2.4   What do they currently buy from us/our competitors, and why?

Warning: It's now time for readers with weak hearts or fragile dispositions to sit down and compose themselves before going further.

Customers do *not* buy product 'features', they buy 'benefits', or solutions to problems.

Yes, yes I know you've heard all this before, the very first day of your basic sales training programme or within certainly the first week of any rudimentary marketing training programme you were told that benefits were more important than features. The shocking thing is that it's really true! At the risk of giving Levitt too much exposure, he said:

(1) *A product is what a product does.*
(2) *Customers just need to get things done. When people find themselves needing to get a job done, they essentially hire products to do that job for them.*
(3) *People don't want a quarter inch drill – they want a quarter inch hole.*

Given (at least for the moment) that customers part with hard-earned cash for benefits rather than features, have we any idea at all what our existing customers have been buying from us over the years? Now, before you recoil in disgust at the idea that you may not know your sales results, territory by territory, year by year, quarter by quarter, week by week, line by line, I am confident that you have these figures – and analysed in detail. No, what you should *also* have is an analysed breakdown of the different needs or problems that have been *driving or motivating* purchase over recent years – what 'jobs' have your products/services been 'hired' to do?

For example, a company in the financial services industry specializing in selling pension products would, I would expect, have a detailed breakdown of the most recent year's sales results and would be able to break down the individual pension product sales, by area, by intermediary, by time period, etc. It's interesting and useful data; but on the other hand it doesn't really help us develop a market(ing) strategy. To explain; if the recent three or four-year sales figures were also analysed by the solutions or benefits purchased, we might know:

- How many and which customers were buying pension products for financing their retirement.

- Which customers were buying pension products in order to reduce their tax liability in the current year.

- Which customers were buying pension products because they had a spare amount of money and didn't know where else to invest it.

- Which customers were buying because their spouse had insisted.

Then you can start to see how this data could start to inform future market activity.

Why is such data rarely held? Quite simply, because it is not the easiest data to collect. Checking off sales by model number or by part number is easy because that's what most organizations deal with.

6.2.5   *What benefits are they seeking?*

As the word 'market' is a collective noun used to describe your organization's potential customer base, if we are to understand our market, we will need to understand the customers who make it up.

Practical and profitable market(ing) strategy will inevitably spring not necessarily from doing what we are good at, but from doing what our customers want us to do. From supplying the goods and services that our customers actually want to buy from us. Inevitably then this means that an understanding of the customer (their needs, wants, problems, motivations and generally how they lead their lives) is the most important ingredient of any market(ing) strategy. Without the market information, you are left with a product strategy at best.

In simple terms, what your organization needs to find out is:

(1) *What* do your customers need or want?
   (a)   What jobs do they have to do?
   (b)   Where does it *hurt*?

(2) *What* do your customers actually need or want – from you?
   (c)   What jobs do they believe you can do for them?
   (d)   What do they believe you are capable/incapable of delivering

(3) *What* will your customers need or want from you in one, two, five years' time?

These are deceptively simple questions. Unfortunately, and here comes the really bad news, no one really understands what makes customers behave the way they do. Yes, I know that the (other) books abound with theories and diagrams and complex flowcharts, and as long as these are used to describe past customer behaviour and draw inferences (and sometimes even 'conclusions') based on correlations, then they can do an excellent (if limited) job. Be that as it may, if we are concerned with developing market(ing) strategy, we need to think about future, not the past – prediction may be difficult but we must try to reduce some of the uncertainty involved in planning ahead. Only some form of prediction can lead to a proper allocation of investment – in other words:

- Where do we put the money for maximum return?
- Which customers should we invest our very expensive time and money in?
- Which products and services should we be developing?
- Which ones should we be putting on 'indefinite hold'?

Looking at customers from the inevitable position of internal (organization) and product-based bias, it often comes as a shock to some practitioners that most customers tend to ask apparently irrational questions such as:

- What job have I got to do/get done?
- What product or service can I 'hire' to do the job for me?
- Where can I get it?
- Can I get it now?
- What's available?
- Who am I buying it for?
- What else is affected by this purchase?
- Can I afford it?
- Should I buy brand A or brand B – or no brand?
- What do I know about brand A?
- Do I know someone else who has bought brand A?
- Who can I ask about it?
- Do I like the brand A people?
- Will I feel comfortable using brand A?

Surprisingly few of the questions in B2C or B2B markets have very much at all to do with the detailed technical aspects of any given product or service. Japanese-inspired quality control and production methodologies now adopted by the West have led most buyers to assume that the product/service which they purchase will actually do the job for which it is being 'hired'. This level of expectation has meant that people have started to concentrate much more on the 'softer' aspects of products and services, sometimes described as the intangible elements of a given product or service offering.

The really important questions, at least as far as companies and their customers are (should be) concerned, are issues like:

- What will the purchase and use of this product or service do for me and my status amongst my peers?

- What will other people think of me?
- Will I enjoy consuming this product or service?
- Will I enjoy the relationship which it brings with the producing organization?

6.2.6 Overt and latent needs

Just a brief note here on the work conducted by Hamel and Prahalad (*Competing for the Future*, Harvard Business School Press, Boston, 1994) where they made the important distinction between problems/needs/wants which are evident to customers and those which are not evident or rather 'latent' (Figure 6.11).

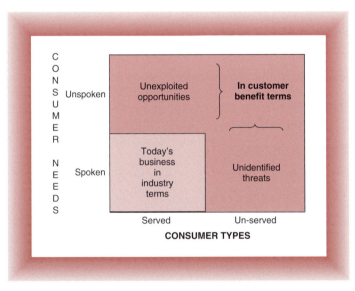

Figure 6.11 Latent needs and wants
Source: Adapted from Hamel, G. and Prahalad, C. K. (1994) *Competing for the Future*.

Hamel and Prahalad made the point that most organizations, when they do conduct customer research, tend to focus on what they have called today's business. On the vertical and horizontal scales you will see that today's business is identified by talking to existing customers about their existing needs. This much is what we have discussed above. They then go on to suggest that the great strategic threats and opportunities for your organization are not to be found in this small quadrant but in the broader area of customer needs and will only be identified by first talking to people who are not yet our customers about needs or wants that they don't yet know they have. Seems impossible? Not really. All you have to do is take a little longer, talk about their lives rather than your product/service – and listen! Such latent needs come in two types.

First, there are the needs that customers and prospects may have but for which no solutions are yet available. Examples could be cars that run without petrol, completely voice-activated computers (just like the bridge of the Starship Enterprise), hangover-free alcohol or safe tobacco products.

The second category of latent needs includes those issues or solutions that people haven't yet thought about but would be popular (and in demand) if the products and/or services were made available. Some recent examples of this category include email, laptop computers, mobile phones and MP3 players.

The Hamel and Prahalad diagram is also interesting as it starts to show the practical difference between tactical market(ing) and market(ing) strategy. While today's business is firmly the preserve of market(ing) tactics the market(ing) strategy should be driven by issues outside of the box that tends to dominate the attention of most organizations.

Dealing with 'latent' rather than 'evident' needs and wants can, at first glance, appear daunting but this needn't be so. Market research methodologies designed to uncover latent needs are well tried and tested. I use them all the time.

6.2.7   Hygienes or motivators?

One final piece of 'theory' that we ought to understand shows that not all needs and wants motivate the same way – or as strongly. We need to leave market(ing) and consider the work carried out by Hertzberg and his *two factor theory of motivation* (Herzberg, F., Mausner, B. and Snyderman, B., *The Motivation to Work*, Wiley, New York, 1959; Figure 6.12).

Originally, Hertzberg was carrying out his research in relation to the motivation of people in the workplace. What Hertzberg found was that there are a number of factors inherent in the workplace which people found essentially *dissatisfying* about their job – for example, salary. He also found that there are a number of aspects to the work and the place of work that respondents found *motivating* about their work. The most important revelation here, to Hertzberg, was that the two lists were not the same.

When Hertzberg started to dig deeper into these two apparently quite different lists he found that the lists did not contain the same items, which is what he had expected, but contained different items (see the first level of items in the figure). Looking deeper, he discovered that there were two separate lists of items which motivated the people in quite different ways. He titled these two sets of items as 'hygiene factors' and 'motivators':

(1) *Hygiene factors* (which include items such as salary and company policies) are items/issues which de-motivate quite strongly as long as expectations are *not* met but once improved to a position where the expectation is met, then merely

	Hygiene factors	Motivators
H e r t z b e r g	Supervision Salary Work environment Company policies Relationships with colleagues	Responsibility Recognition Promotion Achievement Intrinsic aspects of the job
M a r k e t i n g	What everybody offers Expected by the customer Not 'news' Ordinary	Special to you Not expected but prized Worth talking about Makes you special
S t r a t e g y	**Keeping up with the rest**	**Being different from the rest**

Figure 6.12   Hertzberg's (1959) the two-factor theory of motivation

Source: Adapted from Herzberg, F., Mausner, B. and Snyderman, B. (1959) *The Motivation to Work*. New York: Wiley.

become 'neutral' issues and no longer motivate the person. For example, a person who is not being paid what they believe that they are worth is seriously de-motivated by the level of salary that they receive. As the salary moves up to a level which they perceive is 'fair' for the job, so de-motivation disappears. If salary were increased beyond this point, the individual ends up no more motivated than they were once the salary reached the expected level. So hygiene factors will *de-motivate* customers if they are *not* present but at the very best they will only become non-issues.

(2) *Motivators*, on the other hand, consist of items that continue to motivate regardless of the level applied. As Hertzberg noted in his original experiments, the more that responsibility, recognition and promotion were improved, the more productivity and motivation continued to increase.

So what exactly does this mean for market(ing) strategy? Well, there are two primary aspects to the Hertzberg approach which have relevance to our discussions.

First, there is the question of market(ing) investment. Once you have identified which of the groups (hygiene factors or motivators) that the identified needs/

wants/problems may fall into, it is important that any market(ing) investment in these areas matches an understanding of the nature of the need. For example, every time I research this phenomenon, service levels are a hygiene factor for customers – not a motivator. The implication is, of course, that the organization should invest *only enough* so that any perceived deficiency in customer service is removed from the equation, so that customer service becomes a *non-issue*. Any additional investment in this area would be *wasted* as it would not be valued by the target customers. Now, before flinging down the book in disgust, just think about going into a restaurant where you have to wait half-an-hour for the first waiter to come up and take your order – bad service. Now imagine the same restaurant with three waiters assigned exclusively to your table who, in complete disregard for your conversation, replace dirty ashtrays every two minutes, top up half full glasses of wine and ask you whether everything is alright with the meal every other mouthful – you can have too much service!

The second issue here concerns differentiation (see Section 6.4). If hygiene factors can, at best, become non-issues, then they hold *no* potential for differentiation from the competition. In fact, *all* potential for differentiation is to be found in the area of motivators, not hygiene factors. Given that differentiation is critical for profitability, it must be developed wherever it can be found. It will always be found amongst the '*motivators*' rather than the hygiene factors because it is here that you can add real customer value.

I realize that for some, these comments may have come just a little too late. But for those of you who have not yet signed irrevocable contracts for millions of pounds/euros/dollars to implement CRM or loyalty programmes, maybe you should think a little harder before you do! How much money do you really want to spend on hygiene factors such as these? How much more might the same investment attract to the bottom line if it were directed at improving differentiation (and hence margins) through investment in motivational issues?

Of course, you need to be able to tell which is which.

6.2.8   Bi-focal marketing

We always hear that the important thing about strategy of any sort (business, market(ing), corporate or any other) is that it focuses the organization (and the strategist) on the future. This is obviously true but it does not mean that we cannot look at today as well. There is a difference between a strategy which is 'future focused' and one which is 'future exclusive'. The strategists who fall into the latter group are now much rarer than they used to be ten or fifteen years ago. They have been squeezed out of most organizations as competitive pressures have increased and it has been difficult to identify the value they added. The days of large strategy departments, exclusively concerned with developing five, ten and fifteen or twenty-five year (or longer) plans in exquisite detail – while having no interest

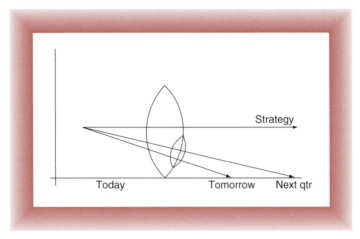

Figure 6.13 Bi-focal marketing

or responsibility for today's results – are gone, at least in the commercial world (Figure 6.13).

A successful strategist in today's markets needs to be focused on the future but also strongly linked to today's reality. This means that as soon as strategic analysis identifies potential opportunities for today's (tactical) market(ing) these should be considered and acted upon as soon as practically possible. There is no dividing line between strategy and tactics; they are not separate disciplines to be kept apart – in different boxes, departments or functions. Present (today) and future (tomorrow, next quarter, next year/years) exist on a continuum. Strategy needs to be rooted in today, but tactics needs to keep an eye on the longer term.

At this point the market(ing) strategist needs to work with tactical market(ing) and start winnowing down the range of potential opportunities into those which might be actionable in the shorter term.

But first a word of warning. Working with the tactical market(ing) organization does not necessarily mean working to short-term objectives alone! While the tactical marketer is, quite rightly, concerned with implementation and the level of individual market or product investment required and the speed of payback on such investment, these are only a part of the criteria which should be used to assess and prioritize the potential opportunities. In addition to the normal 'economic' criteria that will be used in tactical marketing operations, the market strategy must also consider the following:

● Market opportunities which may not pay off in the short term but are required to communicate the organization's future direction;

- Opportunities which should be pursued to differentiate your organization from the competition;

- Opportunities which need to be followed to block potential competitive entry.

6.2.9 *What barriers are getting in the way?*

It will probably come as a great shock to some readers to hear that a large proportion of 'missed' business is deflected not by external competitive or economic activity, but by barriers that the organization *itself* places in front of its would-be customers.

As the driving student was told on his first lesson, if you want to make this car go forward you don't just stamp on the accelerator (gas pedal) – first you release the brake!

Looking first of all into the marketplace, are there any good reasons why we shouldn't be selling more or that sales are going down?

So much for the 'classic' marketing input, nothing there to worry you I am sure. But still we seem to have declining market shares and ever more strident finance directors/CFOs asking, *why?* But that's the trouble with marketing books; they only ever look at the accelerator/gas pedal. What is the point of putting your foot to the floor if the wheels aren't touching the ground? Lots of noise, steam, sparks but no movement – now that sounds like marketing!

6.2.10 *Some barriers are worth keeping*

The needs of sales and finance directors notwithstanding, not every sale is a good one. Not every customer is a good customer. We don't want every customer – we want some customers, not all customers. I shall give you some time to rest after that.

We need to make sure that we place no barriers in front of the customers we want to attract, but barriers that reject the customers we don't want are a good thing.

Barriers that we don't know we are erecting might be termed 'unintentional barriers'. They will create 'unintentional rejects'. These 'unintentional rejects' will fall into two separate groups:

(1) *Customers that we want* (we know them and have designed and produced products/services that they want to buy) but are being rejected by the systems and processes we have in place and

(2) *Customers that we don't want* (haven't targeted and haven't really designed the offer for) and are being rejected by our systems and processes.

The first group of prospects or unintentional rejects we really don't want to lose. We need to understand the systems, processes and behavioural problems they have with our organization – and solve the problems as fast as possible.

The second group of prospects may have been turned off by the quality and precision of the organization's targeted market(ing). If you are in the situation of having a clearly defined market position with unique, differentiated and clearly communicated brand values then it is *inevitable* that you will turn parts of the market off. This is the name of the game. Remember, some people will *never* buy a BMW just because it *is* a BMW – they do not relate to the projected brand values at all. That is absolutely fine, as long as those that are attracted to the brand values are sufficient in number and willing to pay sufficient premium prices to meet required profit levels.

If you want to grow your market in these conditions, you have some options:

(1) Establish whether the measurement is still profits or has changed (reverted) to sales turnover.

(2) Dilute the existing brand position. This will likely 'broaden' appeal for your offering, but will also likely reduce the price premium you are able to command – may not be altogether bad, you need to do the analysis.

(3) Stretch the brand with variants into new/different areas of the market. Can be very successful although beware of dilution effects.

Whatever route the organization takes, the secret is in knowing the difference between the barriers you want to keep (intentional) and those that are there by mistake (unintentional) and are costing you dearly in lost profits. Good management is called for.

6.2.11   *Where do customers interface (connect) with our organization?*

These magical points, sometimes known as 'touch-points' and other times as 'moments of truth', have been described over the years by many different authors. In comparison to the amount of time organizations spend thinking, planning, designing, developing, producing and delivering new products or service, the actual points of contact with real customers where benefits and money are exchanged are tantalizingly brief.

Jan Carlzon first used the term 'moments of truth' in his book (*Moments of Truth*, HarperCollins, New York, 1989) on the turnaround of SAS, the Scandinavian airline. His view was, *Anytime a customer comes into contact with any aspect of a business, however remote, is an opportunity to form an impression.*

In his analysis, he looked through the buying/selling process in SAS and tried to identify all the key points of customer organization contacts that were in existence and then attempted to isolate those points of contact that were 'make or break' for the business. These points of contact were the ones that would lead the customers to decide whether to buy or not to buy, whether they were going to be satisfied or dissatisfied with the transaction and whether they would come back or find an alternative supplier for the next purchase.

What Carlzon, and other investigators (such as Tom Peters), found with different organizations, such as Federal Express, is that the organization's view on what is important and which transaction is key to a purchase and repeat purchase situation is often quite different from the customer! The result is often that significant 'moments of truth' for major customers can end up relying upon services or contacts made with staff that are low level, poorly trained, poorly motivated and poorly managed!

Brands, as they will be described in Section 6.4, are expensive, effective but extremely fragile concepts. The customer who normally has a life full of concerns, questions, worries, issues and unknowns doesn't have very much time available to invest in getting to know your brand intimately. If confusion or uncertainty is to be avoided, the organization must insist on (and achieve) *consistency* at every single point of customer contact. But consistency is not enough. It is not sufficient to avoid confusion and be 'neutral' at every customer contact/moment of truth – that is just too 'hygiene'. It might be enough to ensure you don't lose, but definitely not enough to win – when you have a customer contact, the customer is granting you a personal audience and you should make the most of what is a disappearing opportunity.

The real challenge of points of contact is making every single *touch* a true experience of the unique characteristics of the brand. Much of market(ing) tends to be a grey 'art' rather than a black and white 'science' but in the area of branding and consistency there are no grey areas whatsoever. No consistency, no brand.

This is not the place to labour the point, especially given the above-average intelligence of my readership; the need for central, co-ordinated overall control of this important activity is obvious. Equally obvious are the historical, structural and cultural reasons why your organization finds it very difficult to do this.

But don't worry, as long as none of your competitors are actively managing what is arguably the most important area of the business's activity, then you have nothing to worry about. The day that they work it out though . . .

6.2.12   Conclusions – the customer

In this second part of the market(ing) strategy discussion, we have started to scratch at the surface of the crucial question of *who is our customer and what do they want from us?*

The customer is always going to be at the centre of *any* market debate – although some modern texts seem to think that we should start with the models, theories and processes and then try and *do* something *to* the customer. No, the customer is in control – today more than ever – and they know it. And the organization that focuses on encouraging its customers to buy more instead of trying to sell them more stuff will emerge as a clear winner.

It has always come as a surprise to me that the much-vaunted 4Ps, and the 7Ps that followed, never had a P that referred to the customer. The SCORPIO model corrects that wrong.

We have covered a lot of ground in this section, from research to benefits to barriers and moments of truth. We have travelled through different concepts from market versus product research, knowledge management, moments of truth and onto latent needs and hygienes and motivators.

Check your progress against the strategy checklist in the Appendix.

Remember that as we work through the SCORPIO process, you may not have to cover all of the seven elements in exactly the same depth. Depending on your organization and your competitive position, you might be able to simply skate over some sections. Unless you are working in a nationalized industry (SNCF), a monopoly (Microsoft), a utility (British Gas) or a dying company (no examples, it would be too embarrassing) then this section is unlikely to be one that you will be able to skip.

Finally, a few questions that you should now be able to answer:

The customer

1	Who are they?	
2	What do they currently buy from us/ our competitors, and why?	
3	What benefits are they seeking?	
4	What do they want from us now/will they want in the future?	

5	What barriers are getting in the way?	
6	What will make them come to us?	
7	Where do customers interface (connect) with our organization?	

6.3 Segmentation and targeting

The French complain of everything, and always.

All foreign people, but especially the Italians, need severe repression from time to time.

England is a nation of shopkeepers.

Napoleon Bonaparte

We always have been, we are, and I hope that we always shall be detested in France.

Duke of Wellington

Market segmentation (or customer profiling) is one of the basics of good market(ing) strategy. The *mass market* is long dead and today one size no longer fits all (Figure 6.14).

To compete effectively, segmentation is not a 'like-to-have' for practitioners; it is a 'must-have' tool. It has been said that, *if the organization isn't talking segments, it isn't talking markets* (Levitt). Without an understanding of the different groupings of needs and wants in the marketplace, no organization can hope to have the clarity and depth of customer focus required to stay relevant.

There is no 'one way' of segmenting markets; it always depends on:

(1) *The sophistication* of the target market;

(2) *The degree of competition* in the market;

Figure 6.14   SCORPIO market strategy

(3) *The stage of development* (product/service life cycle) of the organization, the product/service and the industry;

(4) *The strategic sophistication* of the organization and its ability to understand the (customer needs) differences shown by the segmentation analysis;

(5) *The ability of the organization* to deal with and implement change and the *new* ways of marketing that are normally implied within different segments;

(6) *The tactical implementation* capabilities of the organization and its ability to market to more than one segment at the same time.

People nowadays, whether buying for themselves or for their organization, are less ready to settle for a mass-produced standard item, be it product or service. The search today is for something special, something different, something that reinforces their own sense of identity as a person, as an individual, as a professional buyer – certainly as someone separate from the 'herd'. The modern day array of product/service choice (just go and find out how many different MP3 players you can buy, how many different forms of coffee/beverage you can buy in Starbucks, the bewildering array of mobile phone tariffs or the range of options open for the buyer of Back Hoe diggers for construction sites) stands witness to this growth in choice which seems to be demanded in many advanced marketplaces in the world.

In essence, the nature of competition has changed over the past twenty years and we now see:

● Greater internationalization of competition so that even the most remote areas are open to international operations.

- Greater competition from outside categories (Porter calls this 'substitute competition' (five forces model, see Chapter 2) as airlines compete with Internet communications for international meetings; mobile phones produce cameras; Boeing, IBM and GE offer finance for the purchase of their own products.

- Customers are more willing to buy products and services from substitute providers. Nokia doesn't have to stipulate who makes the camera that they put in the phone. Sony doesn't have to say (apart from Intel and Microsoft) who provides the myriad of components in their laptops.

In a world where the 'supply side' of the equation now looks as unruly as the 'demand side', segmentation is promising more clarification.

When we are talking about segmentation it probably makes some sense to start with the easy bits. What do we mean by market segmentation? There are very few occasions that I reel out past definitions but market segmentation is one of the rare instances where a definition can be quite useful. One of the (oldest but) best comes from Kotler:

> *Market segmentation is the sub-dividing of a market into homogeneous sub-sets of customers, where any sub-set may conceivably be selected as a market target to be reached with a distinct marketing mix.*

Two, more focused ones are:

> From Peter Doyle:
>
> *To group customers in terms of similarity of need*
>
> From Nigel Piercy:
>
> *...how we identify groups within the market as targets for our products and service*

From these definitions we can see that market segmentation is all about:

(1) The identification of *homogeneous sub-sets of customers*; that is, customers who are alike in some way or other.

(2) Where any of these groups may *conceivably be selected as a market target*, in other words we can go for one or all of these groups but importantly we can treat them as a stand-alone market target.

(3) The final implication, *a distinct marketing mix*, is that the segments, once identified, may demand something different from us as a producer. In other

words, the marketing mix (product/service, pricing, place/distribution, promotion/communication) can conceivably be different from segment to segment.

Such a breaking up of our marketing into a number of different mixes is obviously more costly in market investment and control procedures but the argument goes that with a more relevant and tailored mix you and your organization would enjoy:

(1) *Improved penetration* of the target market segment because the offer is more relevant;

(2) *Increased volume sales* because the offer is better tailored and more relevant to members of the segment than a 'generic' offer would be;

(3) *Higher/premium prices* due to the perception of superior customer value;

(4) These three effects would more than pay off the additional costs incurred and still make greater profits.

Some authors have argued for 'one-to-one marketing' or 'the segment of one'. Individualism is certainly a growing phenomenon but, barring the few odd dot-com and lottery millionaires scattering the Western world and the one in twenty Londoners whose house is now reckoned to be worth in excess of £1 million (€ 1.5 million), the segment of one is unlikely to be financially viable – at least for most producers.

Segmentation offers us a compromise position (Figure 6.15).

Market segmentation is just that – the compromise between 'mass markets', one-offer-to-everyone standard offer, at one extreme and the 'segment of one', every-one-is-different bespoke offer, at the other extreme.

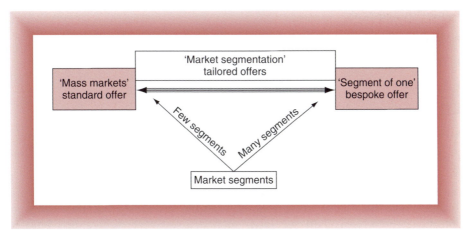

Figure 6.15 The market segmentation *compromise*

How 'bespoke' or how 'standard' your market segmentation solution should be (whether your chosen and defined market requires just two or three different segmented offerings or twenty-five to cover the range of different needs and wants), will depend on a number of variables.

6.3.1 *Customer classification*

The majority of the so-called 'segmentation approaches' are really just methods of customer or client 'classification'. Classification is an internal methodology that an organization uses to describe customers for the (internal) convenience of the organization and its systems and processes. Classification methods (generally) do not identify differences in customer needs or motivations; they describe customer characteristics/descriptors such as (for B2C):

- Age
- Sex
- Ethnicity
- Culture/sub-culture
- Socioeconomic groupings
- Neighbourhood
- Ownership
- Geography

and for B2B:

- Industry/vertical
- Company size
- Location
- Technology
- Company ownership
- Installed base (current owners)
- Standard industry code (SIC).

The advantage of this 'classification' approach is that it is simple, easily identifiable and very 'black and white' even though the world is predominantly *grey*. Unfortunately, as we shall see later, such descriptive classifications tend to present quite weak segments.

All that discriminates is not segmentation!

Look at these two attempts within the airline/flying/travel business

Market segments	Product categories
Business travellers	Wide-body category
Corporate	Long-haul category
Independent	Short-haul category
Tourist travellers	Low-emissions category
Weekenders	Executive jet category
Retired wanderers	City hopper category
Gappers (school and university)	Low-fuel category
VFR (visit friends and relatives)	Low-noise category
Regular travellers	Environmental category
Frightened travellers	Turbo-prop category
Non-travellers	Seaplane category

6.3.2 Customer segmentation

A segment (as we now know) is about a group of buyers (people or companies) in a 'homogeneous sub-set' of the total market that can be selected as a market target to be reached with a distinct marketing mix. If we are to select a target market in this way and are expecting to invest in doing something separate/different/unique for this group of people/companies, *it is important that they react in the same manner to the offer that is made to them,* we would hope positively. This will only happen if the group that you identify has a common need or 'motivation' for the purchase.

The sad fact is that very rarely do descriptive groups actually demonstrate the same needs and motivations.

Before you rush to defend yourself against this outrageous proposition, let's think for a moment about how markets (groups of customers) actually work. Most B2B marketing today is still wrapped around the beloved 'industry vertical' segment – there is no denying that this is neat, practical and a simple way to keep the sales force organized against clear industry boundaries. Nevertheless, what this method of classification suggests is that:

(1) A start-up organization of twenty-five people in the financial services 'industry vertical' with the same issues and concerns as a large, long-established financial

services organization employing 85 000 employees – at least similar enough for the same sales force (with the same offer) to call on both organizations; and

(2) A start-up organization of twenty-five people in the financial services 'industry vertical' will so little in common with another start-up organization of twenty-five people, but in the hospitality/leisure industry vertical – so different that separate salesforces and separate offers are required.

Ah well, efficiency and effectiveness are rarely the same thing!

There is no end to the options for segmentation bases – everybody has their favourite! Figure 6.16 suggests some alternatives for those without their own (sure-fire, works-in-every-situation, guaranteed, 100%-refund-if-not-happy) method.

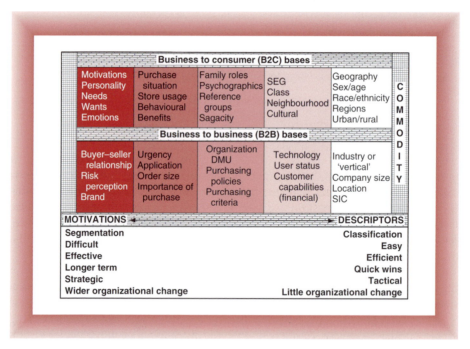

Figure 6.16 Some segmentation bases

To explain the boxes briefly, the top row are bases common in B2C applications and below these are bases more common in B2B applications. Generally, bases in boxes towards the right are driven by demographic and observable facts. As we move towards the left, we start to consider bases that are more needs, wants and motivations driven.

For the segmentation connoisseurs, the far right box (commodity) is the segment-free marketplace where standardization and price have been allowed to reign supreme.

The base box looks at the advantages of the different approaches; the descriptor (demographics) to the right of the continuum:

- Is about classification rather than *real* segmentation;
- Is *easier* to do;
- Is more about making the organization *efficient*;
- Promises *quick wins* especially in marketing communications;
- Is *tactical* rather than strategic in its implementation; but
- Threatens little organizational *change*.

The motivations (left) end of the continuum:

- Is *real* segmentation rather than simple classification;
- Is more *difficult* to do;
- Is more *effective* when it is carried out;
- Works (and pays back) over the *longer term*;
- Is more *strategic* in nature; but
- Threatens wider organizational *change* so you should tread very carefully.

From a competitive standpoint, it is useful to identify which box your organization is currently using as a base for segmentation (if any) and also to assess which box your competitor(s) is/are using. Competitively, it doesn't really matter which box you are in – as long as you are to the 'left' of your competitor(s). If they are to the left of you, you are probably feeling the effects of being at a competitive disadvantage already.

If you need to think about being more competitive (no, I don't mean being cheaper, but offering more customer value) and moving your segmentation approach towards the motivation (left) end of the continuum, experience has shown me that trying to move more than two boxes to the left (in one move) is often too challenging for the organization to consider; the effects on the organization can be too severe. If the competition is more than two boxes to the left, you may have no choice, of course.

6.3.3   What do we want segmentation to do for our organization?

I fully realize that we are talking specifically about market(ing) strategy rather than tactics, but at this point it is important to raise the issue about what we really want segmentation to *do* for us.

The purposes for which you *can* use market segmentation are fairly straightforward. The purpose for which you *should* use market segmentation depends largely upon your current state of activity and, let's be frank, how desperate your competitive situation is.

In slightly more detail then, let's look at the pain–gain issues involved (Figure 6.17).

The pain		The gain
Investment	Tactics	Strategy
• More research • Higher costs of multiple markets • Complicated administration • Possible re-organization costs • 'Inefficient' production system • Lower economies of scale • Changing 'habits' of the organization	• Better targeting • More efficient promotion • Less marketing 'wastage' • Improved retention • Improved 'service' levels • More effective production • Higher prices • Focused NPD	• Unique customer propositions • Clear market positioning • Differentiation • Brand values and personality • Retention, 'loyalty' and 'relationships' • Sustainable competitive advantage • Market influence • Market leadership • Premium prices and margin • Profitability

Figure 6.17   What can segmentation do for you?

The investment
Let no one tell you otherwise, segmentation is not a cheap activity – and the more we are talking about 'real' segmentation (rather than classification), the more expensive it will be:

(1) *Research will be required*: You probably have lots already (what do you mean no?) but this is unlikely to be right for segmentation which usually needs different data from that collected for day-to-day research purposes.

(2) *Different offerings*: Once you have the segmentation solution, you will (I hope) want to deliver different offerings to different segments – expensive.

(3) *Administration costs*: Will rise as you complicate the marketing – you don't want the wrong offering going to the wrong segment after all.

(4) *There may be some re-organization costs*: As the organization rises to new challenges.

(5) *Production costs*: And as the production people will scream at you, the best (cheapest) production comes from long runs of standard products, and you want what?

(6) *Economies of scale will suffer*: But don't worry, the economies of scale argument is nonsense anyway. For greater insight, look up what the economics textbooks say about *diseconomies of scale* and *the law of diminishing returns*.

(7) *Changing the organizational 'habits'* can be the most expensive of all: *But we've always done it that way* and *Well nobody complained before* . . . is all you will hear for a while (see Section 6.6).

The tactical gains

Depending on how 'motivational' your chosen segmentation approach is, in the *short to medium term* you can expect gains such as:

- *Better targeting* of your market(ing) activities to segments that want what you can offer.

- *More efficient promotion* means that you direct the right messages to the right people (even at the right time and place). Not always an easy task.

- *Less market(ing) 'wastage'* in communications, sales activity as well as developing offerings that nobody wants. Some market(ing) will always be wasted but that is normal – minimizing the wastage can mean millions of pounds/euros/dollars saved every year.

- *Improved retention* of customers that you want to retain.

- *Improved 'service' levels* doesn't necessarily mean doing more and spending more money but doing the right things; things that targeted segments value.

- *More effective production* by making products and services that will be sought out and purchased. Rover cars seems to have spent the past twenty-five years making cars that sit in fields – never was a sound strategy!

- *Higher prices* as targeted customers perceive more value and expect to pay higher prices.

- *Focused new product development* (NPD) will reduce risk in another expensive area.

The strategic gains

Depending on how well you apply market(ing) to the identified segments, in the *longer term* you can expect gains such as:

- *Unique customer propositions* that are just that, 'unique'. Your insight gives you a lead in seeing customer needs – and acting on it.

- *Clear market positioning* from the customer's perspective so that they understand how you are different and what you stand for.

- *Differentiation* that is clear and has customer value (not based just on what the organization believes the 'mass' market will buy).

- *Brand values and personality* and your offering starts to come alive. We will talk more about branding later, but the best brands are not planted at random in the 'mass market' – they are rooted carefully in a specially prepared segment (see Section 6.4).

- *Retention, loyalty* and *relationships* is where we start to see bigger increases in margins because real emotional attachment is worth paying for (see Section 6.5).

- *Sustainable competitive advantage* and 'sustainable' is the operative word. Rooted carefully in properly researched and prepared segments, competitive advantage can be grown, protected with brands and (unlike simple techno-logical advantage) cannot be copied (see Section 6.6).

- *Market influence* is much better than being at the mercy of customer 'whim'. Have you noticed that only 'follower' companies describe their customers as *promiscuous*?

- *Market leadership* is the step beyond influence. Not only do customers watch what you do, now they watch to see what lead you are going to take in the market and (almost) learn what is 'right' and what is 'wrong'.

- *Premium prices and margin* and what premiums can be commanded at the leadership end!

- *Profitability* is what it is all about.

6.3.4   *What segments exist in our target market?*

Before we launch off into a slightly more detailed analysis of market segmenta-tion and how to do it, there is one lesson that needs to be learned. That is, we do not segment markets; *markets segment themselves*.

In practice, what this means is that there is little point in us preparing ourselves with 'ideal segmentation bases' or developing grand theories about how the market will segment – and then searching for particular segments in certain areas.

The fact is 'the market just is'. Every organization needs to face up to the fact that the market that they are trying to serve exists as an entity – it has a life of its own and is not somehow our 'creation'. It includes a number of groups of buyers/people/ companies with similar demographic backgrounds and/or similar needs/wants all working or living in similar/different contexts or situations. The idea that the market will reform itself and fit itself into boxes of the organization's choosing is (although worryingly widespread) simply laughable. No, the market is what the market is – it's our job to identify what is going on in the market rather than trying to make the market do what we want it to do, unless of course you are Microsoft.

The only leeway we have is to decide the level of 'granularity' of the market that the organization is able and willing to use. What this means is there is just no point in analysing the market to such a degree that the outputs are either not useful (or actually frightening) to the organization, even to the extent that it reverses away from the concept.

This is very important; I have learned from (bitter) experience that it is very important what information you give to the organization. There is absolutely no point in conducting the most detailed analysis if the implications of that analysis are that the organization needs to undergo greater change than the senior decision makers are prepared to accept. No matter that not changing might mean the demise of the organization, sometimes death *will* be preferred to radical change. Be very careful to present segmentation data only to the extent that the organization (and the senior decision makers) can deal with the change involved and will be willing to implement the segmentation solution. If this means progressing stage by stage over a number of years, so be it.

So how might we spot the segments in the market? We aren't going to look in depth at the mechanics of the market research involved but, by way of illustration, Figure 6.18 describes a process that I have found useful in uncovering existing or natural segments in any market.

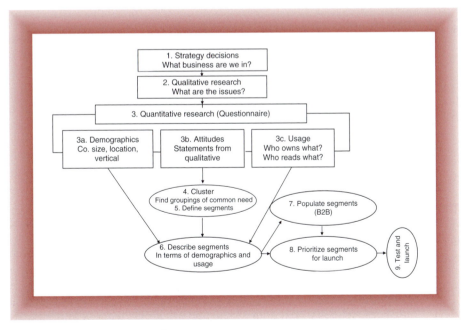

Figure 6.18   A segmentation process

You will see from the figure that there are a number of steps to the process and these can be described quite simply as:

(1) *Agree market definition*: This refers back to the previous SCORPIO section (see Section 6.1) and requires that we define our market in customer rather than industry terms. Why would Rolex attempt to identify segments in the watch business – it isn't in the watch business. This is a point in the process where many organizations go wrong because they attempt to define a market that is described in product terms – never a very successful segmentation exercise!

(2) *Qualitative research*: We need to conduct qualitative research, either focus groups or in-depth interviews or a mixture of both, to determine what are the issues driving behaviour in the target market.

(3) *Quantitative research*: It is about putting real numbers into the analysis. The quantitative research questionnaire, I have always found, can most usefully be described as consisting of three parts:
   (a) *Demographics*: These are all the relevant demographic and descriptive variables that we need to know about as noted earlier.
   (b) *Usage*: This concerns itself with what the respondent purchases on a regular or irregular basis, which products or services the respondent owns or has regular access to, which channels are used, frequency of purchase as well as situations or occasions when/where consumption takes place. We also collect data on different media readership, viewing and listening as well as channel or outlet usage to help with later communications.
   (c) *Attitudes*: Not really 'attitudes' but more accurately defined as 'beliefs, feelings, wants and needs', these are all the key issues that have been taken out of the qualitative research. These will form the battery of questions to set into the quantitative questionnaire.

(4) *Analysis*: Normally this is 'cluster analysis'. Cluster analysis is a statistical methodology that identifies (through a computer programme) the groups or clusters or segments within the data. It creates these 'clusters' by putting respondents into groups that are as alike as possible (homogeneous) *within* the cluster and as different as possible (heterogeneous) *between* the clusters. Which variables are used for the cluster analysis will, of course, define the clusters of respondents. Here you have a *big* choice. You can search for segments in any of the three areas that you have used to collect data:
   (a) *Demographics*: This is a favourite area for B2C and B2B 'classification' – even though it fails many of the key segmentation tests described later. The main *disadvantage*, however, is that when the sales team approaches the identified prospects, they are all unlikely to respond the same way to the same offer because their needs are different. Postcode *segmentation* is also popular in many areas of B2C marketing but you just have to look at the people who live next door to you and ask if they want or buy the same things as you do.

(b) *Usage*: It is another favourite method of certain industries such as IT where the world is split into two broad segments, existing customers (the installed base) and the rest (prospects) – well it's simple. Other approaches include users of different channels or intermediaries (B2B) and light/heavy users (B2C). All still have the problem of whether the 'segments' exhibit similar buying behaviours.

(c) *Attitudes*: It is the other end of the scale. The main *advantage* of this approach is that you are likely to get segments that respond the same way to a (differentiated) offer because you will (we hope) have developed an offering based on the identified and understood segment customer needs. The main *B2B disadvantage* of this approach is the segments are almost certain to be spread over a number of different industry verticals, industry groupings or other key demographics and are very hard for the sales force to identify. The main *B2C disadvantage* of this approach is that the segments may not split as the internal technical or product/service-focused departments 'expect' them to split.

(d) *Mix and match*: You can try to mix bits of all three types of data but that's like putting starter, savoury and dessert in a blender (and the results look like it too) to save time – why would you?

(5) *Define segments from the clusters*: The computer doesn't understand the meaning of the data it is given and is quite capable of producing nonsense clusters as sensible ones. Way back in the 1970s, Yoram Wind (Market Segmentation, *Journal of Marketing Research*, August 1978) devised a series of tests for good segments. We have added to these but not significantly changed the list that Wind provided. These are:

(a) *Is the segment identifiable?* Can you describe the segment?
(b) *Is the segment reachable?* Can you reach the segment with your communication with distribution?
(c) *Is the segment viable?* Is it big enough to make money out of?
(d) *Is the segment recognized by customers?*
(e) *Is the segment recognized by distributors or channels?*
(f) *Is the offering distinctive, does it appeal strongly to the target?*
(g) *Will the offering be premium priced?* – If not, reject.
(h) *Will the offer provide above-average profit margins?* – The acid test.

(6) *Describe the clusters*: At this point what we do depends on which method you have used to segment the market – demographics, attitude or usage. You use the other two measures to describe the clusters that you have produced through the analysis. For example, if you have used attitudes (motivations/needs) and found groups of people with a common need, problem or motivation, then you 'cross correlate' these attitude/motivational segments against the demographic and usage data collected to identify any significant correlations. You just need to be aware that you remember that *correlation does not imply causality*. This means that, should you find that a particular attitude

segment also uses a particular supermarket, it is not *because* they shop in the particular supermarket that they have the same need.

(7) *Populate segments (B2B)*: This is a particular requirement of B2B markets rather than B2C. B2B organizations, which have decided to use segmentation on either an attitude or usage basis, may find it difficult to identify which prospective buyer may belong to each different segment *before* they have been approached by the sales force. Spotting members of particular demographics (such as industry or geography) is much easier. There are methodologies available for this and these will be covered in more detail later. B2C markets don't have this issue because there are (normally) larger numbers of customers and, through communications and promotion activities, customers *self-select* themselves into (and out of) particular segments.

(8) *Prioritize and target*: Whatever the segmentation solution that comes out of the analysis, it is unrealistic (especially in today's competitive market environment) that an organization could feasibly (or credibly – customers just don't tend to believe that an organization can do eveything) think it could attack all segments in the market at the same time. Prioritization is best done using a 'portfolio management model' such as the GE model, the Shell Directional Policy Matrix or the Arthur D Little model – they are all fairly similar in that they focus on identifying and quantifying two key dimensions for any segment. These are:
   (a) *Attractiveness*: Is it capable of delivering what the organization needs (returns) from its market?
   (b) *Company business strengths*: How skilled (or how easily could you acquire the skills) is your organization at delivering on the needs of this segment, as we understand it?

(9) *Test and launch*.

6.3.5   How can we market to different segments?

We have identified the segments in the market and calculated the priority order of those segments according to:

(1) Their attractiveness to our organization and

(2) Our skills and strengths in delivering on their needs.

Now we need to know what to do with the analysis – how many of the segments should we approach? Market(ing) to more than one market segment at the same time is macho but difficult (Figure 6.19). Certainly, doing it *properly* is a major task. Classically the theory tells us that there are three different approaches to market(ing) to different segments and these consist of:

(1) *Undifferentiated marketing*: delivering the same offer to more than one, or all segments;

(2) *Focused marketing*: delivering a specialized offering to just one segment;

(3) *Differentiated marketing*: delivering different offers to different segments.

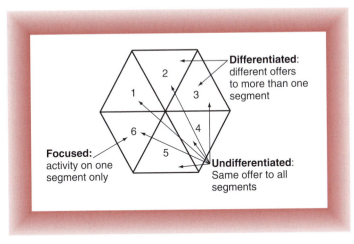

Figure 6.19 Marketing to the segments

Ignoring all the different segments and doing what you were doing before, market(ing) the same offer to everybody is *undifferentiated marketing*. This is not quite as unrealistic as it might seem – you may have identified the segments and their different needs/wants but also calculated that at the moment there is not enough value to justify the additional cost of developing special market(ing) mixes for the different segments, in which case you might decide to keep a watching brief on the market and drive down different market segments with different mixes as and when competitors decide to do the same.

The second approach is known as *focused marketing*. This involves identifying one segment and market(ing) only to that segment – to the exclusion of other segments – very similar to the case of focused market(ing) strategy as described by Porter in his generic strategy theory (see Chapter 3) as well as everything you have probably read about 'niche marketing' (no, I don't know why there are three words for the same thing either). This can be quite a successful strategy. However, it does tend to put all your eggs into one basket. If the segment you have identified really is a 'niche' (technically quite different from being a single or small segment, a niche is defined as a safe and protected harbour that the larger companies would not find it economic to participate in), then you can do quite well.

The third alternative is *differentiated marketing* and here we are looking at developing and delivering different market(ing) mixes to the different market segments.

6.3.6   *Conclusions – segmentation and targeting*

In this third part of the market(ing) strategy discussion, we have broached the unnecessarily tangled question of market segmentation.

Segmentation has been around for a long time now and most managers have heard the word. But it is not easy to do. The analysis is quite costly (collecting the customer data) and takes time to complete. Not only that, but it can sometimes suggest what appears to be quite radical change for the business. Sometimes, it's just too difficult.

Levitt talked a lot about segmentation; he said that, *if you aren't talking segments, you aren't talking markets*. And if you aren't talking markets you can only be talking products.

I hope that this quick review of market segmentation has convinced you that:

(1) It might be difficult, but you don't really have an option.

(2) The 'mass market' is really dead.

(3) Business isn't just a revenue game, it's a profits game.

(4) As your business faces more and more competition, tomorrow's battle will be for segments – that can be defended.

(5) If you don't understand where the segments are (and what they want from you) you won't win the battle.

Market segmentation is not a luxury any longer – it is a key tool in the battle for customers. Of course, the results of the analysis will meet internal opposition, and implementation will be a challenge, that's natural (see Section 6.6). But it will be easier to deal with that opposition now (while we still have a successful business) and we still have some flexibility. *Later*, when we have spent too long doing things the 'old way' and our money and options are more limited, may be *too late*.

Again we arrive at the point of comparing your outputs with the strategy checklist in the Appendix. Now we can add input in the section on market segmentation – we should have the answers to important questions such as: What are the segments in our target market? Which segments do we need to own and defend? What do those segments want from us?

Finally, a few questions that you should now be able to answer:

Segmentation and targeting

1	What is the current state of segmentation in the organization?	
2	What do we want segmentation to do for our organization?	
3	What segments exist in our target market?	
4	How durable are the segments identified?	
5	How can we prioritize the segments for approach?	
6	Which segments should we target?	
7	How can we market to different segments?	

6.4 Positioning and branding

A newborn Government must shine and astonish — the moment it loses its éclat it falls.

Napoleon Bonaparte

So far, on our voyage through the SCORPIO model we have looked at:

(1) *Industry or market thinking?* Is the organization customer/market focused or product/service driven? What business are we in?

(2) *The customer*: Who is the customer/prospect and what are the customer's needs, wants and expectations?

(3) *Segmentation and targeting*: we know that all customers do not want the same thing, so how can we group customers into sets (segments) of people who want the same things so we can target them separately?

Now we are going to add another piece to the jigsaw and look at positioning and branding (Figure 6.20) – how can we make our offering stand apart from the rest and easy to identify and purchase?

6.4.1 Branding

For a subject which makes organizations so much money (and could make them even more), it has always surprised me that branding doesn't sit anywhere in the traditional 'marketing mix'. It is squeezed into all parts of the mix, sometimes it's inserted into product and packaging, sometimes it's inserted into promotion, in fact it's spread all over the place – so thinly nobody gets to concentrate exclusively on the important issues of branding. Brand is absolutely *not* a tactical issue, something that even the writers of tactical textbooks have recognized because investment in brand rarely has an immediate (in the same financial year) return. But neither does it, at least up to now, have anywhere to sit in the overall structure of market(ing) strategy. Of course there are books written just on branding, I know that, but where does it fit in the organization's planning structure? How does anybody know what to do about planning

Figure 6.20   SCORPIO market strategy

brand growth? Now that the SCORPIO concept has arrived (I hope) all this is behind us!

First, let's get a measure of the importance of branding. Every year Interbrand and *Business Week* calculate the value of the top 100 global brands and publish the results online, and most years Coca-Cola comes out as number one with an estimated brand value of around $70 billion (that's $70,000,000,000), the value fluctuates every year because of the method of calculation. We will look at exactly how the brand can be calculated later. Remember, $70 billion is just for one brand. Interbrand's value for the top 100 comes to just shy of $1 trillion (that's $1,000,000,000,000) and of course there are more than just 100 brands alive in the world. In 2005, Interbrand's 100th brand was listed as Heineken, valued at $2.35 billion. Simon Anholt (*Brand New Justice*, Butterworth-Heinemann, Oxford, 2003) has compared this global brand value as:

- *Equal* to the combined gross national incomes of the sixty-three countries defined by the World Bank as 'low income' (where almost half the world's population lives) and

- *Almost* one-third of the entire value of global wealth.

I take it that I now have your undivided attention? Then imagine that almost *all* of this value exists off-balance sheet, as most 'intangibles' are not yet included under the list of the company's assets. Hmmmmm.

What are brands? Well, they are nothing really. A brand isn't a name, a product or a service, it is more precisely:

(1) *A set of consistent meanings* which belong to and exist separately from the product or service offering and

(2) *A set of feelings and beliefs* that exist in the customer's mind.

Even though brands are intangible, several aspects of the brand offer real value to the customer. Some writers with a utopian agenda would really like to prove that brands are a form of confidence trick aimed at overcharging the customer – these writers simply insult the intelligence of customers – who know what they get for their money. The 'death of brands' was announced (prematurely) in 1993. On 'Marlboro Friday', Friday, 2 April 1993, Philip Morris, the maker of Marlboro cigarettes, announced that it would be cutting the price of Marlboros to compete with generic cigarette makers. The company's stock fell by 26% following the announcement, losing about $10 billion off its stock market value in a single day. The day was hailed as a landmark moment in the 1990s consumer movement away from name brand products in favour of cheaper generic products with prices sometimes up to 50% lower than their branded competitors.

Needless to say, brands did not die on Marlboro Friday because customers value them and buy them. There are (hopeful) claims of the death of brands on a regular basis but to no avail. Not only are brands not dead, but they also show absolutely no sign of dying in the near future. So why is this? The answer is quite simple – customers really like brands.

Why is this? There are three extremely good reasons why customers buy brands today and will be buying brands well after you have stopped reading market(ing) books and I have stopped writing them:

- *Statements*: We use the brands we buy to make statements about ourselves to other people.

- *Customers actually enjoy brands*: Brands often have some form of fun value to them such as sensuality, romance, self-indulgence, nostalgia, etc.

- *Brands make our life easier*: They make decisions easier so that, for example, when I am confronted with an entire aisle of coffee in the supermarket I am not forced to spend half-an-hour weighing the pros and cons of competing products and promises, I know what I want, I know what I like, I can see it, buy it without having to spend an entire day doing the weekly shopping.

Where do brands come from? As you can imagine, a lot of work has been done by a lot of researchers spending a lot of money and the answer is well . . . 'it sort of depends'. As far as we can make sense of the detailed, fastidious and costly research which has been conducted, brands are built over a period of time from the following sources:

- *Experience* or perceived experience of the product and/or service offering;

- *Advertising* and promotion history;

- *Word-of-mouth communication* in its various forms;

- *The customer's perception* of how the brand owners actually appear to behave;

- *The importance and role of the brand* in customer's everyday lives.

And which of these various bits and pieces are the most important elements for your brand? Well, you know the answer really, don't you – *it all depends*. Let's face it, if researchers could get inside the complexity of the human mind and understand which bits of experience and perception actually created which bits of behaviour and therefore which brands worked and which brands failed then they would be millionaires – rather than researchers.

We will discuss brands and branding in much more detail in the following sections but before we do that, we need to concentrate on one other important but often overlooked aspect, that of market position.

6.4.2 *Positioning*

Much of the work on positioning comes from advertising and marketing communications research and especially the books written by Al Reis and Jack Trout, (e.g. *Positioning: The Battle for Your Mind*, McGraw-Hill, New York, 2001). The basic idea behind positioning is it's about big money! There, now I've got your attention again. Positioning is not what you do to your product or service but *it is all about what you do to the mind of the prospect*.

Simply put, positioning is about owning a word or a concept in the customer's mind. As you can see from Figure 6.21, the whole idea of positioning is really based on trying to help resolve the chronic *over-communication* that is happening in today's complicated consumer and industrial markets. Customers are bombarded with messages. Research (often rather vague) suggests that we are bombarded by something between 600 and 1000 separate messages every day of our life. In the USA, the estimates rise, according to some researchers, to 1600 messages a day. These are messages that come from a growing number of sources as the shortened list in the figure demonstrates.

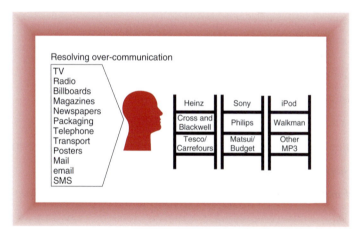

Figure 6.21 Positioning

How, practically, do customers deal with this deluge of data that comes at them unbidden and unannounced? While we simply screen the data so we don't go mad Reis and Trout suggest that what is actually happening is that the customers are forming short 'ladders' in their mind for each product or service category which has any relevance to them. The figure suggests what the ladder positions might be for tinned vegetables on the left through TVs to mobile music on the right. Different customers have different ladders but generally the top position is the one that customer believes 'owns' the word or the category, the second position is that owned by the runner-up and the third position is often either a local or a budget supplier. People tend to lose interest in most categories after three positions on the ladder. For areas or categories which we have a particular interest in, it is suggested that the ladder can reach a maximum of seven rungs.

So what does all this mean? What it means is if you can own the top position on the ladder you can make serious amounts of profit! If you have started to realize that branding and positioning could be the secret to the creation of more organizational wealth than any other method, you could be right. If you've also worked out that positioning and branding is definitely not about trying to work on a 'level playing field' but about finding ways of tilting the playing field so that it works in our favour, you could be right here too.

If you think it might be worthwhile learning a bit more about some of these techniques, then read on.

6.4.3   *Differentiation or* commodity *marketing?*

Levitt said that there is no such thing as *commodity markets*, only *commodity marketing*. In other words, markets don't insist on consuming commodities, that is done by 'bad marketing'.

Before we go any further, we need to establish a few facts:

(1) Commoditization of markets is *not* a foregone conclusion.

(2) Commoditization is *not* something that is out of your control.

(3) Because everyone else is reducing prices does *not* mean that you have to follow.

(4) Continual price reduction is *not* an immutable law that must be followed.

(5) Customers do *not* always buy on price alone.

(6) You are *not* serving your organization if you let profits slide – even to maintain market share!

(7) Lemmings are *not* the brightest animals in the world.

(8) If the market price collapses *on your watch* and you collapse your prices to match the market, you *are* at fault.

The very first thing we must do here is to ask you whether you realize that every time you look at '*reducing prices*', '*becoming more competitive*', '*employing aggressive pricing*', or any other euphemism that you may care to use, you could actually be taking your organization one step further towards its death?

The commodity slide is the most dangerous ride in the amusement park and it's waiting for you (Figure 6.22).

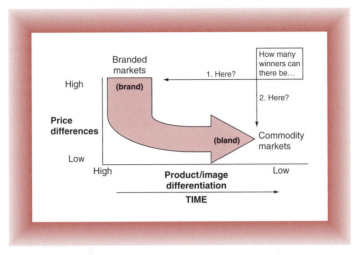

Figure 6.22   The commodity slide

The commodity slide is an idea that has been around for a very long time although it does not seem to have penetrated the day-to-day lives of many (certainly not enough) practising market(ing) managers. From the figure, you can see that all products and services exist somewhere on a continuum between 'brand' and 'bland' – between highly priced and highly differentiated offerings at the top left-hand corner known as branded offerings and low priced with little or no differentiation in the bottom right-hand corner called the commodity markets.

Over the years that I have been working with different organizations, it always appears to me that practitioners generally seem intent on driving business towards the bottom right-hand edge of the figure – commodity offerings seem to attract organizations like mythological sirens calling Odysseus (a very small piece of culture there for our classically trained readers).

But, before you start to curl up in the foetal (yes, I had to use spell check for that one) position as you realize what you have been doing all this time, let's look at what's really going on in commodity markets. These are markets (and there are *far too many* of them) where the products or services competing are – to all intents and purposes – the same; at least most customers find it almost impossible to see any real differences between the offerings and are forced to judge the competitive range just on price!

As soon as price is the only difference that customers can see in the range, then of course they use price to guide their choice. Remember, they may not have been looking to choose on price, but they can't see any other differences. Nevertheless this, it seems, is all it needs for the price-driven practitioners to say that the market is obviously driven solely by price – so we have to be the cheapest if we want to sell the most. It's what the psychologists call a 'self-fulfilling prophecy'. Before you all say, *yes, that sounds like my business*, let's see what happens down this dreary and depressing end of the market.

6.4.4   A word about price

Before we go on, a brief word about the nonsense that is talked about price. You really need to spend a little bit of money to prove to yourself – and your fellow managers – that *customers do not want to buy on price* (Figure 6.23).

All the research I have ever conducted for clients (a lot) and other research that I have seen (more) show the same message every time (read this list carefully):

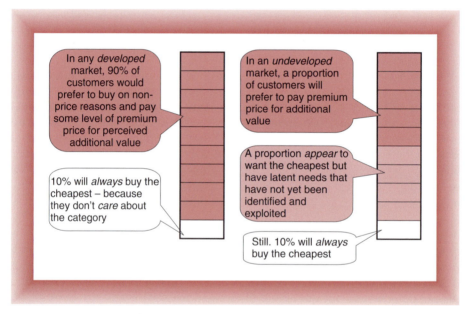

Figure 6.23   A word about price

Price

(1) In a developed market, 90% of customers would *prefer* to buy on non-price value issues (as long as companies can be bothered to offer them).
(2) In a developed market, 10% of customers will (always) buy on price because they *don't care* about the category and are not engaged in the issues (me and washing powders, I'm afraid).
(3) In an undeveloped market, a given proportion of customers would *prefer* to buy on non-price value issues.

(4) In an undeveloped market, 10% of customers will (always) buy on price because they don't care about the category and are not engaged in the issues.

(5) In an undeveloped market, a given proportion of customers will *appear to buy on price* because nobody (even the marketers) has worked out what additional benefits they would be willing to pay a premium for. This is *latent* need. And it only exists because of *bad market(ing)*. I could have softened that bit but then . . .

Professional, practicing managers have a complete market(ing) mix at their disposal; price is *not* the only element they can use.

Commodity markets

Ultimately, success at this end of the market is about being able to produce at the *lowest cost*. As everyone is competing on the same variable – price – there can only be *one winner* in this battle. The player that is the last one able to scrape any profit when everyone else is making losses is the winner. Winner of what, I don't know but everybody seems to want it so . . .

Now, the really difficult question – are you (or can you become) *the* lowest cost producer in your business? If the answer is *Yes*, then you can play the game with a good chance of winning. You just need to ask yourself a few questions:

(1) Can you remain the lowest cost producer?

(2) What do you plan to do when you have removed all the competition?

(3) Do you want to invest your profits this way?

I have only ever worked for one lowest cost provider and that experience was enough to last a lifetime – everything must be devoted to achieving the lowest possible cost and to living off the thinnest margins imaginable. Faced with such dedicated obsession (absolutely no space for mediocre thinking here), the *almost lowest cost producers* and the *I like to think of myself as a low cost producer* simply don't stand a chance.

If the answer to the question is an honest *No*, you really can't become the lowest cost producer, then you have absolutely no reason to reduce prices now because that can only take you to somewhere you already know you cannot win.

Branded markets

If we look at the other end of the continuum, we see the branded markets. These are characterized by a rich assortment of product and service offerings that are recognizably different in the customer's perception. All offer clear and distinct benefits and together make for a sensible range of choices, in that the customer isn't forced to choose on price; there are other variables that can be used as well. For example, if you happen to be in the market for a new car or a new mobile phone, there seems to be a fairly wide range of choices, at an equally wider range of prices. Before I am assailed by the cries of, *yes, but that's OK for B2C and baked beans but it just doesn't happen in my B2B market*, it does, but first, let's tick off the advantages of looking at this end of the slide:

(1) *Reduced sales volume*: First it is true that sales volume is likely to be smaller at the branded end of the market than it is at the commodity end. However, as we all really know from experience:
(a) Revenue is 'vanity'.
(b) Only profit is 'sanity'.
And at the branded end of the commodity slide we would expect to see profit margins far in excess of those which allow organizations to eke out a survival living at the commodity end.

(2) *More than just one 'winner'*: It's also worth considering how many different organizations can be classed as 'winners' at the branded end of the commodity slide. Unlike commodity markets (where there can only be one winner) at the branded end of the continuum, there will be as many potential winners as there are credible market positions (in customer's perception) to be owned. Depending on the market, there can be three, ten, even twenty or more viable and profitable organizations, all making a good living in a properly branded environment. Not only that, customers are happier too because they have more options to choose from and they are not just forced to use price as the discriminator.

So why do organizations appear to be driving, lemming-like, to create a significant market position in a commodity business? As far as I can work out, there are a number of reasons for this strange 'death wish'. These are:

● *The sales culture*: An unreformed sales culture in a business will only allow anyone else to see sales revenue as the ultimate measure of the organization's success.

● *Rewards and assessments*: Often a hangover from the rapid (rabid) growth stage of an organization's development, if management's appraisals are based on sales turnover and sales turnover growth rather than on customers, satisfaction, commitment, retention or even profits, then a commodity business is what you are going to get.

● *The prevailing business model*: Some organizations (I find these often in IT) have a business model where they can survive for four or five quarters without making a profit but they cannot survive one quarter without meeting their revenue targets.

● *Inappropriate benchmarking*: Rather than benchmark their activities against the only measure that really matters – satisfying customer needs – too many organizations benchmark performance against others in the industry where everybody is cutting cost, price and value. The cliff beckons . . .

● *Laziness*: The big one. For too many organizations and managers, it's just easier to do what we have always done than to think about new ways of doing things.

● *Fear*: For some managers, it is simply fear of the unknown. Fear needs to be confronted – preferably before the money runs out.

6.4.5   Differentiation

Differentiation is a term that we all know, we all use – and some of us understand.

Being different from the competition is always a good thing to do if for no better reason than it panders to our ego to see our organization's name on our service or product in the market. But, is putting our name on a standard offer really all we need to do to be differentiated? Like the old SWOT analysis, it's not what *we* think our strengths are but what the market thinks. Too many organizations think they are different and that all they have to do is put their name on an otherwise undifferentiated offering. It needs more than just a name change to be different – it needs the customer to believe that the offer is different, really different in terms of the benefits that it promises. That might seem a daunting challenge to any organization that is not used to looking outside its walls for input and inspiration and anyway, why should we bother? Well, there is research that suggests that there is real money at stake in differentiation.

One of the many pieces of research comes from the UK's Chartered Institute of Marketing (Great Marketing Drives Great Business, Chartered Institute of Marketing (CIM), http://www.cim.co.uk). In 2003, the CIM worked with PA Consulting to research some 6000 companies worldwide – the highlights of what they found were:

(1) 97% of Chief Executive Officers (CEOs) believed their priority was to create long-term value for shareholders.

(2) The interviewed CEOs realized that there are two ways that value can be created within companies:
 (a) by operating at a cost advantage compared to others and
 (b) by creating a superior differentiation that supports a price premium over others.

(3) The research found that, on average, the latter (differentiation) was *three times more influential* than the former (cost advantage) in creating value.

The 'three times' effect tends to be a theme that runs through much of the research on differentiation. It means that:

Differentiation

Provides about three times the payback for the same (but differently directed) effort.

– now does that make you want to try the idea?

Building on the work done by Porter, Nora A. Aufreiter, David Elzinga and Jonathan W. Gordon (Better Branding, *The McKinsey Quarterly*, November 2003) looked at what makes good brands compared to just names and commodity offerings. I have adapted the Aufreiter *et al.* approach and have used it very successfully with clients (Figure 6.24).

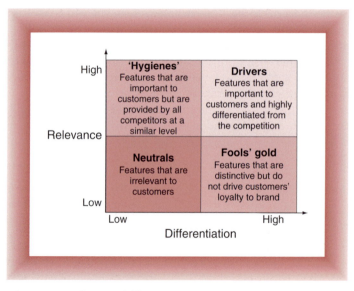

Figure 6.24   Invest in being different
Source: Adapted from Aufreiter et al. (2003).

The work harks back to Hertzberg's work (see Section 6.2) and suggests that being different isn't the whole story. Customers (as always) are the key. We can make our offer(s) different in two main ways:

(1) *Differentiated*: From the competition in the customers' perception. That means different in terms the customer can understand (for example, not just clever technology that they don't understand). Also, customers may compare your offering with offerings from another technology (substitute competition) – you need to be different from these too.

(2) *Relevant*: Your offering needs to have some form of relevance to your customers' lives. This means possessing some information of your customers' needs, wants, aspirations, lifestyles and culture. Again, technological or scientific knowledge is unlikely to be enough.

Within these two categories, offerings fall, broadly, into four categories:

(1) *Neutrals*: These offerings are typical basic commodity offerings. They are not different to any other offerings and have no features that are particularly relevant to your customers. They do the job but are, well, boring.

(2) *Hygienes*: These offerings have all the right features – and they are what customers want, but they are the same as everyone else. This is better than the neutral offers but there is still no way of telling these offers from the other (also good) competition. There is nothing 'wrong' with offerings in this box; it's just that you need to do more to stand out – and reap the financial reward.

(3) *Fools' gold*: These offerings are different, there is no doubt about that. But, perhaps because you have given the R&D boffins their head, you are now launching offerings that are packed with clever 'gismos' that no customers understand, want or ever asked for.

(4) *Drivers*: These offerings are not only clearly different from the competition, they are different with features that customers really want – and value! The 'drivers', if they have been properly identified, will be the 'motivators' identified by Hertzberg. Remember that customers really can't get enough of these additional features, each time more value is added.

Just in case anybody missed the point of all this, *the real money is in the top right box*. The value is here because segmentation works in our favour. We have talked about market segmentation previously (see Section 6.3) and seen that it is an essential technique for extracting maximum value from any market. We also saw that the great debate is (and remains) which segmentation bases to use – demographics, which are easy but give poor segments, or motivations, which are more difficult but give better quality segments (Figure 6.25).

The different drivers in the top right box in the figure are the building blocks of successful (and profitable) marketing. Attempting segmentation from any other box is a fruitless exercise.

How are you going to be different?

If I really have got you thinking about how to be different rather than being the same, the question is, *how* are you going to be different from the competition?

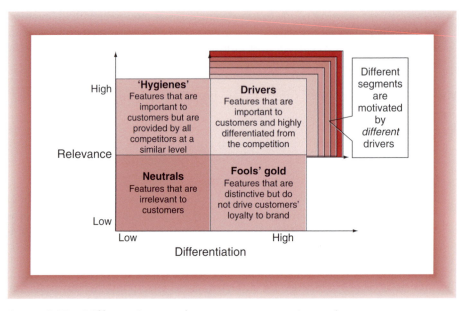

Figure 6.25   Differentiate to the target *segment's* needs
Source: Adapted from Aufreiter et al. (2003).

Yet again (no, I never did promise originality) the answer is not going to be found inside your organization or its history, but is going to be found in the market, in the minds and hearts of your target customers and prospects.

You should be asking yourself a few key questions:

(1) *Which market segment(s) are you targeting?* As we have discussed already, the 'mass market' is dead – it is now a thing of mystery and folklore – you should not be attempting to market to it. To be successful, you need to move away from *same* towards 'different' and aspire to 'unique'. The further you get away from 'same', the more value you add to the offer, for the right people – but the more potential prospects you alienate because they don't value the differentiation. You know this is going to happen, so choose your target segment(s) with care and make sure you know what they value – and what they don't.

(2) *Where does your customer/prospect perceive the most value?* It's important that from all the possible ways that you 'could' differentiate your offer, you choose the ways that actively support the needs of the market segment and the market position that you wish to own. For example, a food company wishing to own the 'pure/purist' position in its category would be unlikely to differentiate itself by adding more chemicals and/or preservatives than anybody else. Aim to target the greatest store of market value with the fewest attributes or features.

(3) *Where is most of your competition concentrated?* Simple strategy is called for here – and some intuitive thinking. Look for gaps in the marketplace and exploit them. Only attack competitors' positions directly if there is no alternative.

(4) *Where is your offer most/least credible?* Unless you are coming to the market for the very first time, you will have a track record, a history and many customers will already have experience of your offer. It is important, when you differentiate, to make sure that you don't add aspects that the market simply does not believe. Relate the differentiation to your perceived strengths and weaknesses. Always aim for credible (to customers) areas first.

(5) *Where is the differentiation easiest for your company to maintain?* Markets (made up of customers needs and perceived value) tend to change over time. Don't move unless you are sure that you will be able to 'keep up the payments'.

(6) *Where is the differentiation easiest for your company to protect?* There is simply no point in spending money to differentiate your offer if the competition can copy what you have done in a matter of weeks.

(7) *Where are the opportunities that fall outside your technical/scientific expertise but within your 'market' definition?* If you limit yourself to the technical/scientific/product aspects of your offer and consider only potential differentiations that you are (technically) able to create and deliver, you will expose yourself to technological leapfrog (copying) as well as missing more profitable opportunities.

6.4.6   What is a brand?

A brand is described properly as a set of 'consistent meanings' which exist in addition to the product or service offering. This means that a brand is not the same as a product or service. Branding is something that exists over and above the physical product or service. This also means (get ready for this) that doing more and more work on the product or service won't necessarily enhance the brand – working on what your customers' think the brand 'promises' them will.

So we can see that a brand is really a set of 'beliefs and feelings' existing in the customers' minds (rather than in the fabric or workings of the product or service) that convince customers that they will receive certain 'specific benefits' from using the brand rather than a competing offer.

Where do these beliefs and feelings come from? We believe (no, we don't 'know', we're dealing with people here, not products) that they are derived from a complex of:

● *Actual experience of the product/service*: Using, testing and living with the product or service will certainly communicate what it does and how it is different or unique from other offerings. Of course, you might want to communicate to customers and give them an idea of what differences to look out for.

- *Word-of-mouth communication*: Talking to others and hearing what their experiences were. We take word of mouth to include telephone and Internet communications too.

- *Advertising and communications history*: And what 'promises' you have been making. The general rule is under-promising and over-delivering is better than over-promising and under-delivering.

- *What the brand owners do more than what they say*: Much more important. Remember the sad stories of Barclays and South Africa, Nike and child labour, Nestle and baby formula in Africa, Mercedes and the 'elk test', the list goes on. How the brand owner behaves is becoming more and more important to the success of a brand in more cynical times.

- *The role of the brand in our lives and purchasing behaviour*: The big one. Forget what the brand is; understand what the brand *does* for the customer. Every successful brand has a role in the customer's life (things without a role are peripheral and are just products, services, stuff, who cares . . .). Find the role, understand its importance, design your brand to fit the role – easy!

Importantly, *a brand is not the same as a name*. Just putting a name on a product (even as good as my snappily named printer the *7301*) does not automatically confer a set of consistent meanings, beliefs and feelings to a standard (undifferentiated) product or service. No really. Just because you know all about your product service and could pick it out of a crowd at a hundred paces does not mean the customer can or wants to. Don't continue deluding yourself; ask the customers what they see in the offer. The sooner you find out whether you have a brand or just a name the sooner you can start the marketing job proper.

B2B has brands too

3M	Hewlett Packard	Pfizer
Accenture	IBM	Pratt & Whitney engines
BAE systems	Intel	PriceWaterhouseCoopers
Boeing	International Harvester	Reuters
Caterpillar	JCB	Rolls-Royce engines
Chubb security	Komatsu	SAP
Cisco	Lloyds of London	Salamander Grills
Dell	Merrill Lynch	Sikorsky helicopters
DHL express	McKinsey	Smith Kline
GE	Oracle	Sun Microsystems
Group 4 Security	Otis Elevators	Tetra packaging
Heidelberg printers	Perkins engines	TNT delivery

Different types of brand

There are brands and, well, brands. Unless you have a range or portfolio of brands you probably won't need to worry about this. But, if you have more than one brand in your care – or more than one segment to market to – and you really don't want confused customers, then pay attention.

It's all about how you organize yourself and your brands. There are a number of ways to arrange the 'portfolio' (a big word if you only have two brands, but bear with me). It's important because we need to make sure that the story is as simple as possible for the customer. You remember I'm sure that we need to make it simple, not because the customer is stupid, but because they have a busy life to lead and no time to invest in understanding subtle differences. Your options are:

(1) *Monolithic brands*: Here we arrange all (both) the brands under a common monolithic name. Examples would be Siemens, BT and British Airways. A monolithic approach then conveys a guarantee of overall corporate excellence (or failure) and differentiation. Just think what guarantees are promised by monolithic brands such as IBM, Dell, Google, Microsoft, Lidl, Marks & Spencer, DHL, Parcelforce, Amazon and Tesco. This is a 'swings and roundabouts' game:
   (a) *Advantages*: Any investment in communications or research benefits all the products/services under the common banner.
   (b) *Disadvantages*: A failure in one area can have effects in all other areas with the same name. Makes segmented marketing quite difficult because works on a standardized approach.

(2) *Umbrella brands*: They are different from monolithic in that there is more focus on the individual brand's meaning and specific promise but the customer knows that it exists within a broader range and the parent brand exists as an overall quality endorser. Examples would include Dulux paints, Heinz, Airbus, Virgin and Ford:
   (a) *Advantages*: This approach is popular because it allows a degree of variability in the promises but also permits some economies of scale as investment in communications and distribution can be spread. Can be a useful way of addressing more than one segment if not too different.
   (b) *Disadvantages*: It can limit the degree of individuality you can create in the brands; for example, it doesn't help working in segments that are very different, only those that are more common.

(3) *Single line brands*: They are where each brand is a stand-alone offering and no connection or lineage is provided. The usual example here is Van den Berghs (who they?) who produce a wide range of edible oils (margarine to you and me) that you probably have heard of – they own all these brands – Flora, Stork, Echo, Krona, Outline, Olivio, ICBINB, Becel, Blue Band, Rama, Country Crock, Doriana, Family, Delma and many more:
   (a) *Advantages*: This allows the brand to provide maximum focus in its meaning. It's not a cheap approach but you create a lot of separate brand

value and a failure in one brand does not affect any other. The best way of addressing many segments – each segment gets its own, unique offer.
(b) *Disadvantages*: It is expensive, especially with more than one brand to worry about.

(4) *Brands and sub-brands*: This approach rather falls in between the two previous approaches, umbrella and single line. The *parent* brand can have different relationships with its sub-brands; some parents are public parents (Heinz and WeightWatchers) while others are less obvious (Toyota and Lexus). Sub-branding works best when the parent brand has a broad meaning and can encompass a wide range of 'offspring' without negative effects on its own brand:
(a) *Advantages*: Allows the sub-brand to develop its own life while creating some 'back office' economies of scale. In the future and can be sold at a later date if required. Can be a useful way of addressing different segments.
(b) *Disadvantages*: Only limited economies of scale in market investment.

(5) *Brand 'halos'*: Brand 'halos' describe a special 'attribute' or 'promise' that has a meaning that can be used across the entire brand range to enhance offerings. Classic examples who really started the trend are Saab 'Turbo' and Audi 'Quattro'.
(a) *Advantages*: Enhancing every offering attached to the halo can improve differentiation, penetration and profits.
(b) *Disadvantages*: If you haven't got it, you haven't got it. Lots of companies have tried to emulate the Saab/Audi success but haven't done quite so well.

(6) *Brand portfolios*: Where the organization owns and markets an interlocking range of separate brands, which together give reach to all or most parts of the marketplace. Classical examples include VAG with VW, Audi, Skoda, Seat, Bentley, Lamborghini, Bugatti and Royal Bank of Scotland with RBS, Coutts & Co, Child & Co, NatWest Bank, Isle of Man Bank, Ulster Bank and Direct Line Insurance. Often the result of consolidation as a sector moves from rapid growth to maturity stages of the life cycle, the acquiring organization can decide whether to bring all the acquired companies into the main brand – or it can keep the acquired brands and use them to position in different segments. However, treading the line between 'real' differences between the brands and just 'packaging' differences can be difficult – especially with knowledgeable customers:
(a) *Advantages*: If organized properly, can create enormous economies of scale in production and distribution (but not necessarily in market(ing)). Can deliver routes to most segments with different offerings and deeper penetration than with more shallow offerings.
(b) *Disadvantages*: Can be expensive, depending on how different the needs of the segments and how much adaptation is required. Can be tricky stopping the organization not driving for the low-cost routes automatically and destroying any difference between the brands – the customer will notice and margins will suffer.

(7) *Ingredient brands*: Many brands are successful, unique and never purchased on their own. An ingredient brand exists only as a part of another brand or offering. Examples would include: Intel, Goretex, Nutrasweet, Lycra, Teflon, Triplex, and Rolls-Royce (aero engines). Consider the role and power of these important brands and how they affect the perception, sales and margins of the brands that they are in:

   (a) *Advantages*: Good way for B2B brands to get exposure in other and even B2C markets. Help fight constant price pressure from powerful customers who probably buy in large volumes. Low costs of distribution.

   (b) *Disadvantages*: Still require large investment. May not make your B2B customers very happy as you stretch beyond them to create a brand franchise with their customers. If you can live with the extra business and unhappy immediate customers who will look for ways of avoiding having to buy your ingredient if they can get away with it, you will be fine. Difficult concept for many B2B cultures to understand.

Why do brands work?

Brands work simply because customers really like them.

Brands, in different guises, have been around for a long time. They have been delivering customer value for a long time. So what exactly do customers like?

- *Brands make our decision-making easier*: It was fine all the time that we didn't know just how many products and services were out there to choose from. With the arrival of hypermarkets, supermarkets and the Internet, we now know for a fact that there is *too much* choice. Without brands to guide me, I wouldn't get out of the supermarket inside three hours – and frankly there are better things to do with my life:
  - *Brands act as 'shorthand'*: They help me choose within a category and for specific purposes. If I am looking for a hotel in an unknown European city, I can choose one I have never heard of before (for the excitement) or I can choose among Hilton, Ibis, Sheraton, Formule 1, Holiday Inn, Meridien, Novotel, Intercontinental and Travelodge as well as others – each brand gives me a faster way of understanding what I will get if I buy.
  - *Brands help me reduce the risk in the purchase*: If a box of paperclips are not fit for purpose there is not too much problem, if a new car fails to live up to expectations then I am badly out of pocket. The bigger the purchase, the bigger the risk, and the more we worry. Brands can help us reduce some of the risk (see Section 6.7). In a straightforward re-purchase there is little or no risk. Buying something for the first time is very different and brands that we know can be a guide. For example, buying the first MP3 player, iPod, the leader or Sony where my Walkman comes from? Does my regular brand make a good decaffeinated coffee too? Does my preferred car brand do a people carrier for the growing family?

- *Brands allow me to buy on 'automatic pilot'*: Especially for everyday purchases. With an entire supermarket gondola dedicated to tea and coffee and another to washing powders (why?), if it wasn't for brands we would have to make a new set of decisions every week!

● *Brands make statements about ourselves to others – and to ourselves*: On a more personal level, brands are public property and when we buy into a brand, everyone else is likely to see. If I drive a Volkswagen, a BMW or a Mercedes it says something about me and the type of person I am. Within certain circles (or 'contexts') the same could be said about the food I eat, the shops I use, the holidays I take and the clothes I wear:
  - *I am what I buy*: Many people use brands to project their identity and to signal the type of person they are to others, both friends and strangers. In case you think we are getting too carried away with the over-emotional consumer, what do you think the road maintenance companies are doing when they use (branded) Volvo, Caterpillar and JCB diggers and earth-movers beside the busy roads? Or the local printing company that places its least used machine (the Heidelberg) closest to visitor reception?
  - *I would like to be what I buy*: Aspiration is a wonderful thing. It explains why the '3 series', its entry level luxury car, is the best selling model.

Brand leadership

There are lots of reasons why everybody wants to be the brand leader, most of them obvious and to do with ego, money and power. So we won't waste time explaining all that. What I do want to do is to show you how there can be 'more than one winner' in the leadership game. There are three types of brand leadership:

(1) *The brand leader*: The one that everybody thinks about, the biggest in the market or the category, the one that makes all the profit, the one that spends its days fighting off the young pretenders.

(2) *The niche brand leader*: Another option is to differentiate away from the brand leader and become leader of a sub-category or niche. Companies such as Porsche, Bang & Olufsen and Club Med are good examples.

(3) *The thought leader*: The one everybody is talking about. The one that people are watching. The one that people are interested in, even if they haven't tried it yet. BMW has been doing this for years and holds a reputation far above the relatively small numbers of cars produced.

Brands and segments

Finally, some insight into a crucial area that the branding books don't often cover the role of market segmentation in the branding discussion. *Branding and segmentation cannot be separated*; any calculations on brand need to include a deep understanding of the target audience for the brand or all will be for nothing. Let's follow the logic:

(1) *A successful brand* will be one that is *different* and has specific promises attached – the more specific the offer the more some people will be attracted, and others repelled – the rules of segmentation.

(2) *An unsuccessful brand* will have a fairly *undifferentiated* offer – one that sort of attracts a wide number of people but only slightly – the un-segmented approach.

(3) *The most successful organizations* first identify the segments (see Section 6.3) in their market, prioritize the segments they want and then design the branded offer required to penetrate the segment.

Failure comes from a number of routes:

(1) *Planting a brand in any number of segments* – and watching it die;

(2) *Planting a brand in all segments* (the 'mass market') – and watching it die;

(3) *Developing a brand and not knowing where to plant it* – and watching it die;

(4) *Developing a brand from a segment and trying to plant it in another segment* – and watching it die.

6.4.7 Conclusions – positioning and branding

In this fourth part of the market(ing) strategy discussion, we have broached the question of positioning and branding.

Positioning has not really escaped the realm of advertising, although it deserves a wider audience.

Branding, on the other hand, has attracted so many words; books and articles continue to flow from the pens of authors who know what they are talking about – and those who don't. But for the hard-working practitioner the story never seems to get any clearer. But, given the advantages of establishing a clear and distinct position/brand, I hope I have convinced you that it's worth trying. I hope that this section has encouraged you to have a little more patience with your branding activities, the 'Fifield's dozen' is, I believe:

(1) There is no such thing as commodity markets – only commodity marketing – you *are* in control.

(2) If you are not the lowest cost producer, then you must read on.

(3) Customers don't want the 'same' or even the 'cheapest', they want different (believe me).

(4) Everybody can be different, you just have to investigate the market and be prepared to do something 'unusual'.

(5) Success comes from 'owning' a word or concept in the customer's mind – and not for being the cheapest or most boring.

(6) And – there are more 'different' positions than just one of the cheapest.

(7) A brand 'packages' the difference into a promise to the customer.

(8) A brand is not the same thing as a 'name' – you need to do more.

(9) There are different types of brand for you to understand, they are not complicated, you just need to choose the route that is best for you.

(10) Brands can't work without 'segments' to take root in.

(11) Branding is not about products or services, it is about 'relationships' with customers.

(12) Branding is seriously good business – once the finance bods work out that it may not happen with the 'single financial year', you can grow the bottom line dramatically.

Now you need to check the strategy checklist in the Appendix; this time you should see that we can add input in the section on positioning and branding – we should now have the answers to important questions such as, *How am I going to be different?*, *How do we develop brands?* and *How do we avoid price competition?*

Finally, a few questions that you should now be able to answer:

Positioning and branding

1	Are you going to pursue Differentiation or *commodity* marketing?	
2	What market positions exist?	
3	What market position do we own or do we want to own?	
4	How are we going to be different from the competition?	

5	What is a brand? What are its unique *values* and *personality*?	
6	What are the costs and benefits of building a brand?	
7	How do we invest in the brand and a differentiated market position?	

6.5 Customer retention

A great European federative system alone can be favourable to the development of civilisation.

Napoleon Bonaparte

Now we move SCORPIO on to the (sometimes) less exciting areas that don't involve all that macho *hunter* style customer acquisition stuff – but might make you even more money (Figure 6.26).

The 'challenge' of customer retention has always been with us but not really brought to centre stage, at least for larger organizations, until the arrival of

Figure 6.26 SCORPIO market strategy

Frederick Reichheld's book (*The Loyalty Effect*, Harvard Business School Press, Boston, 1996). Reichheld, a member of the consultancy Bain & Company, conducted some simple research among typical large organizations and discovered what happened if these companies managed to lose *less* customers every year.

The now well-known results varied from industry to industry depending on costs but the numbers managed to attract everyone's attention – at least until they worked out just how difficult customer retention can be. The problems that organizations uncovered were (and are) created simply because customer retention is normally approached with a 'tactical' rather than 'strategic' mindset. Retention is too often attacked with a short-term 'fix' in mind by managers intent on making a return on the retention investment within the same financial year. As many of the so-called CRM (Customer Relationship Management) programmes sold over the past ten years have shown, you can get the 'return on investment' by just automating customer service activities and then reducing headcount. The last ten years has also shown that this does little for 'retention' (getting customers to come back/stay longer). Customer Retention is a strategic issue and must be addressed in combination with the other issues of market(ing) strategy.

The examples cited by Bain/Reichheld were all based on US organizations but were impressive, based on the firms increasing retention by just 5%. What this means is of all of the customers that they expected to lose in a year, they retained 5% (they still lost 95%), then:

● Credit insurance was the lowest benefiting industry with just below 20% increase in profits (not bad).

● Credit cards was the highest benefiting industry, increased their annual profits by 120% (doubling profits by losing only 5% less customers should impress us all).

● Other industries (software, office building management, industrial laundry, industrial distribution, insurance brokerage, business banking and automobile service) all fell between these two extremes.

● The average was over 40% improvement.

How would you like to increase your annual *profits* by just the lowest figure of 20%? I always hope to have people's attention by this point but some people just seem to take a lot of impressing.

In this chapter, we will look at a few key questions that might help you jump your annual profit levels significantly:

● What is retention all about?

● Why is it important?

● How do you do it?

● What gets in the way?

6.5.1 First, catch your customer

Marketing is about customers. Levitt said that the *purpose of every business* is:

> *To create and keep a customer*

'Create' is obvious; everybody reads that far but not many people read to the end of the six-word sentence.

This focus is probably because we all think we know how to create customers (it's called sales in some businesses) and everybody in the organization sees the value in more customers, so the plaudits lie thick on the ground. Generally managers think so narrowly that as long as the organization is acquiring more customers every year they believe that they and the organization must be doing well – when it all falls apart underneath them they are genuinely surprised and instantly start looking for the saboteurs in their midst. They don't for a moment imagine it could be their fault, they have done their bit and brought in more new customers every year – all those experts in accounting and production had to do was to keep service up. It's not that difficult, or is it?

Well, no. There is a larger problem of organizations, 'silos', organizational design, 'empires' and 'baronies' involved here as well as appraisal, reward and bonus systems that make it very personal – and deadly. The moral of the story is simple; catching more and more customers is *not* the name of the game. Unprofitable customers you don't need – the problem is, they are often the easiest to find. Too many customers are not necessarily unprofitable – they just need to stay long enough to 'go into the black'. The more investment (discounts, incentives, intermediary/channel costs, lower prices, sales and promotions activities) you lavish on acquiring customers, the longer they have to stay before the investment is paid back.

Second, keep your customer

How do you keep your customers? Customers will stay with you as long as they believe they are getting something out of the deal. Just to be sure we understand each other here, customers will stay with you *as long as* they *believe* they *are getting something out of the deal*. I know you need something as well but that is not doing anything for the customer. Tune into the famous radio station – W11*fm* (What's 1n 1t for me?; Figure 6.27).

Imagine that you are trying to get fair trade products to differentiate your offer (they have been around for a long time); you know that you won't succeed just by making morally correct claims like:

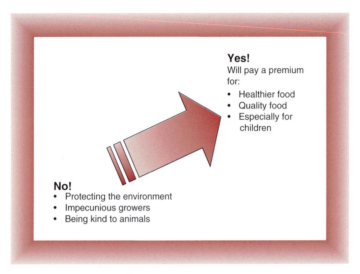

Figure 6.27   Tune into 'W11*fm*'
Source: Institute of Grocery Distribution (2002) and Cooperative Bank (2002).

● Protecting the environment;

● Caring for the rights of poor, third-world growers;

● Being kind to animals.

Everyone *will* agree but *won't* buy – what's in it for them? Making claims that offer something for them (or better, people they love) will be much more successful:

● Healthier food;

● Quality food;

● Especially for children.

So, the steps in retaining customers are really obvious:

(1) *Constantly add customer value*: That means delivering offers that make sense to them and clearly contain something for them (*W11fm*). Bear in mind that 'what they want' changes over time (see below). To do this:

(2) *Find out what they want*: Not complicated, I'm sure you'll agree. Don't guess or assume, ask them what they want. Then:

(3) *Satisfy their needs and wants*: Or, give them what they want. Don't give them what you 'think they want', what 'they should want' or 'what you would want if you were them'.

(4) *Make sure that they can get more of what they want with you than anywhere else*: If you are really intent on adding customer value, make sure that they really can't get more of what they want anywhere else.

(5) *Make sure that they know it*: Then, and only then, bring the marketing communications to bear on the target customers – make sure that they all 'know' what you have and that nobody else does it better.

If you can do this more than once in the face of constant change in customer needs, wants and perception, not only are you very good, you have a strategy!

Third, beware value migration

There is a book you need to read (after you have finished this one of course), *Value Migration, How to Think Several Moves Ahead of the Competition* by Adrian Slywotzky (Harvard Business School Press, Boston, 1996). Briefly, Slywotzky suggests that:

(1) *Market(ing) strategy is the art of creating value* for the customer.

(2) *Customer needs*: This can only be done by offering a product or service that corresponds to customer needs.

(3) *Change*: In a fast-changing business environment, the factors that determine value (customer perceptions of what they think they need/want) are constantly changing.

(4) *Value migrates* from outmoded business models to business designs that are better able to satisfy customers' new needs/wants. For example, yesterday's customers were fighting to own Walkmans, colour televisions, video recorders and a second home in Wales. Today it's MP3 players, HDTV, DVD recorders and a holiday home in Switzerland or Croatia.

According to Slywotsky, there are three phases of what he calls *value migration*:

(1) *During inflow*: The initial phase, a company starts to grow by taking value from other parts of its industry because its business design proves superior in satisfying customers' priorities – it has more of what the customers want now than the other players (iPod takes value from Sony?).

(2) *During stability*: The second phase, business designs are well matched to customer priorities and by overall competitive equilibrium – the organization grows on its successful base and spreads its offer through the innovation diffusion categories from the early adopters to the rest of the population (now everybody has a mobile phone).

(3) *During outflow*: The third phase, value starts to move away from an organization's traditional activities toward business designs that more effectively meet

evolving customer priorities – today's early adopters are on the move again, looking for the next big idea (interactive gaming? voice over IP? hybrid cars?).

We all knew that nothing lasts forever – now we know what it's called – *Value Migration*. Value migration is an unstoppable force but it needn't be a lethal one. For the product-focused organization, value migration will likely prove fatal but there needs be no fear for the organization that keeps its focus firmly on its customers. By focusing on perceptions of needs and wants (customer value), it should be able to move with its customer base, not away from it.

6.5.2   How important is retention in our market?

We have already seen from Reichheld's work that customer retention, while valuable for all organizations, is more valuable for others. But so few organizations have any idea where they stand in the retention stakes or how bad the 'lapse' situation is currently. It's because it looks a bit like accountants' work I suppose, but bear with me . . .

Picking Figure 6.28 apart to make some sense, we can see:

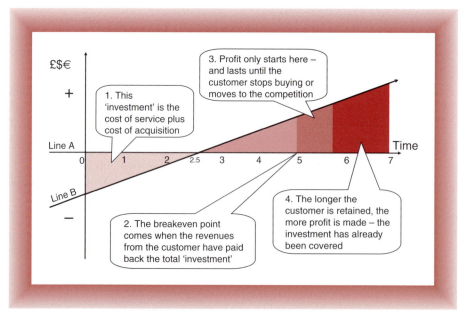

Figure 6.28   Retention – why bother?

(1) *Line A*: It is the time line and shows the progress of an organization measured in years (for a common B2B organization) or in months (for a fast-moving B2C organization).

(2) *Line B*: It shows the money. At the very beginning, time '0', say the launch of the product or service, there is a negative balance (it is below the horizontal year line). This is because of all the special costs associated with acquiring customers in the first place.

(3) *At time '2.5'*: With the passage of time, the organization gradually acquires new customers so that by the time '2.5' (years or months) the figures stabilize and the organization stops losing money. After this time, there are enough customers (and they are not leaving yet) that the money 'inflows' match the money 'outflows' on a daily basis. But the capital investment in acquiring customers (the first shaded area to the left of point 2.5) remains.

(4) *At time '5'*: By the time the organization gets to time '5', the second shaded area equals the first shaded area (between points 2.5 and 5) and, finally, the investment has been paid back – the activity has *broken even*.

(5) *Beyond time '5'*: As soon as customers stay (keep buying) beyond time 5, the profit per customer goes positive because there is no longer any acquisition costs to offset.

(6) *Beyond time '6'*: Moving beyond time '6' or '7', the profitability accelerates further.

(7) *Longer*: The longer customers stay with us, the more profitable they become.

Let's look at the departing customers.

There is normally no shortage of information on the newly acquired customers – you are told even if you don't want to know, but leaving customers – who are they?

Some customers should leave, it is best for them and for the organization. Their needs and wants will naturally migrate and sometimes this will be beyond what we want or are able to offer from our unique market position. You will remember our discussion on positioning (see Section 6.4) and the need to keep to our market position rather than succumb to the all-things-to-all-men approach; sometimes customers must leave because they naturally move to the positions controlled by other organizations.

For those that shouldn't be leaving, where are they going? Importantly, can you tell the difference between the two types of leavers?

6.5.3   Is retention just about customer satisfaction?

The short answer here (in case you were in any doubt) is *No*. There have been lots of research over recent years to show that the so-called 'satisfied customers' are likely to 'defect' about as readily as dissatisfied ones. So just focusing on 'keeping the customer satisfied' (did the strains of Simon and Garfunkel sound in your mind there?) is no longer enough. But, as we have already seen, not very many organizations seem to be doing much about it (Figure 6.29).

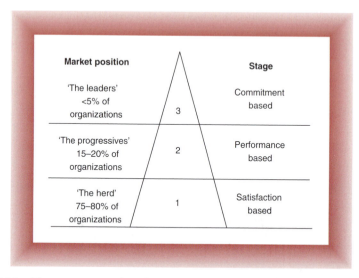

Figure 6.29   The customer loyalty pyramid. Adapted from Lowenstein, M. (1997) *The Customer Loyalty Pyramid*. Westport: Quorum Books (US)

Lowenstein showed that less than 5% of organizations were even bothering to measure commitment (to come back and buy again) among its customers. Granted it was 1997 but things really don't change that fast in the real world where many of the organizations I meet are still grappling with whether to/how to add 'flaky' measures like customer satisfaction to the measurements they take. Other (very large) organizations measure customer satisfaction on a regular basis but still do nothing worthwhile with the results. By worthwhile I mean incorporate the results into everybody's staff appraisal and reward systems – so that satisfying customers get rewarded. When selling stuff (to whoever is in the firing line) adds so much bonus to the annual salary, which turkeys are going to vote for Christmas? So much for progress.

Despite all these, we are told by every organization that they are investing 'fortunes' in creating loyal customers. Show some people a bandwagon and they can't help but clamber aboard. What too many organizations don't seem to realize is that loyalty is about more than 'bribery'.

If you want mindless 'loyalty', then buy a dog.

If you want committed customers who keep coming back, then you have to give them a very good reason to be 'loyal' – and that means much more than being who you are or selling what you happen to sell. Even knowing what the 'good reason to stay' might be, all depends on how well you understand them and their needs. Here we go again . . .

Barcodes do *not* make customers (Figure 6.30). Understanding your products to an insane level of granularity is *not* the same thing as understanding your customers and empathizing with their needs, wants, fear and aspirations.

Figure 6.30   Where to start? Know your customers

Loyalty is what you want, but how do you get it? Issuing everyone with a discount card has nothing to do with either 'loyalty' or 'relationships'. Loyalty is about customers coming back because they want to. How do we get there?

Maybe a better way of posing the question is to ask, what gets in the way of customers coming back? The answer, unsurprisingly, is a lot of things – which ones are driving your business will depend on you, your organization, its unique market position and its customers. The (not exhaustive) list of items to think about might include:

● *Competition*: Have there been any moves by the competition that may have put you and your offer at a disadvantage? Has there been any evidence of competitive entry, perhaps from outside the industry or in the form of substitute competition?

● *Value migration*: Is there any evidence of value migration in the marketplace? Are customers being attracted away to a new, more satisfying solution?

● *Changing customer needs and wants*: Are customers' needs changing? Have needs and wants changed so that your offering no longer has the same interest or following that it used to enjoy? Are you the 'Sony Walkman' of your business who thought your dominant reign would go on for ever?

- *Changing customer circumstances*: Customers are on a journey. They change, grow older, pass through life transitions (school, work, marriage, children, empty nest, divorce, retirement, illness, wealth/poverty) and as they do, their needs, wants and perceptions of (what constitutes) *value* change too. Not only will they possibly leave, they may also significantly change their purchasing behaviour, buying more/more often or less/less frequently as a result. These are 'intermediate stages' between being a customer and defecting, sometimes called upward migration (buying more/more often) or downward migration (buying less/less frequently). The attentive organization will be tracking and *understanding* these changes closely. Firstborn children are notorious at changing their parents' perceptions and buying behaviours.

- *Internal changes*: Finally, check inside for something that your organization has done that has caused (or contributed to) the decline in loyalty. We all know that we ought to check these things out with customers before we do anything, but we all know that we just don't. Sometimes simple administrative changes or minor cost efficiency changes can be enough to tip the scales for a customer who was *just thinking* about changing. Range rationalization is a well-known irritant for many, often long-standing, customers who feel they are no longer valued as their regular purchase is suddenly withdrawn – with no explanation.

Customers change like everything else. Loyalty requires different actions at different times; if you believe you have found the sure-fire-silver-bullet you are bound to be disappointed.

6.5.4   *Do accounting and reporting systems impede retention activities?*

Possibly the shortest section in the book, this part is less like reading and more like an internal project assignment.

If you read the Reichheld book carefully (and subsequent writings by Reichheld and other commentators), one problem comes through all the work – there is not very much chance of customer retention happening in an organization – at least a large, shareholder-owned organization.

The success stories of customer retention all tend to showcase organizations that are private, owner managed or co-operative – examples of successful retention projects in listed companies are as rare as hens' teeth. Why is this? The answer seems to lie in the accounting and finance systems and procedures which once served these organizations and now controls them. Once again we are faced with an external (customer) versus internal (company) argument.

(1) *The external view*: The customer is the name of the game and profits only come from happy customers – who come back. We maximize the profits by

maximizing customer commitment. To do this, we have to take a customer view of the world to be able to empathize with their needs and wants and to be able to develop new products and services that always meet their changing needs. If we can keep the customer committed, the bottom line will look after itself. Profits and margins are all about brands, market position and relationships. Customers who *prefer* to do business with us are committed, profitable customers and (reasonably) safe from competitive poaching. Our investments are always investments in customers, not just products, because customers give us our best returns. We maximize the return on customers by taking a view of the investment over the lifetime of our relationship – some investments in our customers might not pay back for five years, in this way we are sure to maximize the *lifetime value* of every customer.

(2) *The internal view*: The shareholder owns the business and need to receive ever-increasing returns on their investment. Business is about being lean and mean and constantly looking for ways of reducing costs and being price competitive in the market – there is *no loyalty that 10% off can't overcome*. The secret to our success is simple – keeping a very close eye on the bottom line and making sure the costs are under control. Everybody knows that they have a part to play in keeping the share price high and the returns on investment attractive – we do that by fearless control of spending and rigorous monitoring of every investment – either it comes good by the end of the year or we cut our losses fast.

(3) *Your organization – your choice*: Where does your organization fit on this continuum? The returns from customer retention activities will accrue more to the externally focused organization because it, rather than the internally focused organization, will be able to do what needs to be done to secure those returns.

6.5.5   *What is the strategic role of customer relationships?*

So much nonsense has been written about 'relationships' and 'relationship management' over the past few years that it is barely credible (Figure 6.31).

Managers obviously love bandwagons, especially very expensive ones.

In this section, we are not going to criticize all those very expensive CRM systems that organizations have purchased and now complain about – I have done that elsewhere. Here we will look at the basics of relationships and relationship building and leave you to make your own mistakes.

The big idea behind 'relationships' (not a very good word really) is that if we work at moving beyond the simple transaction to a 'deeper', more 'relationship' basis, we will make more money from customers who buy more, better and more often.

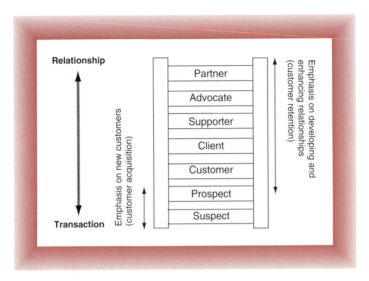

Figure 6.31   The big idea behind 'relationships'

Different commentators have chosen interesting labels for this phenomenon but always it is presented as our view on what should happen, little account is taken of the customer.

Also, where most attempts at forging relationships go astray is in the implementation. One day organizations are going to get used to the idea that customers are not happy just to have things imposed on them without being asked by organizations that think they know best.

If we really want a relationship with our customers, we are going to have to stop 'doing things to' customers without asking them. A relationship needs two parties to be successful, not just one. Relationship is a two-way bridge that allows customers the freedom to take what they want and need from our organization, not just to soak up what we want to give them (Figure 6.32).

I can see the high-need-for-control managers running for cover already.

One of the few books that makes some sense about the whole relationship area is called *The Customer Differential* by Melinda Nykamp (Amacom, New York, 2001). Nykamp keeps reasonably clear of the whole CRM debacle and focuses on what relationships are all about and how to build them, but without the normal obsession with heavy IT systems that allow the whole relationship process to be de-personalized. Has nobody else seen a flaw in that argument yet? Has nobody else worked out that 'relationship' is a human process, not a systems one? Has nobody else worked out that people are better at differentiating your offer than

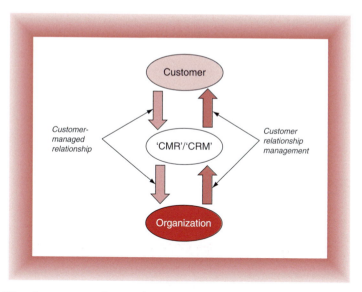

Figure 6.32 Customer relationship is a two-way bridge

systems? Has nobody else worked out that customer service is not excellent if delivered by automated call systems and cheap outsourced call centres on the Indian subcontinent with a language problem? But the bottom line has improved this year, so why bother?

Nykamp explains that the relationship process (Figure 6.33) starts with:

(1) *Understanding the customer*: We need to know all about the customer as we have explained above – there really is no escape from this. We also need to know about the customer's normal purchase cycle.

(2) *Understanding the purchase cycle*: Next, we need to know how the customers needs affect the purchase cycle, for example, how different levels of information, convenience, efficiency, price and reputation might affect purchase behaviour.

(3) *Understanding opportunities for customer interaction*: Next, we need to understand the opportunities we might have to interact with the customer. Nykamp suggest that we look for opportunities that are: Some of these interaction opportunities can be seen in the figure.

Finally, Nykamp draws out the idea of the 'virtuous circle' and places the important 'strategic' arrows in and we can see a flow of investment in:

(1) Driving for customer satisfaction, that leads to

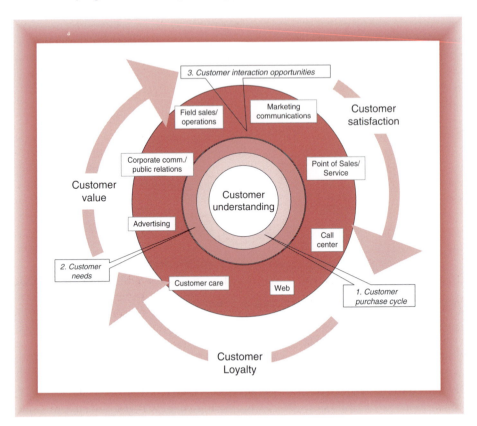

Figure 6.33   Customer relationship requires interaction
Source: Adapted from Nykamp, M. (2001) *The Customer Differential*. New York: Amacom.

(2) Driving for customer loyalty, that leads to

(3) Driving for customer value, that leads to ...

One more time

Just in case you lost sight of things in that run-through of key steps, this does *not* have to be done by a large and very expensive IT system. Nor is this just for the bigger companies; although the smaller companies will be wondering what all the fuss is about, they know that they have relationships with their customers or they have no business.

6.5.6   Conclusions – customer retention

In this fifth part of the market strategy discussion, we have looked at the whole (possibly over-sold) area of customer retention.

Retention, in the guise of CRM, has become one of the big bandwagons of the past decade, which is unfortunate. Retention and relationships (and to some extent even CRM) are definitely not a waste of time like some of the band-wagons we have seen in the past. Dealt with properly, the returns to be gained from good retention practice are astounding. But every task needs the right tool.

Experience teaches us that if you give a powerful IT system to a junior manager, they will expect it to be able to solve all the organization's problems (and then answer the great question of 'Life, the Universe and Everything'). There are some things that IT cannot solve and building human relationships out of silicon is one.

The biggest problem with retention is that 'it is a strategic issue, not a tactical one'.

Organizations think they know about tactics, they play with them all the time. Unfortunately, tactics tend to give a fairly fast response (instant gratification) and strategic issues (like retention) don't. Retention activities cannot be expected to pay back in the short term, not because they are bad or slow but because it takes the customer a long time to notice what is happening and then to react to it. Retention is a strategic issue, like all the SCORPIO elements, and needs to be addressed and assessed over the strategic time frame (about three years), not over the tactical time frame (about three months). It also needs to be developed in coordination with the other SCORPIO elements so that *your unique* retention approach matches *your unique* target segments and *your unique* brand personality.

Typically with relationships, it will take as long to fix as it took to be messed up in the first place. Short-term obsessed managers who believe their future hangs by a quarter-by-quarter thread will just make life increasingly difficult for themselves if they don't deal with strategic issues like retention, on a strategic timescale. Approach it as a tactical problem, it won't pay off within the year and you scrap it – the problem only gets worse as customers defect because they absolutely believe you don't care about them any longer. And they're right.

Finally we arrive at the market strategy checklist again, and this time you will see that we can add input in the customer retention section – we should now have the answers to important questions such as: *How big is the retention 'problem' and the potential gains for our organization? Is retention just about customer satisfaction (no)? What is the strategic role of customer relationships within our business, market and organization?*

Finally, a few questions that you should now be able to answer:

Customer retention

1	How important is *retention* in our market?	
2	How big are the *problem* and the potential gains?	
3	Is retention just about customer satisfaction?	
4	Do accounting and reporting systems impede retention activities?	
5	How good is our marketing information systems (MkIS)?	
6	What is the strategic role of customer relationships?	
7	How are we planning to invest in our primary asset?	

6.6   Organization – processes and culture (with Hamish Mackay)

A man does not have himself killed for a half-pence a day or for a petty distinction. You must speak to the soul in order to electrify him.

Napoleon Bonaparte

Ever since the SCORPIO approach first appeared with 'organization' as one of its integral components, people have been asking why a subject area that is obviously outside the traditional confines of 'marketing – the MBA subject' is included in a model/approach that is obviously all about the customer (Figure 6.34).

Figure 6.34   SCORPIO market strategy

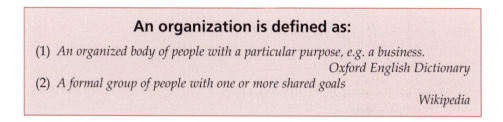

An organization is defined as:

(1) *An organized body of people with a particular purpose, e.g. a business.*
                                                    Oxford English Dictionary
(2) *A formal group of people with one or more shared goals*
                                                                        Wikipedia

The answer is frighteningly simple. Strategy that isn't implemented is a pointless waste of everybody's time. Market(ing) strategy that does not include the organization will not be implemented. You will note the unusual lack of ambiguity in that statement; you will need to get used to that as this chapter is all about the organization. As we take a brief foray away from the 7Ps, we start to see why the book should have been titled *Market(ing) Strategy*. The dying breed of old fashioned 'marketing managers' still tend to believe that how the organization works (or doesn't) is none of their concern. They are somehow above all that because they are responsible to the customer. This is dangerous nonsense. Past and current marketing's obsession with the intricacies of marketing communications has blinded it to the critical importance of investing time inside the organization so that everyone (not just the marketing department) is responsible to the customer. This important oversight has produced 'marketing organizations' that are *excellent* at communicating promises – that the organization is only *mediocre* at delivering.

What we are trying to do in this chapter is give you an understanding of the 'organizational levers' so that you can relate these levers back to the rest of the SCORPIO content – and maybe get things done!

The key elements of organizational processes and culture that that you should focus on are:

(1) *The organization*: It needs to be understood for what it is; a group of 'people' who come together with shared 'objectives'.

(2) *Management*: Management clearly have a role but it is not in delivering benefit to customers. For those of you who are *in* management, here is what we believe management were put on this earth to do:
   (a) Determine strategy – or as Edith Penrose from the LSE elegantly phrased it a long time ago – *the search for profitable business plans*.
   (b) Put the machine in place to deliver strategy.
   (c) Make the organization optimally efficient.
   (d) Resolve conflict.
   (e) Manage change.

(3) *Staff*: Staff are the people who do the work, who deliver the benefits that satisfy (we hope) the customers. What matters is that the four 'natural laws' of organizational life are respected. These are:
   (a) Staff need to understand *why* they need to do certain things, in certain ways.
   (b) There needs to be a common understanding of *the why*.
   (c) Staff need to understand in what way they are contributing to *the why*.
   (d) Staff means all staff.

(4) *Process*: It is the 'glue' that holds the organization together and the easiest way (by far) of affecting and changing what is done in the organization. Process (properly identified and managed) allows the customer and the staff to be united.

(5) *Competition*: Every organization competes for the attention of the customer and seeks to give itself as unfair an advantage as possible.

(6) *Change*: It is the lifeblood of the organization and those that are very good at achieving seamless and efficient change will always be among the most successful organizations.

6.6.1 The organization

Organizations are about people. An organization is a group of people who come together with shared objectives. Most of what an organization does is to 'organize' (see?) the energy of those inside the organization – the staff or employees – to deliver benefit to those outside the organization – the customers.

What we know about how all these people (inside and outside) think and behave has everything to do with how successful the organization will be in the short, medium and long term.

The organization needs first to recognize what it is in business to achieve (see Section 6.1) and that does not mean 'handsome returns for shareholders' (see Chapter 3). Financial returns are clearly necessary, but they cannot guide the organization. An organization needs to be striving to be something.

[That is what Paul is explaining in this book – how you arrive at what that *something* is – the market objective – HM.]

This 'something' gives a purpose and a rationale to an organization. If the organization is customer focused (we have not yet come across an organization that didn't *believe* it was customer focused) then this must guide you to the goal of delivering benefits that the customer wants, values and is willing to pay for.

Is the organization focused on internal or external issues?
Ideally, an organization needs to be focused externally and internally – not just internally.

As with 'customer orientation', all organizations tend to claim that they are externally focused, even if their strategy and their product development have been developed totally from inside the organization and their KPIs (see Chapter 5) are all internally focused. Organizations are naturally internally focused. We are not saying that this is how it should be but in most cases that is the way it is – people go to work and meet the same people every day; many staff never see, much less talk to, a customer as long as they work in an organization. This makes involving staff to implement market(ing) strategy very difficult.

A market(ing) strategy requires that the internal focus should be driven by external (customer and competitive) issues – they are the most important issues, are they not? Ultimately, we have to be concerned with how an organization 'organizes' itself to deliver the market(ing) strategy – by delivering on customer needs. To do that we need to pay attention to the *natural default* of people (and so organizations) to be concerned with what is immediately around them, rather than what is perhaps more important but further away and less visible.

The right focus can be created and supported by internal marketing programmes and will be delivered more by process than by structure – an organizational structure can help to make an organization more efficient in the delivery of customer benefit but it will not ensure that the focus is maintained (effectiveness).

The focus of the staff/organization's activities will be set first of all by the market(ing) objectives and these, as we saw in Chapter 5, should be translated directly into the KPIs. The organization's performance is then measured and compared to the KPIs so informing the organization whether it is on track or not. In the same way that the objective should not be financial (see Chapter 3), neither should the KPIs; they should be about what matters to the organization if it is to succeed in achieving its strategic goals.

Assuming the decision makers (you?) have followed the process outlined in this book, the objectives are customer based and the market(ing) strategy has been drawn from this understanding of perceived customer value, then the organization will have a clear view of what it wants to be and how it wishes to compete. This organizational 'self-view' should demonstrate to all staff how the KPIs reflect the market objectives – imagine the power in that. Bringing the unique identity and business purpose alive for the staff is critical, unless you are intent on running an undifferentiated, price driven business. Each element of the organization has a role, not only in achieving its technical purpose but in communicating to the staff as a whole how the organization is unique, what the organization is setting out to achieve and their invaluable role in that process.

But so much for Utopia.

It is an unfortunate truth that life is not always as we would wish it to be. Too many organizations will short-circuit the objective setting process and some will even simply decide empirically what the objectives are to be – *that is management's job after all isn't it?* The problem with this (traditional) route is that, unless a reasonable process is followed, it will be almost impossible to convince anybody that the objectives are sensible – or that the objectives have anything to do with them or their job. That sounds more like the organizations we know ...

[The process that Paul describes in this book is in my view a reasonable process, it is not overbearing and is very logical — I have followed it myself to great effect in more than one business — HM.]

What is the organization really good at ... and does it matter?
Customers are not all the same and do not all want the same things. It follows then that customers will prefer to buy from organizations that are different in some important way (see Section 6.4).

Most organizations have aspects of their business which they consider themselves to be particularly good at. This is what marks them out as an organization – an understanding, an expertise or a methodology that is unique to them in terms of the extent and depth of that competence. The question is, are these competences core to the customer propositions that the organization has developed?

If organizations are to be (really) different from each other, then it follows that they will be better (and worse) at doing certain things. (Are you following this so far?) Then, different organizations will have what Hamel and Prahalad have called 'different core competences' (see Section 3.5).

This idea was first floated by Hamel and Prahalad in a *Harvard Business Review* article in 1990 and then followed up in a book (*Competing for the Future*, Harvard Business School Press, Boston, 1996).

A core competency is something that an organization can do well – and that meets the following three conditions specified by Hamel and Prahalad:

(1) *It provides customer benefits*: The most important, the competence must add customer value. This means that if the organization is particularly good at doing something that the customer doesn't want or isn't interested in, then it is *not* a core competence. Core competences are the special skills that should enable a business to deliver a differentiated customer benefit. Core competences are what should cause customers to prefer one offering over another.

(2) *It is hard for competitors to imitate*: So it has a life that is longer than a simple process or technology lead that gets copied quickly. A genuine core competence should be 'competitively unique' – if the organization just has the same special skills as every other player in the same industry, these are not unique. A core competence must be something that other competitors *wish they had*.

(3) *It can be leveraged widely to many products and markets*: The idea that the competence is not just specific to one product – but belongs to the organization rather than just a single product, service or brand. The key here is that the core competences allow/enable the creation and development of unique new products and services.

The organization must invest in what makes a difference

A competence may be central to the organization's operations but, if it is not unique in some way, it is *not* a core competence – it will not differentiate the organization within its marketplace. It follows from this concept of core competences that internal skills/resources that are standardized or easily available to all organizations will *not* enable a business to achieve a sustainable competitive advantage over rivals.

You can't be good at everything. Much of the research in the area suggests that if you have more than two or three core competences, then the focus of the organization will be diluted and the 'core' part of the term will change to just 'useful', which is just not good enough.

Some organizations delude themselves that because they are good at something, what they are good at is also important to the customer. These tend to be the product-orientated organizations that produce what they think the customer 'ought' to have. We have spoken long and hard about the need for a clear differentiation (see Section 6.4). Core competences are the means by which the organization becomes different, the customer receives superior customer value and the organization commands superior returns. None of this is possible without (a) identifying, (b) investing in and (c) developing the right core competences.

There is a strong link between the brand and the core competences of the organization – *we are the people who . . . .* If you needed a good reason to command most of the resources available for investment, there it is – the brand needs it.

On the other hand, if you find that you have some competences that no longer make a difference, then you need to be equally ruthless and cut off the investment flow and maybe jettison the expertise completely. Generally the most challenging role for senior management is moving on from former core competences that probably what made them the senior management in the first place – you are asking senior managers to discard their own history. Good managers can do this but inferior managers may need to be replaced by new management (often from outside the organization) to do the job and save the organization. Venture capital organizations are particularly skilled at this.

Core competences are not fixed in time. The organization and its management's job is to manage the 'competence portfolio' (Figure 6.35).

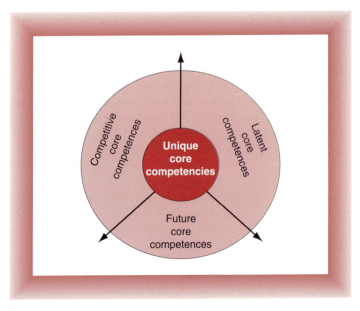

Figure 6.35   Managing core competences

There are in fact four different types of what is commonly called core competence:

(1) *Unique core competences*: If these are what you think they are, they are the unique, uncopyable 'skills and knowledge bases' that sets you apart in the eyes of your customers and allows you to deliver superior customer value for superior returns.

(2) *Latent core competences*: Every organization will have competences that are 'latent' but allow it to operate in its chosen market. For example, hotels will cite 'competitive competences' (such as location, supply chain management and reservations systems) and 'unique core competences' in abundance. However, the people management skills within the hotel business are both complex (different people with a wide range of skills and abilities for a very wide range of time-critical tasks) and simply assumed – the organization's 'latent core competence'.

(3) *Competitive core competences*: Every organization needs core competences that simply allow it to compete in its chosen market. If you wish, these competences are the 'hygiene factors' (see Section 6.2) that permit the organization to 'be in the game'. For example, today's retail organizations need strong core skills in supply chain management simply to survive in the business – but supply chain skills, on their own, do not qualify as unique core competences so will not be sufficient to 'win' the game against the competitors (see Section 6.4).

(4) *Future core competences*: Markets customers' needs change over time and value migrates constantly. This is not unusual and this must not come as a surprise. The organization that is intent on retaining its unique position will have understood the inherent transience of its market and will be busy developing the core competences that it will need to dominate *tomorrow's* markets.

If you have some competences that are fundamental to the delivery of the proposition and the organization's differentiation from the competition, then you need to put them at the very heart of the business. If possible, you should structure around them to give them the importance that they deserve. You need to invest in them – heavily, not just in terms of investment projects but also in terms of the acquisition of skills and the development of those skills. In short, they need their own development strategy. The whole organization should understand what the competences are and why they are important. They need to be built into the very fabric of the organization.

If the organization really wants success badly, then it will not only know what it is good at today, it will also have a good understanding of what it will need to be good at tomorrow. There are very few market disrupting phenomena that are invisible to the *alert* organization. Unless a new entrant has some new and totally proprietary technology, what the competition can see coming should be just as visible to you.

As always, flexibility is the key, the organization needs to be constantly reviewing the environment, the market and its objectives to be sure that its core competences remain relevant and aligned to customer value and, where necessary, make changes.

Earlier changes are always less dramatic than changes that have been ignored, postponed or discarded as 'too scary' – evolution is always better than revolution.

6.6.2 *What is going on with culture?*

What is culture? In the good (and not so good) old days, nobody talked much about culture, now it is a *management science* and we are told that it goes to the very heart of what the organization is and is about. Get it right and you are half-way there, get it wrong and you have no chance at all. So, what is culture?

Culture

Culture consists of patterned ways of thinking, feeling and reacting acquired and transmitted mainly by symbols, constituting the distinctive achievements of human groups, including the embodiments in artefacts; the essential core of culture consists of traditional (i.e. historically derived and selected) ideas and especially their attached values.

Source: Kluckhohn, C. (1951) The study of culture. In *The Policy Sciences* (D. Lerner and H. D. Lasswell, eds). Stanford: Stanford University Press.

The way things are done around here
Source: Anon

Culture is not what management say it is

There are some important 'lessons' here for the (would-be) market-focused manager and market(ing) strategy:

(1) *The culture of an organization is like an iceberg* – most of it is invisible below the *water-line* just waiting to cause an accident (or sink the 'unsinkable' strategy). Culture is all-pervasive and most people who are part of *it* have difficulty seeing 'it' or explaining what 'it' is.

(2) *Culture is self-protecting* and will resist attempts (threats) to change it. New staff (and managers!) are generally not listened to until they have been in the organization for about three months. The process of 'enculturation' (becoming part of and displaying the behaviours required by the culture – or leaving) takes about three months.

(3) *The culture of an organization is not what managers say that it is.* Whenever we have carried out an audit of a business and analysed what managers think is the culture of that organization and then looked at what the staff say it is, there is always a sizeable gap between the two. Just because managers are in charge doesn't mean that they control culture, they don't. They can influence it, but they can't ordain that a certain culture should exist and simply have it happen.

(4) *Culture is best described as 'the way things are done around here'.* It is an expression of the attitudes and behaviours of the staff – not the management.

(5) *Culture is desperately important* because it affects every aspect of how customers are engaged (by staff who are part of the culture) and service is delivered (by staff who are part of the culture) and customers are retained (by staff who are part of the culture). Your organization can't engender trust with the customer if the staff who are dealing with the customers don't feel that they are trusted by the organization. It just doesn't work; somehow or other the feelings and internal relationships always get through to the customer.

(6) *You need to behave internally as you want your staff to behave externally.* If you are intent on delivering a low-cost solution (see Section 6.4 if you still think this is a great idea), then management cannot behave as though it is in a high-margin business and money grows on trees. Staff will see through the veneer and soon customers will see through the offer too.

What should culture actually be?

Theory is all very well, but what should you be doing about your culture? There are a number of factors that need to be considered in arriving at the 'right' culture for an organization

(1) *What do the customers want?* Well it had to be number one. Customers will want to deal with a certain type of organization when they are looking to *hire a product (or service) to get a job done*.

(2) *What does management want and how do they behave?* Management need to understand what the culture should be (as determined by the target customers) and then need to act the part themselves.

(3) *What do the staff want and what do they believe?* Staff are the culture and what they believe *is* 'the way things are done round here'.

Culture can be much worse than a 'negative influence', when it is no influence at all. If management chooses to ignore culture altogether, what it gets is little cells of culture throughout the organization (based on functional background, geography of 'baronies') which are totally inconsistent with each other and a disaster for the customer.

At best, the wrong culture will stop the organization being excellent; at worst, it will stop the organization.

6.6.3   Process – is the organization joined up?

Now we get to the 'organize' part of organization. Organizations are primarily self-serving edifices – such is human nature. They are structured mainly for efficiency (doing things right) rather than for effectiveness (doing the right things) and so we tend to build functional units around similar tasks performed with similar skills and experience, such as operations, accounting, human resources and even, market(ing). To get anything useful done, the different functions need to work together – or, be joined up.

Unfortunately, functions can take on a separate existence within an organization and will naturally default to being inward looking. This can give them a 'silo' mentality (like missiles, things go up and down very fast but nothing goes side to side), lacking in communication with the world outside of their function as well as outside of their organization.

Organizations will attempt to manage the different functions by way of the 'group strategy', which will have a functional strategy showing how each function should fit in and develop with the whole.

All this 'serves' the system that is the organization, but may not provide the outputs that the customer requires. Luckily, there is another facet of organizational life that we can focus on when we consider whether we are joined up and how we deliver a customer benefit – *process*.

Process

A series of actions or steps towards achieving a particular end

AskOxford.com

A series of actions that you take in order to achieve a result

Cambridge Dictionary

A particular course of action intended to achieve a results

Webster's Dictionary

What is process?

Process is the term given to a continuous stream of tasks which are designed to deliver a given benefit (generally to the customer). Because of the functional structures used in most organizations, a customer process will tend to flow through several functions.

So a process, in its simplest form (say, a sale), may start with a customer order (in the sales department or call centre), be passed for fulfilment (in deliveries) and end with a payment for the benefit (in customer accounts) following the successful delivery of the product or service.

Each function may have several 'tasks' in which it is involved, and the process may move back and forth between the functions – thus accounts may be involved at the outset to ensure that the customer has an account with the organization or to set one up and then at the end to send out an invoice and collect payment.

Process is the 'glue' between the functions. For an organization to be joined up, each function has to understand the role of the other functions – and member of staff in each of the functions needs to understand what he or she is required to do to in order to fulfil the customer benefit to the required (*differentiated*) standard. Process is, therefore, the way in which an organization joins up its functions, it is the glue holding the organization together.

Process is also the way in which the strategy and the 'customer value proposition' (CVP) (see Section 6.7) are reflected into what people do in the organization. A process defines the tasks, how those tasks are performed, why they are performed, what the particular task delivers and how they contribute to the end delivery of the customer benefit. Remember the four laws of organizational life seen earlier.

(Macro-)managing the process

Understanding processes can give the market-focused manager a wonderful tool for helping the rest of the organization to focus on, and work towards, creating customer value (Figure 6.36).

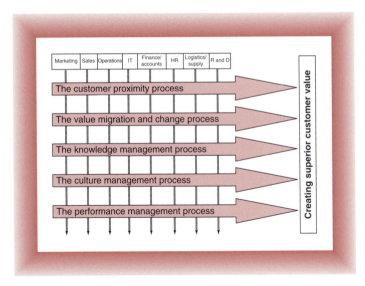

Figure 6.36   Functions and processes
Source: Fifield and Mackay.

Organizations are, by their very nature, input or product focused.

Customers are, by their very nature, output or benefit focused.

Processes are the only way we can hope to channel input-focused functions into meeting the needs of output-focused customers.

Working across any organization are a small number of macro processes which, if managed carefully, can focus the whole organization on delivering what really matters – customer value. These *macro* processes are:

(1) *The customer proximity process*: More than just 'data', 'information' or 'knowledge' (although all these play a part), the process by which we position ourselves *closer to our customer than the competition* and so are able meet their needs and wants well enough that the customer comes back again – and again. Enough of this book is spent on this subject not to need to explain it all again here. What is critical is the process of transferring and translating that sense of customer proximity to everybody else in the organization – sufficiently well that they know what they have to do to create differentiated and superior customer value.

(2) *The value migration and change process*: The process by which everybody in all the functions understands the current customer value as well as the likely future shape and directions of value (migration). Consequently, the organization (and its functions) not only understands the need to change on a regular basis but contributes positively to the constant organizational change process.

(3) *The knowledge management process*: The process by which the organization collects data and information from the market environment and converts it into knowledge (data made meaningful). And then pushes specific parts of the knowledge to those people (in all parts of the organization) who need it – to improve the quality of the differentiated customer value they create.

(4) *The culture management process*: The process by which the most appropriate culture for delivering benefit to the customer is understood and sustained throughout the organization. Bearing in mind that customers (bless them) will change their minds on a regular (or irregular) basis.

(5) *The performance management process*: The process by which the organization tracks performance towards the market(ing) objectives and manages the situation as and when the organization deviates from the chosen path.

6.6.4 Is the organization driven by the right information?

We (should) have reached this point in the market(ing) strategy by carefully sifting through reams of data on the environment, the market, our segment customers and the competition. We have been working through the data carefully, sifting and sorting out what was relevant and what was not. What we believed to be relevant was translated or transformed into information.

What we have to be concerned with now is whether the organization is using or being driven by the right (or the wrong) information.

Definitions

From AskOxford.com:

- *Data*: Facts and statistics used for reference or analysis
- *Information*: Facts or knowledge provided or learned
- *Knowledge*: Information and skills acquired through experience or education

And for those who like the unexpected, from Wikipedia:

- *Data*: The plural of datum. A datum is a statement accepted at face value (a 'given')
- *Information*: In terms of data, it can be defined as a collection of facts from which conclusions may be drawn
- *Knowledge*: Information of which a person, organization or other entity is aware

I hope that clears things up.

Management of 'knowledge'

Typically, the 'information' that an organization concerns itself with is what is needed to inform the organization about itself and the outside world. There is another form of information which is increasingly important; we can call this information 'knowledge'. This is distinguished from 'information' by the way it is used as an essential ingredient in the customer offering and business purpose.

Knowledge management:

The explicit and systematic management of vital knowledge and its associated processes of creating, gathering, organising, diffusion, use and exploitation. It requires turning personal knowledge into corporate knowledge that can be widely shared throughout an organisation and appropriately applied.

Skyrme, Knowledge Management: Making Sense of an Oxymoron (*Management Insight*, 2nd series, no. 2, 1997)

Knowledge is a fluid mix of framed experience, values, contextual information, and expert insight that provides a framework for evaluating and incorporating new experiences and information. It originates and is applied in the minds of knowers. In organisations, it often becomes embedded not only in documents or repositories but also in organisational routines, processes, practices, and norms.

Davenport and Prusak (*Working Knowledge: How Organizations Manage What They Know*, Harvard Business School Press, Boston, 1998, p. 5)

Gradually and inexorably, organizations will differentiate themselves by how they retain and manage knowledge. A relatively new management area, knowledge management (KM) made an appearance at the end of the 1990s. A simple concept but one that is desperately difficult to implement, it is growing – but slowly – as organizations discover that the market(ing) advantage it can bring offsets the investment in developing internal KM processes.

The essence of KM is about creating a competitive advantage by:

(1) *Collecting* relevant data from the environment;

(2) *Analysis*, turning that information into knowledge;

(3) *Pushing* that knowledge to staff that need it to be used in the market;

(4) *Using* the knowledge to enhance the customer offering and experience.

KM is slowly trying to bring together a collection of recent 'good ideas' proposed in different business and management articles and provide a good home for 'orphaned ideas' such as intellectual capital, the knowledge worker, the learning organization, communities of practice, knowledge bases, expert systems, help desks, corporate intranets and extranets, content management and document management. So if you see these buzz-words in your wanderings . . .

Knowledge management is one the keys to the future and all organizations would be wise to give this some airtime in their businesses. Modern technology has changed the way people support each other; there is a great opportunity for organizations to capture the attention of the customer by providing some of that vital support.

Which metrics are used to manage and drive the organization?
Things are starting to get detailed. The specific metrics used will go to the heart of how and what is being managed in the organization.

This is not about a handful of market(ing) objectives/KPIs that are the principal focus of what the organization needs to achieve. The metrics are the measures that tell the organization how it is 'performing' in relation to any and every aspect that the organization considers important.

Albert Einstein

There are things in life that you can count that are not worth counting and things you cannot count, that count.

It's obvious but – the best metrics are not always the easiest metrics. Sometimes, the easiest metrics to use will be the wrong ones – they will create the wrong behaviours and will displease customers.

Maybe, it might be worth thinking about things a little – that measure you have been using since, well forever really, is it creating the *behaviours* that customers say they want and you have promised them? No, we're serious. Are you absolutely sure that that traditional quarterly sales budget (and associated bonuses and rewards) doesn't ever result in customers being sold something on 33 March that they didn't really want or need – and maybe didn't support your brand promise of only providing 'solutions', never selling stuff they don't want? While you're there, you might want to calculate the financial advantage of being on sales target in Q1 against the brand investment that you may have just destroyed.

In their article on 'Creative Destruction' (*The McKinsey Quarterly*, **3**, 2001), Foster and Kaplan had it exactly right when they determined that organizations should *Control what you must, not what you can and control when you must not when you can.*

We need to react to the results. If we are deviating from the path of meeting our objectives, then we need to react and do something about it – as fast as possible. The whole point of metrics and the resulting management information is the call to action when we are off-course.

We call this the control process (Figure 6.37).

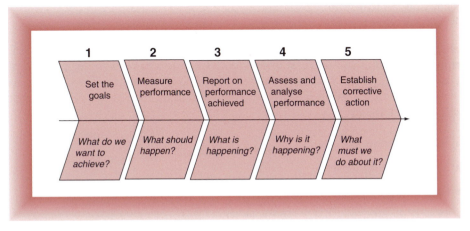

Figure 6.37 The control process

Source: Adapted from Kotler, P., Wong, V., Saunders, J. and Armstrong, G. (2005) *Principles of Marketing*. New Jersey: Pearson.

We will cover the control process in more detail (see Section 6.7), but for now all we need to see is that there are five key stages in any project of activity – and each has a very simple but serious question attached:

(1) *Setting goals*: What do we want to achieve?

(2) *Measuring performance*: What should happen if everything goes to plan (we can dream)?

(3) *Reporting on performance*: What is (really) happening?

(4) *Assessing performance*: Why has it happened? No, don't get excited, these things happen, but we can't do anything about it unless we know *why* it happened differently from what was expected.

(5) *Establishing corrective action*: What should we do about putting it *right*? If anything?

Without the processes in place to answer these questions, only an amateur manager (or one that has already landed the next job) would consider wasting resources by starting the activity in the first place.

6.6.5   Change management – what is that?

There's nothing like finishing a section on Organization on a real high.

You (and your organization) have no choice, you will have to change. Customers change and value migrates – when value moves, either your organization moves to follow the value or you starve. Allow visions of the Lapp herders following the wandering herds of reindeer and you are probably not far off the mark! Further survival guidance can be found in *Who Moved My Cheese?* (Johnson, S., Vermillion, London, 1999).

Change management is the most important of the management disciplines and unfortunately it is also the least understood. Change is never simple; if you think it is, then it is likely you have missed a trick or two, somewhere. If you are changing an organization in however small a manner then at the very least you will have to look at:

● Working practices;

● Measurement metrics;

● Staff communication;

● Project monitoring.

Changes in process or tasks within a process need just as careful a management as large and complex change projects; everything is just conducted in microcosm.

It is the role of management to effect that change and manage the required transition in that part of the organization. The problem is that management will almost always underestimate the effort required and the difficulty involved in making change.

Change always involves people

You will not be able to change the organization successfully in the manner required unless you can not only take the people with you but actively get them on your side. It is accepted generally that 66% of change projects fail and mostly because the impact on staff is either not recognized or underplayed. If you do not change behaviour in some way then you have not changed the organization.

You will be able to make changes in working practices or systems but if care is not taken with the people side of things then the organization will regress and you will be worse off than before. This part of a project is sometimes called 'internal marketing'. Often, this is just a fancy term for communicating what is happening, when and why, what is expected of staff involved and how they are impacted when the change is made. It should be much more.

Like any good story, a change project needs a beginning, a middle (muddle?) and an end:

(1) *The beginning is the plan*. This should be formally documented and is sometimes known as the 'project initiation document'. This ensures that what is intended, how it is to be carried out, what the intended impact is and what the resultant costs and benefits are, are agreed by all the relevant parties. The plan needs to indicate who is involved and what resource is required to achieve the change.

(2) *The middle is the management of the change itself*. A complex project will need a programme office to track all the sub-projects which go to make up the entire event – and a project plan. Smaller projects will need the same methodology but not necessarily with a dedicated team or specialist project management. A complex project will require regular and frequent management reporting on progress. As the changes are put into place then metrics will need to change, management reports will alter and new processes may need to be understood. The organization should have changed and therefore management and controls need to reflect the changed state of the organization.

(3) *The end is the realization of the benefits*. This takes place after the changes have been put into effect. It is surprising how often major projects leave out this aspect of change management altogether. The benefits need to be positively managed or they will not happen. This is the point where regression is a serious threat. Even if the benefits are realized, it is still possible for the organization to regress to its former state.

Organizations must change (and constantly) to stay healthy – there is little real choice in the matter. It is imperative, therefore, that organizations learn how to do this effectively. Business and people are naturally static, seeking firm ground on which to get organized; markets, customers and the business environment are not.

What is really important is that change is taken on willingly and, wherever possible, managed without pressure. It should be timely and appropriate. If the organization has waited until the last moment to make a change then it will always be under pressure and will not have the luxury of doing it properly. Corners will be cut.

[In my experience, whenever I have delayed a change decision, because I thought that later would be easier or less traumatic or that the organization would be more ready to accept a given change . . . I have regretted it. If change is needed then get on with it — HM.]

So the principles of change management are:

(1) Plan the changes well

(2) Communicate and explain the changes

(3) Monitor the change project

(4) Redesign the organization for the impending change then

(5) Monitor carefully, the areas of the organization that have been subjected to the change and finally

(6) Manage the benefits positively, do not expect them to happen of their own accord.

Above all, if everyone in the organization understands that *change is normal — steady state is dangerous*, you will not only have less resistance, you will also have help.

6.6.6   *Conclusions – organization – processes and culture*

It seems as though all roads lead to Rome and in a way they do; that is the magic of this process. If you adhere to the process, the answers to these questions are self-evident; if you do not have the structure of this strategic process, then answering these questions (which are in reality, only the normal issues faced by management every day) and life become very difficult indeed.

You will have noticed that many parts of the chapter link closely to other chapters or even overlap. This is hardly surprising given the pivotal role of the organization in implementing (or not) the market(ing) strategy. As is common with the SCORPIO approach, quite a few of the subjects could be tackled in several of the sections.

This overview of *organization* is a thumbnail sketch of how to implement market strategy. It touches on the main elements of the management skill-set and shows how the actions of managers can and should link together – and to the market(ing) strategy. All subjects can be looked at in much greater depth from the operators' point of view, from the market(ing) strategist's viewpoint; you don't want to get too detailed, you just need to understand why and how.

If your organization is growing up in management and strategic terms and is not that experienced at being truly customer oriented, then this overview should help you to ask the right (and often awkward) questions. Do not make the mistake of getting too involved; ask the questions and when the response indicates a lack of market understanding, keep asking why or how any action will meet the strategic market objectives; you will become a pain in the neck but you will get to them in the end!

We can now add the important question concerning organization, core competences, staff, culture, metrics and change to our strategic checklist (see the Appendix).

Finally, a few questions that you should now be able to answer:

Organization – processes and culture

1	Is the organization focused on internal or external issues?	
2	What is the organization really good at – and does it matter?	
3	What is going on with culture?	
4	Is the organization joined up?	
5	Is the organization driven by the right information?	
6	Which metrics are used to manage and drive the organization?	
7	Change management – what is that?	

Hamish Mackay

Following a successful career in financial services, Hamish has been involved over the last ten years in creating and implementing market(ing) strategy for different companies, many with Paul Fifield. He now acts as a consultant ensuring operational effectiveness and alignment with market(ing) strategy. Email: hamishmackay@springate.co.uk.

6.7   Offerings

He who makes war for National independence must be enabled to count upon the union of all resources, all the wishes, and the concurrence of all the National authorities.

Napoleon Bonaparte

What is this section doing in a strategic concept like SCORPIO (Figure 6.38)? Surely it's all covered in the 'product' section of the marketing mix? Well. No.

Figure 6.38   SCORPIO market strategy

How can I break this to you? Products and services are key to any organization's survival and growth – but only as far and as long as they continue to deliver the solutions and benefits that the customers want from them. At the risk of repeating myself (Levitt can bear plenty of repetition) Levitt said, *Customers just need to get things done. When people find themselves needing to get a job done, they essentially hire products to do that job for them.* You will notice (I hope) that the emphasis here, at least from the customers' perspective, is on the *job* that needs to get done – not on the products that they may hire to get the job done.

This means that, over time, customers might just move from one product to another to get the same job done – but maybe better, cleaner, easier, faster, more environmentally – or whatever differential the customer or segment feels has additional value.

This in turn means that, no matter how good your product or service might be, if the customers believe that there is a better (they define 'better') way to 'get the job done', then your organization and its superior product or service is history. And don't for a moment think that it can't happen to you. The pages of history are filled with organizations and industries that believed they were so important to their customers that they were 'indispensable' in day-to-day living. From agriculture to coal to steel to shipping and shipbuilders to railroads to clothing manufacturers to flag-carrier airlines to who knows what next have been secure in the knowledge that they are the pinnacle of demand and life would be unthinkable if they no longer existed. But they exist no more.

And the problem is product (/service) management is not a *strategic* activity. Product management is taught and practised as a tactical activity aimed at owning market share and creating revenues (sometimes profits) on a quarterly or annual basis. Filling 1% drop in the UK Northeast suddenly becomes the product manager's world. Worrying that customers might eventually (at some undefined future point – *can't anyone be a bit more specific up there?*) start substituting the product with a competitive offer does not figure in the annual appraisal or bonus scheme, so does not get worried about. What? Who designed the rewards system then? What did you expect? It's a dog-eat-dog world out there and a dog that starts wasting time on things that aren't in its personal targets and won't affect this quarter's results had better start looking for another kennel.

Not that I am knocking the system you understand. It's just that there are some issues to be dealt with here, and it is never too clear who is looking after them.

Precisely to help with that issue – and to save the organization from premature death – we have the Offerings category in the SCORPIO process.

If we are going to concern ourselves with strategy at all (that lets a few organizations and managers off the hook), then we will also need to work across some of the internal 'silos' that seem to dominate so much organizational thinking. Given that 'offer' and 'product' are not the same word, maybe there is more going on here than it might seem – indeed there is – we need to look at the whole 'system' of thinking, planning and implementation that attempts to meet the customer's need to 'get a job done'. That includes:

(1) (Another) review of customers and their needs;

(2) A review of the product or service;

(3) How it needs to adapt over time;

(4) The development of new offerings;

(5) The organization's Customer Value Proposition (CVP);

(6) The organization's business model (how it plans to make money from the transactions);

(7) Assessing risk;

(8) Managing the life cycle;

(9) Working with the most appropriate routes to market;

(10) Controlling tactical implementation of the market(ing) strategy.

6.7.1   *Always start with* Value

Let's take a 'refresher' look at the market(ing) process (Figure 6.39). The overall idea is to make money (cash, profits and revenues) from satisfying customers' needs and wants. Ideally the process includes information flow from the customer to the organization (so that we get a better idea of what the needs and wants are) and a flow of communication from the organization to the customer giving the market good reasons why they should prefer our offer over the competition's. But that is just the surface noise.

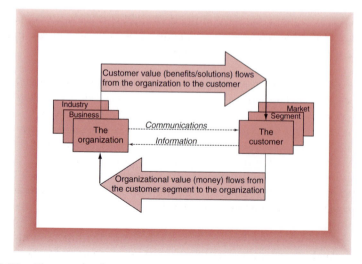

Figure 6.39   The marketing process as an exchange of *value*

Underneath the surface we have the real game:

(1) *The organization receives 'value'* from the transaction (more if it's a *relationship* – see Section 6.5) in terms of money. The very successful organization will receive much more money back than it has spent (profit) because the customer believes that it solves their problems best. The mediocre organization will receive more money back than it spent, but less than the best organizations. The failing organization will receive less money back than it has spent and will be wondering why . . .

(2) *The customer receives 'value'* from the transaction or relationship because they perceive some special benefits or solutions in the offer that allows them to 'get a job done' in precisely the way that they want it done. The more 'value' that the customer perceives in an offer, the more willing they are to pay for it.

Michael Porter on value

A firm is profitable if the value it commands exceeds the costs involved in creating the product.

Understanding value

Customers understand 'value' intuitively – which makes it difficult for us to measure dispassionately. Customers buy value and they spend much of their active consumer lives searching for it. Smart customers actively search it out and weigh up the relevant 'pros-and-cons' of each 'proposition' to be able to judge 'best value' – to them.

We already know (unless you have jumped straight to this chapter of course) that *best value does not mean cheapest price*, despite some commentators continuing to confuse the *value end* of the market with the *cheap and nasty* end.

Customer value can involve small or large amounts of money. All that matters is what the economists call the customers' perception of the overall 'utility' of the product/service – or what *they* believe the offer will do for 'them'.

Customers (just like you and me) will spend lots of time 'trading off' different 'perceived values' of different offers against the price demanded.

For all these reasons, the term 'value' is probably one of the most over-used and misunderstood terms in business today. Why?

The first reason is because value is too often simply linked with the issue of pricing, which itself is a subject that is hugely under-researched. We don't understand enough about pricing yet either.

Also, 'value' means different things to different people, and it is not easy to define and quantify – but we must, it is the reason why we are all here.

But help is at hand.

Customer value

Customer value is the ultimate in insight and bankable profits (Figure 6.40).

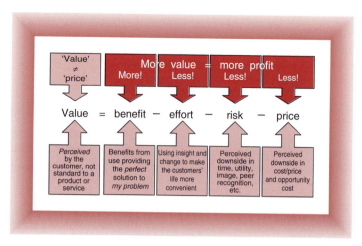

Figure 6.40 It's all about *Customer Value*
Source: Adapted from Osterwalder and Pigneur (2003).

If you know what your customers 'value' and can deliver it, you have success within your grasp. But customer value is more intuitive than scientific and that makes it more difficult to measure.

Developing some work carried out by Osterwalder and Pigneur (University of Lausanne, 2002) I have created a practical equation that enables organizations to do something practical about measuring and plotting changes in customer value. This is not meant to be the quickest or simplest model, but the one that constantly reminds you of the components you have to play with.

The basic equation is:

Customer Value = Benefit – Effort – Risk – Price

This means that any customer's perceived value (what they see in the offer that they are willing to pay for) is made up of separate elements, usage, effort, risk – and price. The key elements of the equation need to be explained:

- *Customer value*: This is *not* about price and especially not about being cheap. Customer value is about the value that the customer perceives in the offer (and its promise) and the value that the customer sees in getting the job done in the particular way that the offer promises. The perceived customer value is made up of four separate components.

- *Benefit*: By 'using' the product or service the benefit or solution becomes obvious. Customers are always looking for one thing – the *perfect solution* to their problem. The closer the offer to the perfect solution, then the greater the perceived customer value and the greater the price the customer is willing to pay. Easy. All you need to find out is (a) the nature of the customer's problem, (b) what the customer believes would be the perfect solution to that problem, (c) where exactly you fit on that scale and (d) where you fall short. It goes without saying that every customer's perception will be unique, every problem will be unique and every solution will be unique. Aren't you glad you're in market(ing)?

- *Effort*: How much effort will the customer have to put into solving the problem? Life generally is about ease and convenience. The customer will take a view on all the offerings (and different ways of solving the problem) and will see greater value in offerings that are more convenient than ones that are inconvenient. Generally, there will be greater customer value attached to those offerings where the organization has spent time, research, effort and insight into finding new ways of making the old jobs easier. This perceived value will extend to acquiring the product/service (channels and route to market decisions) as well as the usage of the product/service itself.

- *Risk*: The interesting question. Customers see 'risk' in all sorts of choice and purchasing situations. Much risk is caused by lack of experience or knowledge. The greater the level of risk that the customer sees, the lower the perceived customer value – got that? Some of the risks that you should investigate here might include perceived downsides (things that could go wrong) in time taken in choosing, waiting for delivery or for the benefits to flow (set-up times and problems with 'learning' to use new products), image risk (what others will think of me) and utility (the product or service doesn't do what it promises, then how will I feel?).

- *Price*: The obvious one, but last in the order of things, just where the customer places it. This component does *not* just cover the price being too high – a producer perspective – but from the customer's perspective covers more complex and interesting issues such as paying too much (obviously) seeing the same thing cheaper elsewhere, paying too little (inferior quality or maybe not fit for purpose), opportunity cost (if I buy this, what offerings can't I buy), not buying early enough and missing out (waiting too long for the price to fall), spending too long searching for the lowest price (opportunity cost of time).

Applying the equation in non-traditional settings

This book is not the place to delve too deeply into other areas that the Customer Value approach will work, although I have done so – and it works extremely well.

The approach works better than any other I have tried because it forces the organization to focus on what really matters to the customer – on where the customer sees real value.

In the case of the not-for-profit sector, for example, many of these are not only sizeable organizations, but are often highly skilled at market(ing) and the sector is becoming ever more prominent. Here the organization can gain valuable insight into 'donor behaviour' by understanding the real 'customer/donor value' in the transaction – the value might be a salve to the conscience, an emotional tug at the purse strings although no actual 'price' enters the equation or even a need to belong. Charities will have to be increasingly adept at distinguishing their offerings and expressing what they stand for and as donor fatigue inevitably creeps in the market gets tougher and more 'competitive'.

Maximizing customer value

There are a number of ways of doing this – not just price cutting – the one way favoured by the dinosaurs. As we are dealing with an 'equation', the alternatives are:

(1) *Reduce price*: The obvious one and one we have already spoken about – it is a way of increasing customer value – getting more for less – but less successful than most people seem to think (see Section 6.3). There are customer costs in reducing the price too far, too unevenly or too fast, so think it through before you act. Price reduction is not only a very crude way of competing; it is also very expensive compared to other ways of increasing customer value. Before you take a lemming-like lunge at price reduction, look to see if there isn't a better way; for example:

(2) *Increase benefits from usage*: Adding more benefits (make sure that they are real benefits, things that customers really want) will increase perceived customer value.

(3) *Reduce effort*: Make it easier to use and acquire the benefits.

(4) *Reduce risk*: So much time is spent worrying about price that the non-price risks seems to fade away – but here are the even bigger issues. You can reduce these risks by offering guarantees and warranties, free-trial periods and above all, a *brand* to believe in. Branding is the most effective way of reducing perceived risk (by making valued promises that will be kept, see Section 6.3) and so of increasing perceived customer value.

To broaden out the issue of offerings, we will look at the most important aspects. As always, not every organization will have the same customer, market and competitive situation to deal with, so not every aspect of offerings will be of equal importance, or even relevant.

Look at each one and discount the parts that don't matter – at least not yet – and focus on the ones that do.

6.7.2   *Where is the value proposition?*

We really, really need at least one value proposition. By *we*, I mean that:

- Your target customer needs a value proposition.

- Your target prospect needs a value proposition.

- Your market(ing) department and brand/product/segment groups need a value proposition.

- Your internal staff need a value proposition.

- Your sales force needs a value proposition.

- Your intermediaries/channel partners need a value proposition.

- Your agencies all need a value proposition.

- Your shareholders need a value proposition.

What do you mean you haven't got one?

What is a value proposition?
The key to successful market(ing) and successful business is 'preference'. If we can somehow make customers prefer our offering over the competition's then we have done our job. But how exactly do we do that if we are larger than a one or two person business? The more people that are involved in the process, the greater the chance is that things can go wrong. We have seen (see Section 6.6) that this is not malicious, it is how things happen. But the customers are not concerned with our problems, they just insist on capturing as much customer value as possible and will go wherever the value seems greatest.

How do we ensure the customer comes to us? By being clearly different (see Section 6.4) from everyone else. And how do we do that, with people on the inside all trying to do (what they think is) their best and customers on the outside not knowing where to go – and changing their minds over what constitutes customer value over time?

You put pen to paper (or finger to key, but it doesn't really have the same ring to it) and you create a clear, concise series of factual statements on what the customer can expect to be the tangible results from purchasing and consuming your products or services:

(1) *Externally*, a value proposition (VP; also called a CVP) is an offer to the target customers/segment in which the purchaser gets more value than they give up, as perceived by them, and in relationship to competitive alternatives, including doing nothing.

(2) *Internally*, a value proposition is an internal statement summarizing the customer targets, competitor targets and the core strategy for how you intend to differentiate your product/service from the offerings of competitors.

Treacy and Wiersema define a value proposition as

An implicit promise a company makes to customers to deliver a particular combination of values

They have identified organizations as offering three (generic) kinds of value propositions (see Chapter 3):

- Management efficiency/operational excellence
- Product leadership
- Customer intimacy.

Treacy and Wiersema's definition of a value proposition is about *the very least* you should expect your CVP to achieve. Their approach is rather more external communications led than I would like. For the CVP to drive the organization as we need, it absolutely must also:

(1) *Relate* to all the different suppliers, agencies, staff and other 'stakeholders' that are listed at the very beginning of this chapter and earlier in the 'stakeholder' map (see Chapter 1).

(2) *Integrate* all these essential 'stakeholders' so that they are *aligned* to meet the customers needs.

(3) *Inform* all the essential 'stakeholders' where they fit into the customer value process and how they relate to each other and to the customer.

(4) *Specify* (exactly) *how* the organization (and each of the stakeholders) will create customer value. The differentiated organization will do this in a *unique* way; this must be carefully specified within the value proposition.

A successfully tested and proven value proposition is essential to a successfully differentiated business. It can:

- Align all those (internal and external) people who are involved in the customer satisfaction process by generating (and policing) the fabled 'single hymn sheet'.

- Open more doors and close more sales.

- Create strong customer propositions that deliver results.

- Increase revenue from clearer positions.

- Speed time to market as internal staff align their efforts.

- Decrease costs as agreed 'wastage' (in customer-value terms) is removed.

- Improve operational efficiency from agreed and understood customer-centric targets.

- Increase market share.

- Decrease employee turnover as staff identify with the differentiation – and the customer value.

- Improve customer retention levels.

Creating your own value proposition(s)

If the value proposition process is going to work, you really need a 'cascade' or 'hierarchy' of value propositions that follow that of the brand(s) and/or market segment(s) and position(s).

The format for each value proposition needs to be the same, although you can chose your own format that best suits your internal and external needs. Remember though, that to be successful, your value proposition must be differentiated, compelling and clearly communicate best value to all your audiences.

To get you on the road, here are a few 'worksheets' that I have used to start the process inside an organization.

The basic version is given in Figure 6.41 and a slightly more detailed version is given in Figure 6.42.

Who is your target market?	
What jobs do they need to 'get done'?	
What will your product or service do for them?	
How is your offering unique? (in customer perception terms)	
Why should they prefer your offer over the competition?	
The 'elevator pitch"	

Figure 6.41   The value proposition worksheet

Issue	Question	Answer
Market description	Who is our target market?	
Market sizing	How big is our target market (segment)?	
Needs and wants	What are this particular segment 's needs and/or wants?	
The benefits	What will our product or service do for them?	
Differentiation	How is our offering unique (in customer perception terms)?	
Competition	Who is the closest competitor?	
Preference	Why should they prefer our offer over the competition?	
Brand	What will be the brand promise to this market (segment)?	
Offering	The (minimum) key elements which are fundamental for any offering to be credible	
Route-to-market	What are the (customer) preferred routes to market/channel partners?	
Alliances	What are the critical partnerships/ alliances required to launch?	
Price	The strategy of pricing the service packages	
'Elevator pitch'	Strip the proposition down to the essentials	

Figure 6.42   Another version

If neither of these worksheets do it for you, please compile your own. But, the first worksheet really carries the *absolute minimum* of questions you need to answer (for every separate product/service variant, market segment and brand. You can add more questions to worksheet one, but don't try to remove any. Even if it would be a lot easier!

6.7.3   What is the most appropriate business design?

The most appropriate business model is the one that allows the organization to extract the most value from the marketplace.

As customers and their perception of what constitutes customer value changes over time (value migration), an organization will need to look at whether it needs to change its business model to keep up.

This is not an easy matter for the organization, but also not as difficult as many organizations would have us believe. Anyway, unless the organization wants to face bankruptcy, it is very unlikely to be able to run forever on the same model – customer needs and competition will see to that.

For those who wish to investigate all the potential business models, a good selection of twenty-two of the most common can be found in *The Art of Profitability* (Slywotzky, A., Little, Brown & Company, 2004).

Assessing the business design

Before we look at some of the options, we need to think through the best way of assessing whether we have the most appropriate design for extracting value currently. There are a number of steps in the process:

(1) *Identify the target customers*: Which customers are we targeting?

(2) *Create the value proposition*: The value proposition will clearly define the nature and quality of the value to be delivered – and extracted.

(3) *Identify how value is captured currently*: How does the organization capture value/profit from its customers at the moment?

(4) *Identify potential strategic market control*: How is your target market influenced or controlled to create and protect profit flows over time?

(5) *Identify the critical activities required by the value proposition*: What does your (unique) value proposition require you to deliver to customers?

From these analytical steps, you should be able to assess whether you currently have the most effective business design for what the value proposition requires you to do, whether competitors are doing it better, whether you should think about moving to a new business design.

There is more than one way to skin a cat – and many more ways of making a profit. But you would think that most organizations have only one way of working and making profits – and that if it stops working everybody is out of business. It is rare for an organization to think about its business design – it started with it so . . . . But it isn't necessarily so. What was a good way of working years ago won't necessarily last forever – equally, there is no reason why an organization should be saddled with the same design for the duration of its business life – change is possible and should be considered.

6.7.4   *Where are the new offerings?*

That's the trouble with customers, they're never happy – just as you think you have them in the palm of your hand, they are queuing up to buy what you are very happy making, then they just decide that they want something else.

Or worse, you try to keep up with your customers, you look after, you talk to them regularly and invest good R&D money in developing and improving the product or service to make sure that you keep up with their needs – then they decide that they don't like the new model and they want the old one back, and you have carefully run the old stocks down because you don't want to be left with any and you have warehouses of the new stuff and communications campaigns ready to break and . . .

There is a message here:

(1) Innovate or die, *but*

(2) Don't make a big thing about it, change *is* business as usual (see Section 6.6).

(3) Not everything that is new will sell.

(4) No matter what you do or how good you are, you will still mess up from time to time because customers will never be predictable.

Still, we can't just sit back and accept what comes, that's not the Western way, we have been trained to predict and anticipate rather than just react – but we haven't been trained to accept that anticipation is never 100% accurate.

Sources of innovation for new products and services

Most of my clients and people I talk to are not so much interested in what 'types' of innovation to look for or whether to worry about *discontinuities* but what they can do, within an already too busy schedule, to try and keep up with what customers might want next. *Exactly*, I hear you cry, *Delighting customers is fine but I have my work cut out just keeping up with mine.*

How then do we integrate innovation within the normal 'managing' day job? To put you out of your misery, there are four main market(ing) ways of thinking about this:

(1) *Redefine the business you are in*: This approach takes us all the way back to the very first part of the SCORPIO discussion, 'industry or market thinking' (see Section 6.1). Imagine that you are re-defining the nature of the business/market you are in from the left (industry/product) definition to the right (market/ customer) definition as Harley Davidson or Swatch have done. If you haven't already done this, start by listing all the possible 'businesses' that you might be in. For example, Mercedes might list its 'possible businesses', such as cars, tracks, prestige cars/trucks, business transport, supply chain, engineering, status or moving. Looking at the problem through these different lenses can give valuable customer insight and stimulate new product/service ideas.

(2) *Re-segment the market*: This approach also takes us back to the earlier parts of the SCORPIO discussion, market segmentation and targeting (see Section 6.3). There are many ways that a market can be segmented. To use this approach, you need to ask how you currently segment your market and what other ways you might look at segmenting the market. Looking back at Section 6.3, you will see another 'lens' that will help you see previously invisible opportunities.

(3) *Track customer value*: If in doubt, follow the 'customer value'. Obvious, but sometimes it gets lost in the excitement. I think the role of research and customer insight is best explained by the *Kano* model (Berger, C., Blauth, R., Boger, D., Bolster, C., Burchill, G., DuMouchel, W., Pouliot, F., Richter, R., Rubinoff, A., Shen, D., Timko, M. and Walden, B., Kano's Methods for Understanding Customer-Defined Quality, *Centre for Quality Management Journal*, **2**, 1993). Here we see that any offering can be split into its component parts and these components assessed in terms of the amount of customer value that they deliver.
The *Kano* model (Figure 6.43) suggests that certain components/features have more customer value than others and, over time, perceived customer value will decline. If you can plot the components/features that have moved from 'delighters' to 'must-haves' in your market, you may be able to start plotting the speed and the 'triggers' of movement, the nature of the customer value in your market as well as the likely nature of future value.

(4) *Work with your customers*: Finally, we can look at how we might use some of our customers to help us uncover innovations. Many years ago, Everett Rogers developed the 'innovation diffusion' model (it's in all the books) that suggested that a new idea, concept, product or service would pass through a population (segment) of people (customers) in an understandable way. Of all the groups identified, the innovators are the most interesting and, if properly researched, can help us spot innovations that may be worth investing in. I use this method quite frequently and some research organizations specialize in this type of research.
Innovators, by their very nature are more aware of tomorrow's customer value in an offering than the later groups – it is what they are attuned to (Figure 6.44). If we can identify these customers from our existing base and talk to them more deeply, we might gain some valuable insight in tomorrow's products and services.

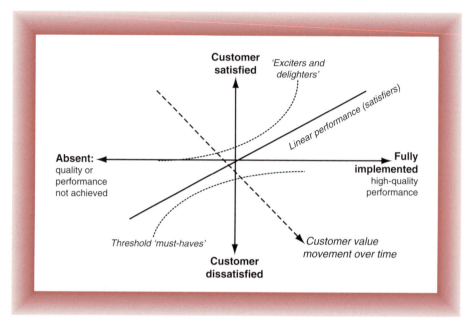

Figure 6.43   The Kano model
Source: Adapted from Kano in Berger, C., Blauth, R., Boger, D., *et al.* (1993) *Centre for Quality Management Journal*, **4**.

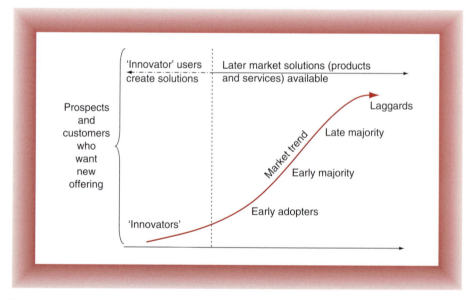

Figure 6.44   Innovators as sources of innovation
Source: Adapted from Von Hippel, E., Thomke, S. and Sonnack, M. (1999) *Harvard Business Review*.

6.7.5 *What is business* risk?

'Life is risk,' I hear you cry, and you are right. The nature of business is all about risk. In fact, the Oxford English Dictionary defines an 'entrepreneur' as *owner or manager of a business enterprise who through risk and initiative attempts to make a profit.* I particularly like the use of the word 'attempts'.

Today life is more controlled and managers and directors need to demonstrate that they have assessed the business for risk and carried out all reasonable and necessary measures to reduce business risk. For good or bad, the days of *laissez-faire* are past and have been replaced with 'accountability'.

So, what is this risk business all about? Essentially it is about you taking some time to think through the things out there that could mess up your plan(s) – and then think about what you might do about it, before it happens. Sounds quite professional to me.

There are many different definitions of risk, one of the more common is:

Risk

Is an event or action that may adversely affect an organization's ability to survive and compete in its chosen market as well as to maintain its financial strength, positive public image and the overall quality of its people and services.

Can arise from failure to exploit opportunities as well as from threats materializing.

All becoming clearer?

Types of business risk

As always, one of the best ways of understanding a concept is by breaking it down to its component parts. The UK Institute of Risk Management (IRM) has done this and suggests that there are four key areas of business risk:

(1) Financial risk;

(2) Strategic risk;

(3) Operational risk;

(4) Hazard risk.

They also suggest that the risks can be broken down into:

(1) Those driven internally within the organization and which should be under the organization's control and

(2) Those driven by external events and forces that are outside the organization's direct control.

The individual risks in each of these categories are self-explanatory.

	Types of business risk			
	Financial	**Strategic**	**Operational**	**Hazard**
Internally driven	Liquidity and cash flow	Research and development	Accounting controls	Public access
		Intellectual capital	Information systems	Employers
		Mergers and acquisition integration	Recruitment	Properties
			Supply chain	Products and services
Externally driven	Interest rates	Competition	Regulators	Contracts
	Foreign exchange	Customer changes	Culture	Natural events
	Credit	Industry changes	Board composition	Suppliers
		Customer demand		Environment

Source: Institute of Risk Management (UK), 2002.

You can see immediately that business risk, defined this way, goes far beyond simple finance/money risk and covers all aspects of business activity.

Apart from just complying with government regulations (a stand-alone activity in its own right), managing business risk better can lead to clear and obvious business benefits for the organization. Some of these might include:

● Stronger and better quality *growth*;

● More *stable* business and less prone to environment/market changes;

- Better quality *staff* as clearer responsibilities emerge;
- Stronger *suppliers* attracted by more stable business;
- Better quality *channels to market* as business stabilizes;
- Better *customer acquisition* and stronger, more stable brand;
- Better *customer retention* through consistency of operations;
- Obtains *cheaper finance* through lower perceived business risk;
- Drives *lower costs* (for example, insurance).

What about market(ing) risk

There is more to risk in the market/market(ing) area than you might imagine although there should be no surprises, apart maybe from the format. There are two key areas of market(ing) risk that really fall into your area:

(1) *Primary demand risk*: These risks are quite similar to financial risks in that they are based on factors largely 'beyond the control of marketers' and other managers. The 'primary demand risk' relates to the general level of effective demand in the marketplace and the ability to pay. This will be driven by factors such as:
   - (a) economic life cycles;
   - (b) currency and exchange fluctuations;
   - (c) government regulations;
   - (d) technology changes.

(2) *Market share risk*: Market share risk is different from the organization's primary demand risk in that it is not 'absolute' it is 'relative' – to the competition. The organization might be world class in the way it identifies, assesses and manages market(ing) risk but if its competition is even better it will still be at a disadvantage. These risks should be within the control of the organization and better organizations will reduce these risks further (and make more profits) than poor (less customer-focused) organizations. The factors included in this section are:
   - (a) the possibility of not acquiring customers and
   - (b) the possibility of not retaining (losing) a customer.
   The market share risk will be directly affected by the amount of consideration and company investment (time, attention and money) in:
   - (a) customer research and understanding;
   - (b) product and service development (offerings);
   - (c) price maintenance (not discounting);
   - (d) brand and differentiation;
   - (e) communications activities.

As you work to first 'assess' and then to 'reduce' the risk in this area, you need to remember that your activities are affected not only by your actions over time, but also by the quality and quantity of our different competitors' investments in customers, product/service, pricing, brand/differentiation and communications. The solution: The best way of reducing market(ing) risk is to focus on three activities (as if you didn't know already):

(1) Get closer to your target customers.

(2) Improve the quality of your organization's market(ing) efforts.

(3) Increase the share of market(ing) investment – relative to your competition.

6.7.6   Are we managing the life cycle?

What on earth can the venerable product life cycle model tell us about Offering strategy? Probably more than you thought. We dealt with the basics of the PLC in Chapter 2 when we were looking at the business environment.

Now that we are looking at how to develop and manage the offerings part of the market(ing) strategy, we can start to use the PLC in a more creative way (Figure 6.45).

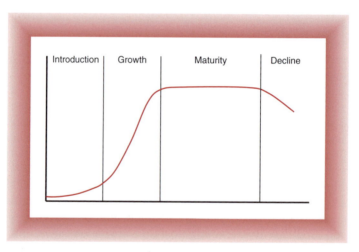

Figure 6.45   The product/service life cycle

The product life cycle is a model, it is not a fait accompli

The way that the PLC is taught and written about (just as I did in Chapter 2) always gives the impression that the PLC is a 'given', that it is almost cast in stone and that our products and services will, if we are lucky to get beyond the introduction stage, pass through the different stages until it eventually passes into decline and death. The very first thing to realize is that this is not so. You do have some power to play with the PLC for your benefit.

The first question facing you though is the 'big' question, where are you now on the curve? I know it's a big issue and we never know for sure until we are past the stage and can say for certain where we 'were', but take an educated guess. You can always replay the ideas if you find that you were wrong. Go on, what have you got to lose?

There are four 'games' you might want to play with the PLC to support your offerings (Figure 6.46):

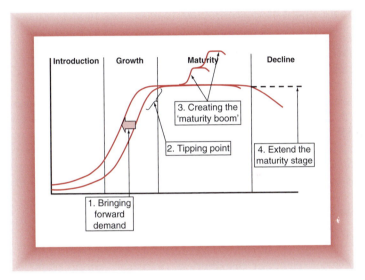

Figure 6.46 Managing the product/service life cycle

(1) *Bringing forward the demand curve*: The first 'game' involves shifting the whole curve to the left and bringing in more demand earlier than would otherwise be expected.

(2) *Getting to the 'tipping point' first*: In Chapter 2, we looked at the problems with the move from 'rapid growth' stage to the 'maturity' stage. It is a time for 'consolidation' and many organizations do not survive through this difficult transition. Knowing this, and being prepared for the inevitable transition from rapid growth/sales emphasis to maturity/customer emphasis, if you can get to the transition stage (tipping point – named after the book by the same name *The Tipping Point* by Gladwell, M., Abacus, Altrincham, 2001) before the competition, you will make early and significant wins in the maturity stage.

(3) *Stimulating demand*: Just because the product or service has moved into the maturity stage does not mean that subsequent growth is now impossible. We can create sales 'booms' within the maturity stage. Good examples of maturity booms over the years would include:

(a) manual to automatic transmission for cars;
(b) black and white to colour TV;
(c) vinyl to CDs for music;
(d) videotape to DVDs for films;
(e) coal to diesel for shipping;
(f) coal to gas for electricity generation.

Maturity booms are not the same thing as normal product/service development that continues throughout the maturity stage. A maturity boom must be important enough to encourage a significant proportion of the customer base to 'trade up' and exchange or replace their existing model well before normal replacement would be expected.

(4) *Extending the maturity stage*: The maturity stage is recognized as being the longest of the stages. How long depends on the organization's closeness to the customer and the resulting quality of the marketing involved. Products and services do not have *to* die, it is not fore-ordained by some superior law, it all comes down to the skills of managers in keeping the offer relevant amid changing customer perceptions and needs. Why should your organization survive and others go to the wall? The answer is 'relatively' better market(ing). The longer the offer is seen as worthwhile, having a role in the customers life and possessing value to the customer, it will survive and even flourish.

6.7.7 How do we take the offerings to market?

This may be the single, most important part of this chapter.

This section is *not* just about 'distribution', 'logistics', 'supply chain' or 'routes to market' or whatever is the next definition of moving stuff and people around the country or the world.

How we get the offerings to market is about implementation in its broadest sense. Having the best ideas and the most creative insights amounts to nothing (a 'hill of beans' for the pub trivia people) if we don't get the offerings to the customer. Why is this important?

(1) Strategy is a pointless exercise without implementation.

(2) A strategy that cannot be implemented is just a management *whim*.

(3) The best plan cannot be expected to implement itself.

(4) Implementers will not implement as *you* wish without some involvement from *you* in the process.

(5) A complete strategy includes a plan for its implementation.

(6) The market strategy *will not happen* unless you protect and nurture it during its early stages; why go to all the hard work of creating a differentiated market strategy just to 'orphan' it when it needs you most?

Have I got your attention? Good.

> *If you start to take Vienna — take Vienna.*
>
> Napoleon Bonaparte

The key strategic aspects of taking the offerings to market (Implementation)

There is no end of things you can worry about when looking at implementation – just look at how many people are paid to worry about the tactics of life. But, implementation *per se* is not our problem.

What is our problem is setting the critical implementation issues that will ensure that the strategy is a success – not a failure.

Every business, market and organization will be unique and the very idea of prescriptive cure-all remedies is laughable. You will have to decide for yourself which of the issues could be critical to your strategy. The critical areas of implementation you need to consider are included in 'the market(ing) mix', especially (and traditionally):

(1) *Product* – or service that carries the benefits that have maximum customer value;

(2) *Pricing* – to extract maximum value from the market;

(3) *Place* – routes to market, channels, distribution . . . ;

(4) *Promotion* – communications.

Your job is not to implement there are people much better at that than you (or there should be) and you have other things to worry about.

Your job is to highlight areas where implementation can make or break the strategy and to make sure that the strategy isn't broken.

The tacticians know their job, but differentiation is rarely achieved by doing what everybody else does. Remember that some functionally driven idea of *best practice alone will never create superior customer value* – that's where you come in and what this section is all about.

The market(ing) mix

Today, everyone is an expert; whether it is in packaging, supply chain, communications or just knowing who to talk to, everyone knows more and more – about less and less. Everyone has heard of the market(ing) mix, most people know it's about lots of Ps and some people can name them.

Referencing the market(ing) mix

(1) Bordon, N. H. (1965) The Concept of the Marketing Mix. In *Science in Marketing* (G. Schwartz) pp. 386–97. Chichester: Wiley.
(2) McCarthy, E. J. (1975) *Basic Marketing*. Boston: Irwin.
(3) Booms, B. H. and Bitner, M. J. (1981) Marketing Strategy and Organization Structures for Service Firms. In *Marketing of Services* (J. Donnelly and W. R. George) New York: American Marketing Association.

Not enough people know that the most important word is 'mix' and the whole skill is in *blending* the ingredients to create 'differentiated' customer value. Some market(ing) departments even organize themselves by function – ensuring internal competition and no interaction or blending at all. One organization I came across even split the Ps between the sales department (price, place, people, process) and the marketing department (product, physical evidence, promotion) – you can imagine the results (Figure 6.47).

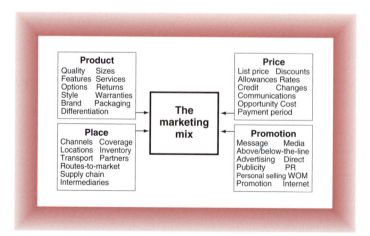

Figure 6.47   The market(ing) mix (4Ps)

1. The product/service

The 'me-too's, the also-rans' and the other organizations heading towards the commodity end of the market will all focus on *making no mistakes with the components* of the marketing mix. Organizations intent on reaping the rewards of differentiation will be focusing their attention on *creating superior customer value from innovative blending of the components* of the market(ing) mix. Which type of organization is yours?

If you have researched the market and gleaned sufficient insight to create a winning value proposition, you must make clear to the organization what needs to be done to achieve success (Figure 6.48). Your strategy will undoubtedly depend on certain components being blended in a certain (and unique) way – you must specify these to the implementers if you are to avoid the possibility of *things being done the way we have always done them.*

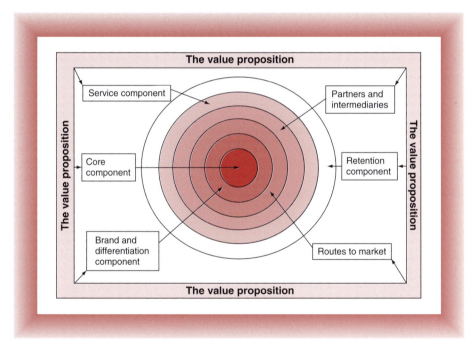

Figure 6.48 The value proposition drives the offering components

Although each organization and market(ing) strategy is different, I suggest that there is likely to be a common theme that ties your strategy together; and you will need to clarify before you pass the strategy over to the tacticians. The best way to do this is to translate the value proposition into market(ing) mix terms that the implementers will be able to use. This is not doing the implementers jobs for them, it is handing over enough detail in a 'specification' that they can do the 'right' job for your customers.

Remember, your job is to specify the benefits that the customer requires – how the product/service delivers these benefits is a tactical issue, what the benefits are (today – and then tomorrow) is a strategic one that you cannot abdicate.

2. The place

The whole issue of routes to market/supply chain/distribution is complicated – it involves a lot of people, a lot of time, a lot of expense and so much can go wrong that it needs looking at carefully, all the time. A more technical definition might be:

Supply chain management defined

Encompasses the planning and management of all activities involved in sourcing and procurement, conversion, and all logistics management activities. Importantly, it also includes coordination and collaboration with channel partners, which can be suppliers, intermediaries, third-party service providers, and customers. In essence, supply chain management integrates supply and demand management within and across companies.

As soon as you meet something that has lots of different variables to control or co-ordinate, then you have something that lends itself to being 'systemized', 'planned' and 'processed'. Organizations seem to feel that a structured approach to these issues is a good and safe way of avoiding costly mistakes. 'Best practice' becomes important – for very good reasons.

However, best practice is benchmarked, copied and measured by everyone. That's excellent for the organization that is driven by not making mistakes, but not so good for the organization that is driven by its need to be different. If your strategy includes a healthy dose of differentiation (I hope it does), then you will need to determine which elements of the routes to market implementation will need to be tailored to the strategy rather than allowing an abstract notion of best practice to tailor the strategy!

Products and (some) services need to get from where they are produced to where they are to be consumed. Some services (such as hotels and laboratories) are fixed so we need to find ways of getting customers to the service – to consume. Every step in the process that is owned by someone outside the organization needs to be paid – and motivated to do things the 'right' way. The more steps are in the process, the more this gets complicated – and expensive.

Some areas you might think about are:

● *Conventional wisdom*: If there is an 'accepted way' of distributing your product or service, do you really have to follow it? Some of the biggest (most profitable) 'innovations' have come from taking another view on distribution. Go on, think different.

● *Customer convenience*: Should be top of the list really but...Where is the customer in all this? Convenience is the name of the game here, how convenient is your system for customers?

● *Customer value*: The *big* one, what value does the customer get from the distribution process? If it's *none*, then you need to cut costs wherever you can. What value *could* the customer get from the process? Who *should be* delivering the additional value? Which leads to:

● *Cost–benefit*: What benefits are we/our customers receiving from the intermediaries in the system, and what is it costing us/our customers?

● *Differentiation*: Differentiation is always complicated, is the distribution system part of the solution – or part of the problem?

● *Segmentation*: Segmentation comes before branding (you can't have one without the other, see Section 6.4). Delivering on the special needs of different segments is difficult without active support from the channels. Do the intermediaries work with you or against you in delivering to different segments?

● *Where is the battle for control?*: Every distribution system has a battle going on – are you winning or losing?

Winning the battle for control: Every distribution system or network has its battle for control – it's where the money is. Who controls the customer, controls the margin (Figure 6.49).

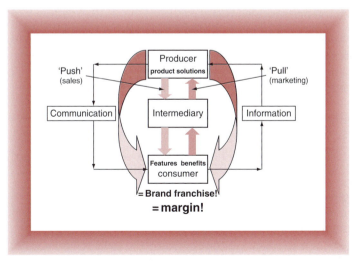

Figure 6.49   The battle for control - and margins

Intermediaries in the system tend to be closer to the end customer (they try to serve them), so should be better positioned to understand and satisfy their needs. If they can do this (some can, some can't), then they can pick and choose which suppliers to support or stock and can effectively control access to customers and revenues. Intermediaries in this position have the power to dictate terms to producers. Often the intermediaries are given this position of power by producers who are not customer or market oriented – they are only interested in making what they make and are happy to rely on the channel to know the customer and inform them of new trends and needs as they arise. 'Slave' producers such as these survive as long as the channel wishes them to survive and tend to be prey to cheap imports.

Where producers are in control of the distribution system, they tend to be customer and market oriented, they don't 'push' their products/services through the system but invest in creating a brand franchise with the customer so that they are 'pulled' through the intermediary system.

If you want to take control of your distribution system, you will need to invest in:

● *Information* – on what your customers want and value;

● *Communication* – to your target customers on the reasons why they should prefer your offering over the competitive offerings.

Not a low-cost route, but an investment that will pay off (if you get it right) in increased margin.

3. Pricing

Of all the Ps in the marketing mix, only one – price – is about revenues (and cash, and profits), the others are all costs.

Give the implementers as much room as possible, by all means, but don't lose control over pricing (Figure 6.50).

If you are wondering at this new idea, you only have to remember:

(1) Price is not, not, *not* just what you drop any time you need to meet some arbitrary product or service sales target.

(2) Price is where all your revenues, profits and *cash* comes from – not something to be *tinkered* with.

(3) Reducing prices has been known to make customers think:
   (a) The item is about to be replaced by another model – so will postpone purchase.
   (b) The firm is in financial trouble, needs the cash, may not stay in business long enough to supply future parts.

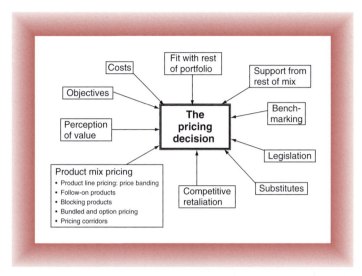

Figure 6.50 Pricing decisions

   (c) Price will come down further and so better to wait.
   (d) The quality or size (or both) has been reduced.

(4) Raising prices has been known to make customers think:
   (a) Price is an indicator of quality.
   (b) They are unsure and require quality reassurance.
   (c) They perceive quality differences in competitive offerings and are prepared to pay for quality (expensive but worth it).
   (d) They are concerned to be seen to buy the most expensive.

(5) Don't mess with prices unless you know what effects it will have over the short, medium and long terms.

(6) If you want/need to increase profits, reducing price is a really *bad* way to try and do it. Increasing sales is better, decreasing costs is better still, increasing price is best!

(7) Creating the circumstances where you can increase prices, and not lose significant sales is what you, market(ing) strategy and this whole book is about.

This won't happen unless you control price as part of the strategy implementation process.

4 The communications

So much nonsense has been written about market(ing) communications over the years that I am always wary about coming near the subject.

When people insist, and to ignore the subject in a book like this would be irresponsible, I fall back on the four questions that have guided me over the years (Figure 4.51).

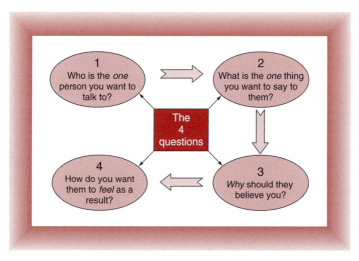

Figure 6.51   Communications - *cutting to the chase*

There is nothing very clever about the 'four questions' apart from the way that they are (still after all these years) able to cut right to the core of any communications problem – no matter how much hubris has been piled on top.

I have also discovered that these questions apply to any type of communications, from the 'above-the-line' advertising (TV, Press) to the 'below-the-line' activities including public relations, promotions, direct marketing and personal sales.

The four questions you should ask of any communications issue are, in order:

(1) *Who is the 'one' person you want to talk to?* Effective communications need to be focused. People are not the same (see Section 6.3) and the mass market is really dead – segments are the order of the day. Different segments want different things and need to hear different things from you – and everyone is an individual, so make it personal or don't talk at all. Don't know who the 'one' person' is? Don't waste money on communication until you find out.

(2) *What is the 'one' thing you want to say to them?* An effective message says one thing only. More than one message just confuses, so better not to say anything

than to confuse your audience. Don't know what the 'one thing' is? Don't waste money on communication until you find out.

(3) *'Why' should they believe you?* If they don't or won't believe you, why would you communicate – just to give the audience an opportunity to recall how untrustworthy you are? You need to give them the reason why you should be believed, they won't necessarily work it out for themselves. Don't know why they should believe you? Don't waste money on communication until you find out.

(4) *How do you want them to 'feel' as a result?* Communicating is all about feelings – that ultimately lead to purchase. Communications needs to generate some key feeling in your audience's mind – that can open the way for the unique benefits of your offering. Whether it is 'peace of mind', 'reassurance', 'relief', 'smugness' or any emotion of your choice, there needs to be an outcome. Don't know what emotion you want them to feel as a result of the communication? Don't waste money on communication until you find out.

The more adventurous among you might also want to try applying these ideas to your internal audiences as well as you external ones – some internal market(ing) will be essential if the old lines of demarcation between strategy and tactics are not going to limit your chances of market success.

Controlling progress

The marketing mix is obviously more complicated and detailed than the points I have covered – I agree. There are (very thick) books dedicated to understanding and manipulating the elements of the market(ing) mix – and they do the job very well indeed. But, they don't worry too much about longer-term market(ing) strategy, and that is my main concern.

The secret though is that what gets measured gets done. If the market(ing) strategy is important to you, then you will absolutely need to measure progress – against the strategic levers that you have identified, communicated and agreed with the implementers – regularly.

If you hold tight to the handful of levers that I have pointed out, you might just succeed in sending your strategy off to the market, intact in the most important parts. Naturally, every strategy changes between formulation and implementation. This is true, but putting down some strong markers about routes to market, pricing and communications will ensure that any changes made are 'necessary' and not just 'convenient'.

6.7.8 Conclusions – offerings

We arrive finally to the end of the SCORPIO modules.

I hope that you have seen now that the order that you take through the seven modules is largely up to you, it's all interconnected and it all leads to the customer.

In this section on Offerings, I have tried to make a sensible link from strategy (three-year thinking) to tactics (this quarter). The differences between strategy and tactics have been picked over too many times in the past to be of any use to anybody. The differences are not going to help satisfy customers, looking for the similarities is likely to be much more profitable for all.

If we (strategy and tactics) all work for the same organization (subject to all the 'issues' highlighted in Section 6.6), then we need to find a way of working together so that the customer benefits – only customer value can create organizational value. In this final chapter, I have tried to look at those areas where a managed handover is needed from the strategy to the implementation. Some of the issues are technical although most are cultural.

How well your organization succeeds with the handover is less a measure of its ability than just how badly it wants to win.

Check you results against the strategy checklist in the Appendix.

Finally, a few questions that you should now be able to answer:

Offerings

1	Do we (really) understand the target market?	
2	What is the value proposition?	
3	What is the most appropriate business design?	
4	Where are the new offerings?	
5	How do we assess the risk?	
6	Are we managing the life cycle?	
7	How do we take the offerings to market?	

Conclusions – Part Two

There are but two powers in the world, the sword and the mind. In the long run, the sword is always beaten by the mind.

Napoleon Bonaparte

This section was never going to be the easiest in the book – nor the shortest. Practically, we have covered:

(1) Setting market(ing) objectives

(2) Developing market(ing) strategy, specifically:
    (a) What business are you in? (industry or market?)
    (b) Who is the customer and what does your customer want?
    (c) What are the natural market segments and which ones must you own?
    (d) How do you differentiate/position your offer and create profitable brands?
    (e) How do you retain customers longer?
    (f) What are the requirements on the organization processes and culture?
    (g) What are the offerings that the market is demanding, and how do you deliver them?

More important than the individual elements of the SCORPIO approach, we have (or should have) seen that:

- SCORPIO is not a 'new' model or theory but is a way of structuring the learning that any good marketer should possess.

- Mintzberg noted that real strategy needs to be 'crafted' rather than 'deduced' according to the hard data available. SCORPIO is exactly the same: move among the elements as you feel most comfortable and seems *right* to you.

- The seven elements are all interrelated, and decisions cannot be made in isolation because there will osolated be effects elsewhere.

- You cannot eliminate any of the elements from your strategy. Experience shows that every organization will need to at least touch on each element.

- The elements will have different importance for your organization. The competitive situation that you find yourself in will make certain elements more important than others – although this will certainly change over time.

● We have to work on all of the seven elements at the same time. Working on one element alone but in depth will ultimately waste time as interactions between the elements are not taken into account as they arise.

● You choose your own order to the process; you don't have to use the sequence I have used in Part Two.

Check your progress against the strategy checklist in the Appendix.

Part Three

From Market(ing) Strategy to Tactics

7 Making it happen

Take time to deliberate, but when the time for action has arrived, stop thinking and go in.

Napoleon Bonaparte

How exactly do we make it happen?

Planning and strategy are important but, without implementation, it is a pointless and expensive exercise which will probably take the organization backward, rather than forward.

In the 1980s and 1990s life, academia and boardrooms were alive with questions about what the organization should or must do. While some of the schemes and theories which had been postulated to aid with our corporate, business and market planning were of grandiose scale, Henry Mintzberg, among others, spent his time railing against this overly intellectual exercise and called for a more practical, implementation-led approach.

Pendulum time.

Late 1990s saw the arrival of the Internet and the dot-com 'revolution' alongside the unnaturally long growth stage of the global IT industry and everybody had to benchmark themselves against organizations who had no strategy, invest in products rather than customers and 'strategize' only when the quarter's sales targets had been met.

Strategy @ Microsoft

It [Microsoft] has a vision but not a roadmap. It can see the peaks but doesn't know how to cross the foothills to get there.

A former Microsoft executive, The Economist, 1 April, 2006

A place somewhere between the two extremes would have been nice. The pendulum is moving again now; maybe it will stop somewhere short of the ivory tower strategy departments of the 1980s this time.

In the meantime, we have a market(ing) strategy; we need to do something with it (Figure 7.1).

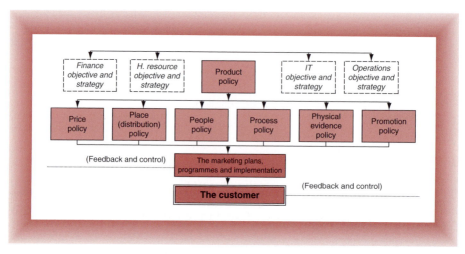

Figure 7.1   From market strategy to tactics

We have spent a lot of time in this book looking at the concepts that will support the 'right' sort of market strategy, so far without worrying too much about what constitutes 'good' or 'bad' market(ing) practice. I have always been concerned that what is often called *marketing* is too often little more than marketing communications, and 'real market(ing)' is still waiting to make an appearance in most organizations. Recently, more commentators have started to agree.

Rather than get embroiled in a discussion about what constitutes good market(ing) practice – who knows? – I will leave that to the heavyweight books that specialize in the area.

Here we will focus on how to shepherd the customer/market(ing) strategy through the organization to arrive at the proper conclusion.

It might still be a bit 'strategic' for the self-limiting marketing communications manager but we will look at the stuff that really makes a difference:

7.1 Market(ing) plans

7.2 Market(ing) control systems

7.3 Strategy evaluation

7.4 Identifying barriers to implementation

7.5 Identifying drivers for change

7.6 Using the system.

7.1 Market plans

> To be a good general you must know mathematics; it serves to direct
> your thinking in a thousand circumstances.
>
> Napoleon Bonaparte

The process of market(ing) planning (Figure 7.2) and market(ing) plans has been
described at some length – and in some detail – in a number of specific and
specialized marketing texts, so I shall not repeat their efforts here. This (unsur-
prising) process is the traditional approach of sequential thinking that proceeds
step by step with back-steps as we adapt through learning.

Figure 7.2   Market planning

From the market(ing) strategy perspective, the market(ing) planning process fills
the gap between the strategic process and specific, market or segment-based

activities. We have seen that the market(ing) strategy process is concerned with taking various elements of it into a strategic market(ing) mix.

The strategic market(ing) mix can also be seen as a set of interrelated sub-objectives which are passed down to the relevant market(ing) function to be turned into more detailed operational plans, with a small number of strategic control levers maintained by the strategy manager or team to control implementation.

It is these later detailed plans, when combined, which form the basis of the organization's market(ing) plans.

While, as I have said, I have no intention of turning this into yet another long book on detailed aspects of tactics, there is one final aspect which market(ing) strategy *must* bring to the market(ing) plans – an effective and functioning control system.

The market(ing) strategy process described so far depicts market(ing) objectives and market(ing) strategy as translating the business strategy into market-based terms. The market(ing) strategy is then translated into a strategic market(ing) mix which is in turn implemented through a series of detailed tactics, activities and programmes. Of course, the process will only be deemed an ultimate success if the organization is able to generate profits (and cash) through creating customer value by satisfying customer needs.

Up to this point, you will probably have seen the entire process as one of analytical thinking and (I hope, intelligent) planning. But so far, we have nothing to prove that our thinking and planning has been along the right lines. The only true test of the market(ing) strategy is marketplace response – the final verdict always lies with the customer. A market(ing) control system is essential if the organization, and its market(ing) strategy, is to be validated by real, unbiased market response.

7.2   Market control systems

> Great ambition is the passion of a great character. Those endowed with it may perform very good or very bad acts. All depends on the principles which direct them.
>
> *Napoleon Bonaparte*

Essentially, the control system will detail the controls that will be applied to monitor the progress of the market(ing) plans and their success (or otherwise) in achieving the market(ing) objectives/KPIs (Figure 7.3).

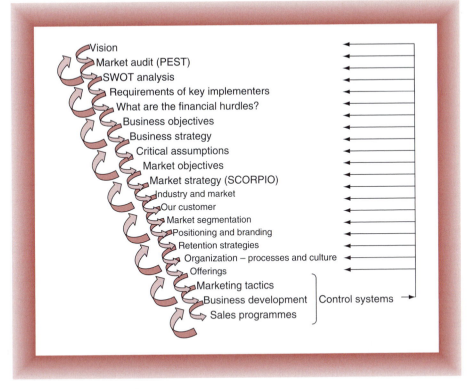

Figure 7.3 Market planning

Often, market(ing) control systems, where they exist at all, tend to be spelled out in budgets and budgeting terms. Product, pricing, distribution and other objectives will have been broken down, on a monthly basis, and transformed into a set of targets. These subsidiary targets are merely surrogates for sales turnover and (sometimes for) profit and profitability. Few control systems even mention profitability (so far I have found none that mention customer value), let alone relate profitability to the various market activities. It is always better to involve the staff in real-life profitability so that everybody has a very clear idea of what the organization is out to achieve and how their activity will play a major part in the broader market(ing) strategy (see Section 6.6).

The ideal control system will also contain some element of contingency planning. A contingency plan is an outline plan for additional or alternate activity which management would initiate if specific correctional activity were required. The idea behind contingency planning is to encourage managers to think forward through some of the difficulties which might arise in the marketplace. It encourages pre-planning in case (albeit extremely unlikely!) the market(ing) strategy and plans do not operate like clockwork.

Because of the fundamental inter-connectedness of the SCORPIO elements, contingency planning of this sort should not be restricted purely to implementation activity. The effects of such contingency plans on other areas of the organization, human resource, finance and operations must not only be communicated to other functions, but their active help in developing contingency plans be sought. If this is not done, then contingency planning is purely an exercise to keep the strategy team quiet – it should be much more than that if it is to be taken seriously.

The last comment to be made on market(ing) control systems is the use to which they are put. Like targeting and forecasting, if control systems are put in place merely to act as a stick for recalcitrant or under-performing implementers, much of the positive potential of the control system will be wasted. Control systems should be seen as a method of improving performance, not a way of identifying and punishing under-achievers. Some organizations even prohibit the development of market(ing) control systems in their market(ing) plan in the belief that this is 'defeatist' thinking and that it will – of itself – produce plans that are bound to fail. Frankly, it is very difficult to know how to respond to this type of organization, apart from saying that it is completely wrong. This thinking is symptomatic of an organization that believes market(ing) strategy and implementation is a science that can be practised and controlled according to well-understood rules. Unfortunately (or fortunately?), customers remain unpredictable. Market(ing) control systems and contingency planning are essential tools. Never leave home without them.

7.3   Strategy evaluation

> Read over and over again the campaigns of Alexander, Hannibal, Caesar, Gustavus, Turenne, Eugene and Frederic...This is the only way to become a great general and master the secrets of the art of war...
>
> *Napoleon Bonaparte*

The primary consideration here is the evaluation of alternative strategic options open to the organization. We have already seen that there are a large number of different routes available that any strategy might take to achieve the stated objectives. Once all options have been uncovered, how do you decide which is the best way to go?

The chance of successful implementation is greatly increased if we choose the right strategy in the first place. Considering both broad business and market(ing) strategies as well as more detailed implementation programmes, the manager is faced with three separate but related problems:

(1) What objective(s) was the strategy (originally) designed to achieve?

(2) What choice criteria should be used?

(3) How can we evaluate alternative options that appear to be open to the organization?

7.3.1 Short or long term?

Before considering the best way to evaluate market(ing) strategy, it is probably wise to think about where we started this journey. What do we mean by strategy? If strategy is about marshalling the gross resource of the organization to match the needs of the marketplace and achieve the business objective, this *cannot* be a short-term activity.

Every organization is complex and any change takes time to accomplish. Strategic decisions, such as the general choosing his battleground, will have long-term implications. Strategic decisions, such as which business area to enter, cannot be reversed at a moment's notice – momentum has to be built up over a planned period of time.

The choice of evaluation methods is critical because they can quickly become the *raison d'être* for the organization's activities – it is interesting how few managers keep a hand on the strategic issues that confront their organization – visible success at dealing with tactical operations (too often the symptoms of strategic problems) is a much safer route to the top of many organizations. We have to be careful that the evaluation methods are aimed at assessing how well the intended strategies will achieve set objectives (may be difficult to measure) and not how well they will meet current sales or revenue targets (probably easier to measure).

If market(ing) strategy is about the long-term success of the organization (that was a rhetorical question), its success or failure must be measured by procedures that take into account this long-term view. A practical evaluation system should note any short-term setbacks in the plan but, more importantly, should be capable of setting these within a long-term context.

7.3.2 Financial versus non-financial measurement

In business texts, generally there is surprisingly little discussion over the difference between those measures which assess 'efficiency' and those which assess 'effectiveness'. Efficiency is defined as *doing things right* and effectiveness is defined as *doing the right things*.

Efficiency measures are by far and away the most common in business and tend to evaluate, often on an ongoing basis, the efficiency or precision with which actions are carried out by the organization – mostly internal. When we look at effectiveness measures – and these are much less common – we will be looking at how well the organization is doing the 'right' things. In other words, how well the organization is meeting its paying customers' needs.

For the rare organizations who manage to be both effective and efficient, that is they are efficient in their operations and are also delivering what their customers want, the future looks very rosy. For those organizations that are neither effective nor efficient, it is just a matter of time until a new company comes along who can meet their customers' needs better. Between these two extremes, however, the situation is more interesting; it is clear that organizations can become more and more efficient, leaner and leaner in their operations but if they still fail to provide the market what the market wants and needs it is only a matter of time before they are supplanted by eager competition. On the other hand, as long as an organization continues to supply what the market wants, the demand remains more or less buoyant. They may not be very efficient in their operations and the way they supply the marketplace but they are likely to survive.

More worrying for organizations is that the majority of measures that are used to evaluate and appraise strategy tend to be of the 'efficiency' rather than of the 'effectiveness' type.

The majority of financial and accountant-driven measures also fall into the efficiency category. While of course there must be a point of inefficiency below which no organization can survive, efficiency of itself is no guarantee of the organization's survival. Unless the organization delivers what the market wants, it will die – albeit slowly.

The answer, as in most strategic issues, is one of striking the elusive (and changing) balance between these two apparently opposing forces. We should be searching out the evaluation and appraisal measures that allow us to pursue both these goals simultaneously.

Financial measures
The more usual measures of evaluation under this heading will include:

- Profit
- Profitability
- Shareholder return
- Cash flow/liquidity
- Share price
- Earnings per share

- EBITDA
- Return on net assets
- Return on sales.

Most of these traditional financial measures concentrate on some notion of 'return' and it goes without saying that profit is essential to the long-term survival of any business. However, as Levitt said, *profit is a requisite not a purpose of business* (see Section 1.4). Profit is essential to any business but is not the only reason why we are here. More importantly, evaluation and appraisal processes which rely exclusively on profitability can overshadow the fact that the only way we make profits is by satisfying customers.

The laws of physics apply to all activities, even financial returns:

- Financial returns can only be created by sales revenue (customers recognizing and purchasing what they consider to constitute value).
- Short-term returns above the average may have to be paid for in the long term.
- When profits continue while sales and customers are disappearing, a company is simply taking value from its brand (which exists off balance sheet) and is mortgaging its future to pay shareholders today.
- Strangely enough, stock markets and investors don't seem to worry about long-term returns as much as the short term – human nature I suppose.

Equally important, if somewhat shorter term, liquidity/cash-flow evaluation is essential. Lack of long-term profitability is not a major reason for the demise of business but cash-flow problems can even eliminate companies with a rising order book. Despite everything we have said about strategy being longer term, the one thing we have to bear in mind is short-term cash flow. Without cash, there is no longer term. See the comments on Bi-focal market(ing) (Section 6.2)

Non-financial measures

The non-financial measures of performance tend to measure the effectiveness rather than the efficiency side of the equation although not exclusively so. Non-financial measures may include:

- Market share
- Growth
- Competitive advantage
- Competitive position

- Sales volume

- Market penetration levels

- New product development

- Customer satisfaction

- Customer commitment

- Customer franchise

- Market image and awareness levels.

Two things should be readily apparent from a review of this list. First, that any one of these measures taken in isolation is unlikely to be sufficient to guarantee the long-term survival and development of the organization. Secondly, implicit (although often not stated) is that growth is always a good thing. The growth aspect to strategy is very much a development of the heydays of the 1970s and remains largely unquestioned in most texts.

Certainly the organization must develop if it is to continue to adapt and remain in touch with its marketplace. But 'growth'? Growth of what? Growth can be a good and healthy influence but if pursued for its own sake can lead to problems. Sales maximization and volume growth can often lead to serious declines in profitability especially in highly competitive marketplaces. Directed and controlled growth based on a qualified and detailed analysis of the marketplace and potential business opportunities can lead to a flourishing organization. However, as author Ed Abbey has noted, *growth for the sake of growth is the ideology of the cancer cell.*

Multiple criteria

In almost every situation, the dependence upon a single criterion for evaluating and appraising strategy is likely to be dangerous. There are two extremely good reasons why we should consider using more than one criterion in our evaluation of strategy. This is because:

(1) Organizations behave ineffectively from some points of view if a single criterion is used.

(2) Organizations fulfil multiple functions and have multiple goals, some of which may be in conflict. It would be inappropriate to assess market(ing) strategy purely on the basis of any one criterion.

Organizations and their market(ing) strategies can best be regarded as living entities. If they follow their markets, they will also need to be dynamic and evolving entities just to be able to survive – let alone flourish. Time, if no other factor, will always act to make certain measures redundant and other measures important in new situations.

We have also seen that conflicts naturally arise in the management of any organization. These require that different performance measures need to be traded off in different situations, for example:

(1) Customers' need for 'value' versus shareholders' need for 'return';

(2) Cost of achieving 'market share' versus need for 'profitability';

(3) Organizations' need of 'efficiency' versus customers' need for 'service';

(4) Production efficiency requirement for 'long runs' versus the markets' need for 'choice';

(5) The organization's drive to 'standardization' versus the consumer's need for 'individualism'.

The choice of the most appropriate measures for evaluation and appraisal will depend entirely on the organization's situation and the marketing strategist's ability to balance internal and external needs.

Industry measures of performance

The IT industry view (Bill Gates)

'If automotive technology had kept pace with computer technology over the past few decades:

- You would now be driving a V32 instead of a V8

- It would have a top speed of 10,000 miles per hour

Or:

- You could have an economy car that weighs 30 pounds and gets a thousand miles to a gallon of gas

- In either case, the sticker price of a new car would be less than $50'

The automobile industry view

'If General Motors had developed the same technology as Microsoft, then we would all be driving cars with the following features:

- Your car would, without any obvious reason, have an accident twice a day

- The seats would require that everyone had the same sized buttocks

- Every time the road markings were replaced, you would have to buy a new car

- Before inflating, the airbag would prompt you: Do you really want to inflate me?

- In order to switch off the engine, you would have to press the "Start" button'

Choosing the right criterion

How can we make sure that we are choosing the right criterion against which to evaluate our longer-term market(ing) strategy? Although there are no hard-and-fast rules for this selection, the application of simple common sense can take us a long way forward. The judicious use of some selective models might also shed light on this problem.

Although you should always treat these models with great care because they can mislead badly, some indications might come from:

(1) *Product life cycle*: It may be worthwhile trying to plot our organization's position on this cycle. Whether we consider the PLC should be applied to the organization, the industry, the product or service category or even the particular brand, it might help us to select those criteria which are of most relevance in the situation at hand.

(2) *Boston Consulting Group (BCG) matrix*: Although there is much debate about the continuing validity of the Boston matrix and much care must be taken in its use, it can still be useful for 'conceptually' placing products or businesses in the organization's portfolio. Different forms of evaluation need to take place depending on the market and business situation of the product or the business considered. For example, 'dog' products or businesses need to be measured according to the net free cash flow that they generate; 'question marks' are best evaluated by the sales volume and revenue that they are able to generate in their particular market situation; 'Stars' are best evaluated by an assessment of net present value; 'cash cows' need to be assessed, evaluated and managed to generate the maximum return on investment.

(3) *GEC/McKinsey matrix*: This and other 'portfolio' models can also be used, with a little common sense, to ensure that we are measuring strategies within a sensible context of the business conditions that the company faces. The common use of a standard set of criteria to assess any strategic option is both naïve and dangerous – of course, that is what analysts do all the time.

What is the best way?

Considering the area of evaluation and appraisal of market(ing) strategy, the question always arises: *so what would one of the best market-driven organizations be doing?* Always a difficult question to answer as much depends upon the environment, the industry and the prevailing competitive situation of any particular organization.

However, as far as it is possible to answer such a general question, research in the 1990s carried out by the Chartered Institute of Marketing (CIM) and Cranfield School of Management identified the following factors as those evidenced by the 'successful marketing company' – they are still valid today:

(1) Start at the top.

(2) Involve everyone in the organization in the marketing philosophy.

(3) Be prepared for structural change.

(4) Use the new structure to feed a 'customer facing strategy'.

(5) Review marketing tactics (4Ps): Do they work from the customer's point of view?

(6) Accept that change is a way of life.

(7) Understand the difference between 'quality systems' and 'quality products and services'.

(8) Focus on the customer, not the competition.

(9) Look 'end-to-end', not piecemeal; customers expect seamless service.

(10) Keep the end user in sight; don't be distracted by the middleman.

(11) Measure the success of the marketing approach and be able to demonstrate the link between customer focus and profit.

This review gives good guidance to the types of evaluation criteria that can/ should be used to drive practical market(ing) strategy.

7.4   Identifying barriers to implementation

> Impossible is a word to be found only in the dictionary of fools.
> *Napoleon Bonaparte*

There are many barriers that stand in the way of successful implementation of market(ing) strategy, some evident, some not so. The barriers fall broadly into three separate categories:

(1) External pressures on the organization;

(2) Internal pressures on the marketing function;

(3) Pressures within the marketing function itself.

We will consider these three forms of pressure independently.

7.4.1   Environmental barriers

To consider the external pressures on the organization first, these are best described under the traditional PEST (SLEPT) headings used to understand and to describe the environment (see Chapter 2):

(1) *Social factors*: Changing demographic and social patterns such as an ageing population, fewer school leavers and the shift in emphasis from manual to white-collar skills will have a major impact on any strategic plans that require implementation over the next five to ten years. British and European society is also undergoing some level of fundamental change and trends such as environment, individualism and immigration need to be accounted for in your plans.

(2) *Legal factors*: There are an ever-increasing number of laws that are affecting business activity on a wider and wider scale. Laws now cover employment, pay and price policies, health and safety as well as specific acts to control particular industries such as financial services, telecommunications, manufacturing/processing and many others. Also, as time progresses we can expect more impact on British activity from European Union (EU)-based laws.

(3) *Economic factors*: The 1980s witnessed an unparalleled level of change in the British economy (Thatcher), and this change continues today. European policy will probably eventually align itself, either with or against free markets too. Strategic implementation of plans needs to take into account the changes that are likely to occur in the marketplace and you should consider changes in your own industry such as mergers, joint ventures, share price movement and investment as well as any union activities, suppliers' actions and changes to include vertical integration and disintermediation (the disappearance of intermediaries in the process). Distribution channels are also undergoing a radical change in a number of industries, and successful implementation will depend upon a good forecasting of likely change in areas such as distribution infrastructure as well as in transportation and supply chain and channel management and control. Internationalization is a major factor in all economic situations and is likely to affect your customers' perceptions of your offer and the entire nature of competition. Competition itself is one of the most important factors to forecast in strategic implementation as no market strategy ever operates in a vacuum. You should be attempting to analyse not only the direct (own industry/business) competition but also the important and often more difficult to predict indirect competition from outside your traditional industry base (see Chapter 2). Competition is expected to increase in all sectors over the next ten years driven primarily by the internationalization of business, the fragmentation of many markets and the continued rise of China, India and eventually Africa.

(4) *Political factors*: There is a general trend in most Western markets for governments to take an increasingly active role in business. Political activities include taxation, lobbying, as well as the ability to pass laws which affect not only your organization's ability to act in a free market but also customers' ability to buy your products or services. In most markets, political activities are often aimed at influencing competitive activity. Whatever the intention

behind political actions, the result is always some form of restriction over the organization's activities in a marketplace and these restrictions need to be forecasted and attempts made to modify implementation of the strategic plan within this developing framework.

(5) *Technological factors*: Technology generally has had a massive effect over the past ten years and we can expect this influence to continue and accelerate. Technology has made radical change in manufacturing possible and has been a major catalyst in the recent proliferation of new products and services. A key factor in the development of technology has been its ability to reduce, if not sometimes eliminate, barriers to market entry. The application of modern technology has enabled small- and medium-sized organizations to operate at cost levels previously the exclusive preserve of much larger organizations. Economies of scale are no longer the barriers they used to be.

7.4.2 Internal barriers

As well as external pressures acting upon the organization, there are a number of internal barriers that will affect its ability to implement its strategic plans successfully. All of these factors act as significant potential blockages to implementing market(ing) strategy and unless these blockages can be overcome the organization has little choice but to amend the goals and strategy to those which the organization is able to implement (see Section 6.6) with the inevitable market consequences.

(1) *Leadership*: There is little doubt that the ultimate success and implementation of any strategic plan will depend upon the degree to which top management buys in to the process. This is especially evident where the strategic thrust of the plan involves any form of significant change. The organization's leadership may be opposed to objectives of the plan for any number of reasons. For example, they may be from non-marketing disciplines, may feel that the need for change is not yet apparent or simply be more comfortable with 'steady-state' management style. Whatever the reasons, unless strong leaders are 'bought in' to the vision and strategy completely, little progress is likely to be made (see Section 6.6).

(2) *Organizational culture*: There are many forms of organizational culture and, in truth, few of these are customer or market focused. In the organization with a non-market-oriented culture, the chances of successfully implementing a true market(ing) strategy must be limited. Market(ing) in this type of organization tends to be all about marketing services, often linked or even subservient to the all-important sales function. In the product- or production-oriented organization, the marketer's role is to provide sales materials, product information and market analysis to support the sales and production functions of the organization. The market- or customer-oriented organization is the only one that sees the marketer's role as that of catalyst and

change agent to focus the rest of the organization's activities on the one activity that really matters – the customer. Changing the culture of an organization is never a short-term task (see Section 6.6). However, as today's markets become more and more competitive, the options are becoming clearer – change the culture or the organization may not survive beyond the medium term. If the culture will not change in the short to medium term then goals and strategies will need to be amended to something which the organizational culture can assimilate. Patience and sensitivity are required to get things done.

(3) *Organization processes*: In many organizations, the existing organization processes are simply not designed to be able to deliver the proposed market(ing) strategy as is intended. Too many processes are designed for the convenience and administrative ease of those that work in them rather than being designed in order to deliver satisfaction to customers (see Section 6.6). It is simply unrealistic to design a customer-focused market(ing) strategy without spending some time looking at the organization's processes and ability to deliver on the promises that you may be making to your customers. When dealing with organizations, it is important to consider the 'soft', cultural elements such as style, skills, staffing and shared values as well as the traditional 'hard' values. Remember, an organization is nothing without the people who work inside it.

(4) *Functional policies*: They are a subset of organization structure; most functions in an organization (finance, operations, human resources, sales – and market(ing)) tend to grow and produce a number of functional policies and procedures which determine how their part of the organization and their staff manage the day-to-day business. The intended market strategy may fall foul of these 'best practice' functional processes and will encounter a blockage on the path to implementation.

(5) *Resources*: The proposed market(ing) strategy may require either the allocation of significant additional resource to certain functions or even the re-appropriation of resource into different areas of the organization. Successful implementation will depend upon these resources either being available for the implementation of the plan or making the appropriate resources available so that the plan can be implemented fully. The potential blockage here is likely to be either in the resources simply not being available or that senior management considers that other causes are more deserving. In any case, this could provide a significant blockage to implementation.

(6) *Evaluation and control procedures*: The lack of appropriate monitoring and evaluation procedures in an organization will be a significant block to the successful implementation of any strategy. It is a truism that what gets measured gets done. No matter that your long-term market(ing) strategy is aimed at improving and developing customer satisfaction levels, if the organization is managed and motivated by monthly or quarterly sales figures, that is what will be achieved. This potential blockage can be less of a problem than

the ones outlined earlier, in that you are not necessarily faced with over-coming perception or resource problems. As long as the proper control measures are installed, there need be no problems in implementation.

7.4.3 Barriers within the marketing function

Not only are there a number of issues internal to the organization which can act as blockages to developing and implementing quality market(ing) strategy, there are a number of aspects of the market(ing) department or function which can also act as potential blockages to the development and implementation of your plans:

(1) *Market(ing)'s interface with other functions*: Delivering satisfactions to custom-ers may be the responsibility of the market(ing) function but it is not a job that market(ing) can carry out on its own. To deliver customer satisfactions and thereby improve the organization's position against competition, the entire organization needs to operate as an effective partnership and deliver required benefits seamlessly. To do this, market(ing) needs to interact positively with other functions within the organization, such as production, purchasing, personnel and finance – the solution is not in 'telling' other functions what to do but in involving them in the process.

(2) *The role of market(ing)/the market(ing) specialist*: The role of the marketer will depend largely upon the organization culture and processes. In the non-market-oriented organization, market(ing) tends to be synonymous with 'advertising and promotion'. The *market(ing) specialist* is often taken on as a necessary (and expensive) evil because the competition seems to be making inroads into the organization's markets by advertising. Other managers in the organization often have little understanding of the market(ing) concept and don't appreciate their role in satisfying customers. The role of the marketer in the production- or product-oriented organization is twofold – to give his or her internal customers what they want and to act as catalyst for organizational change towards a more customer-oriented position. In the case of a customer- or market-oriented organization, the role of the marketer and the market(ing) function is quite different; rather than concentrating on advertising and promotion, the marketer's function is to identify, anticipate and satisfy cus-tomer needs profitably. Doing this needs much more than an in-depth knowledge of advertising and promotional methodology and techniques; the marketer's key area of responsibility is to understand the organization's customers and to feed this information back into the organization and other functions so that people are able to act upon it profitably.

(3) *Market(ing) feedback*: How effective a manager is in his or her job and how well the market(ing) strategy is implemented will depend on how much, how relevant and how good the information is and how well it is interpreted and acted upon. Information (not lots of data) is critical; information and feedback

on a plan's progress is never 100% accurate but it does act to both reduce uncertainty in planning and improve the quality of action. Customer information is the market(ing) powerbase, although too few market(ing) professionals use it as such.

(4) *Market Research*: It is the final, crucial area of market(ing) and market feedback. In many organizations, some market research is carried out but invariably it is insufficient to meet the organization's real needs. Market research should not be regarded as a crutch to support weak decision-making but as an essential 'investment' in the marketplace and future prosperity of the organization. Unfortunately many organizations, often product, production or planning oriented, do not see the investment aspects of market research but rather consider it as a cost.

7.5   Identifying drivers for change

A legislator must know how to take advantage of even the defects of those he wants to govern. The art consists in making others work rather than in wearing oneself out.

Napoleon Bonaparte

Rather than simply paint a completely negative picture, organizations and the current market can be used to actively support the implementation of market(ing) strategy. The astute manager will be able to use these drivers for change (to a more customer/segment/market focus) to enlist help and active cooperation within the organization to implement strategic change.

(1) *Customer expectations*: Customers in all markets are now demanding the 'impossible' on a regular basis. As their needs and wishes are met in competitive markets such as groceries, fast-moving consumer goods and durables, they see no reason why these expectations should not be met in unrelated fields such as banking, telecommunications, travel, business services and entertainment. As customer expectations continue to grow, so concepts such as 'brand loyalty' (see Section 6.4) and retention (see Section 6.5) may appear to be less effective. They are as important as ever but the rules – as imposed by customers – are changing. Customers are becoming less and less loyal to brands and organizations if these fail to provide what is wanted, when it is wanted, at what the customer sees as a reasonable price. The explosion of choice in so many markets means that customers do not have to put up with second best – loyalty has to be earned, it is not given as 'right'. The astute manager can use the changes in customer demand (and forecasts of future demand changes) to drive through internal organizational changes at a rate which the staff would

otherwise consider 'uncomfortable' (see Section 6.6). The manager's ability to investigate and understand market changes will be crucial to an organization's future survival. Knowing and being able to communicate this to others inside the organization are, of course, different matters.

(2) *Revenues*: These (and cash and profits) are the lifeblood of any organization. Senior managers and stock market investors just can't get enough; sometimes analysts look more like junkies searching for the next fix. Recessions drive deep spending cuts that make the thirst for revenues stronger. Booming markets fuel the addiction so that organizations need more and more revenues. Once the cost-cutting (hitting the brakes) and financial manoeuvring (playing with the gears) have wrung out all the spare revenues, every organization, eventually, works out that the only source of further revenue and profit growth is now the customer (time to hit the accelerator/ gas). Customers are the source of all revenues and profits and satisfied customers have now (at last!) started to top the agendas of more and more businesses. The market(ing) manager needs to use this trend to drive through the message that long-term profits do not come from a 'numbers game' (adding more customers at any price) but from a 'quality game' that involves retaining more customers, for longer, by constantly offering customers real value in offerings that meet their needs better than the competition. If you don't build a quality 'top line', there won't be a 'bottom line' to count.

(3) *Competition*: Not only is technology driving down entry barriers everywhere, but markets are also beginning to fragment in many and devious ways and competition is intensifying in practically every business sector. Not only are existing players fighting to gain and retain customers but new entrants are often being attracted by more substantial profits than they can gain in their hard-pressed home markets. Product and service offerings are proliferating and customers are now faced with a greater choice in more markets than they have ever experienced in the past. The only way through this maze is to be able to establish a clear and differentiated position in the market in which the organization operates and to give customers good, simple and relevant reasons why they should come to them rather than the competition (see 'value proposition' in Section 6.7). Effective market positioning (see Section 6.4) is not achieved solely by product or service quality but requires the deft application of all the elements of a SCORPIO-driven market(ing) strategy – we have already played out all the arguments. The market manager's job is to convince the organization, before it is too late, that customer orientation and customer value are the keys to survival and growth. Increased competition must be used as a central driver for change.

(4) *Innovation*: A by-product of the increasingly competitive nature of most markets and the application of modern technology, innovation has become the norm in many industry sectors. Innovation for its own sake is unlikely to create additional customer value, so will not gain market share or profitably

per se. But innovation directed at supplying more relevant products to customers (more customer value) will. In the future, innovation in both product or service delivery and processes and service will be the norm rather than the exception. Unfortunately many organizations tend to find innovation an uncomfortable experience and many prefer the 'steady-state' environment to work in (see Section 6.6). Innovation, like all other potential business 'saviours', is a dangerous path to travel; simply doing new things is unlikely to be enough and could even be a way of hastening commercial suicide. Much innovation does no more than create more choice and complication in customers' lives – is this really what they want?.

(5) *Cheap imports from China/India/and?* They are a good thing (see Section 6.4). Organizations that have 'muddled through' for years must now either decide to change (finally become more customer focused) or try to compete on price with bargain basement costs of developing economies. This is not a bad thing and should not be treated as such – it is exactly what we need to put the customer back at the head of the list and get organizations focused on delivering value-added content, not just any content. Maybe the Chinese can be encouraged to compete with the utility companies next?

Barriers to the implementation of market(ing) strategy are big and intimidating. The drivers that can be used to support change are equally imposing. Ultimately it comes down to people – any organization tends to get the degree of change and success that it wants and deserves.

7.6   Using the system

> The herd seeks out the great, not for their sake but for their influence;
> and the great welcome them out of vanity or need.
>
> *Napoleon Bonaparte*

Apart from the self-employed entrepreneur with no staff (or less than five to keep under the increasingly expensive bureaucracy barrier imposed by government), everybody is likely to encounter resistance to change. And, moving from product to customer focus which will always be at the core of a real market(ing) strategy, will encounter more resistance than most changes introduced to an organization. The market(ing) manager charged with a great sense of the rightness of the cause is understandable, even laudable. But the resistors of change are also fired with what they believe to be the rightness of their cause and will fight hard against what they believe to be a threat to the future of the business – after all, working this way has got them this far hasn't it? And they are particularly good at doing this sort of business.

Head-to-head conflict may be fun, even gratifying, but will it change the organ-ization into what it must become? Unless you are vested with more power in the organization than anyone else, there is no certainty that you will win the battle on these terms and, if you lose, you could even set back the change process to terminal levels. No, the important thing is to achieve the change; the survival of the organization must come first. The best (and most effective) method of achiev-ing change is to use the systems – not fight them. How can this be done?

7.6.1 Control systems

Planning without control simply means that the organization has a nice, sophisticated document. The control systems are essential to make sure that the organization drives through the content of the plans and achieves its objectives in the marketplace (see Sections 6.6 and 7.2). Control systems will be in place in organizations – even if plans are absent; every organization believes that the measurement of particular things is important for advancement. Controls, explicit or implicit, will always be found. As to the nature of control systems, James Bureau in *The Marketing Book* (Baker, M., ed., Butterworth-Heinemann, Oxford, 1994) describes the nature of good control systems. They must be driven by the following principles:

(1) *Formality*: firm rituals that are applied generally and in a standard manner;

(2) *Necessity*: should be seen as useful by the organization and not just a ritualistic process;

(3) *Priority*: to be concerned with those elements which the organization needs to control, not with everything capable of control;

(4) *Veracity*: need to be data based, not based solely on intuition or subjective opinion;

(5) *Regularity*: as regular as is affordable and useful depending on the activity measured and the dynamics of the market situation.

7.6.2 Using control systems to support the market(ing) strategy

Control systems are many and various, and selecting the right method will depend very much upon the market that the organization is addressing, the particular goals and objectives that the organization has set itself as well as the particular organization structure, processes and culture.

Control systems can become the reasons for the organization's existence quite soon after their introduction as both managers and staff focus on the achievement of agreed targets (this is what their appraisals and rewards are all about) rather than the achievement of the tasks-behind-the-targets. The reasons for the exis-tence of the targets are rarely questioned. In some organizations, the accepted behaviour (culture) is to exceed targets, not just meet them. There is often no thinking involved; it is just *the way things are done around here*. Sales (revenue) targets are an obvious example: often in the belief that sales and market(ing) people are simple souls who can't deal with the concept of profit, simple sales figures are handed down as quarterly and annual targets to be met. Sales people too have to pay mortgages and put food on the table and, if that is what they are bonused to do, that is what gets done. If achieving the set sales targets means cutting margins to buy sales or doing deals to meet today's targets at the expense of building relationships that will/might bear (sales) fruit tomorrow, then so be it. This is clearly the fault of those who set targets, not of those who relentlessly achieve targets that should have been set differently in the first place.

Control systems, as we have seen, are a matter of balancing four primary issues:

(1) *Standard setting*: The role of the planning element of the process. The goals and objectives which fall out of the business and market strategy process are translated into 'standards' that drive the organization. 'Ideally', the standards will have been set within an understanding of what the organization is currently able to deliver – to customers.

(2) and (3) *Performance measurement and reporting results*: The key areas of most control systems, most discussion will centre on which performances should be measured and how results should be reported. The measurement activities of the planning achievements can simply be broken down into three (really) broad areas:

(a) *Quantity*: How much was achieved? How much should have been achieved?

(b) *Quality*: How good was that which was achieved? How good was it meant to be?

(c) *Cost*: How much did the achievement cost? How much was it planned to cost?

These basic parameters of the plan can then be quantified through an analysis of one or more of five distinct areas of operation which are:

(a) *Financial analysis*

(b) *Market analysis*

(c) *Sales and distribution analysis*

(d) *Physical resources analysis*

(e) *Human resources analysis*.

Then, the three most common measures also used as reporting tools – are:

(a) *Audits*: One method of assessing market(ing) strategy effectiveness is by the use of constant and regular market audits. The market audit (see Chapter 2) is a robust method of monitoring the successful implementation of market(ing) strategy, plans and policies. No matter which form of market audit is taken (there are a few variants), senior management should ensure that all areas of market(ing) activity are regularly monitored and their performance measured against pre-set standards which, once achieved, will guarantee the successful implementation of the plan.

(b) *Budgets*: Probably the most common form of control mechanism. Although developed for financial housekeeping and management, budgeting is often applied to market(ing) implementation as well. There are a number of disadvantages as well as advantages to using the budgeting process; many budgets tend to be short term, typically based on the annual plan for the achievement of that year's profit and turnover forecasts and short-term budgeting of this nature is not always the most relevant for the measurement and control of long-term strategy. Where the budgeting process is longer term and/or continuous rather than periodic in nature, the feedback results may be more relevant to longer-term strategic proposals. Beware – budgeting is not the same as management. Budgeting is an important aid to management decision-making but budgets are always based on *estimates* rather than reality and are always, at best, someone's idea of how the future will happen. Therefore, when deviations from budgeted figures arise, you must ask yourself not only whether the deviations are significant and require corrective action but also how valid were the original estimates incorporated into the budget.

(c) *Variance analysis*: Another analysis and control procedure which falls out of the budgeting process; the detailed analysis of the variance (difference between actual and expected results) that arises from the organization's activities. Variances of a number of different items can be measured and assessed, but much will depend upon the key parameters used by the organization to assess its performance overall. Typical variance measures will include:

   (i) Sales price variance
   (ii) Sales quantity variance
   (iii) Sales volume variance
   (iv) Profit variance
   (v) Market size variance
   (vi) Market share variance
   (vii) Whatever-you-want-to-measure-over-time variance.

Whatever the method of analysis and evaluation that is deemed the most appropriate, it is important to recognize that analysis on its own is rarely sufficient to monitor and implement market(ing) strategy properly. As well as identifying the actual variances or differences from expected results, equal attention has to be paid to understanding the *reasons* for the variance in the first place. Before any corrective action can be taken (if indeed it is required), the reasons for the variance need to be identified. Corrective action needs to be taken against the reasons for the shortfall (or the overrun) if it is to be effective.

(4) *Taking corrective action*: Once any divergences or deviations from the estimated results have been highlighted, the task is to decide whether corrective action is required – and if so, how to implement this action in time to bring the plan back on target. The options open to the organization in terms of possible corrective action fall into a number of separate categories, depending on the reasons behind the variance:

(a) *Environmental changes*: If the reason for the divergence is caused by unpredicted changes in the external environment, the organization has a number of options. If the environmental factors are expected to be temporary, then a modification to the tactics can be considered. If the external changes are judged to be fundamental or 'structural', then the organization may need to re-visit the original strategy and its objectives.

(b) *Internal problems*: If the variances are caused by internal problems, the organization has to decide whether this is a shortfall in performance or is caused by active blockages in the organization. Corrective action will need to be directed accordingly.

(c) *Faulty estimating*: It may even be apparent that the problem lies not in the market or in the organization's ability to deliver, but in the original estimates that were plain wrong. In this case, the organization needs to re-estimate the rate at which it will achieve its strategic objectives.

Strategic decisions have long-term implications, and organizational momentum has to be built over a planned period. Constant change of strategy produces uncertainty, confusion, misdirection and wastage – not results. Tactics are designed to change on a weekly or even a daily basis in response to changes in the marketplace; tactical change causes no problems of uncertainty as long as the strategy, the broad overall direction of the organization (and the tactics), remains constant.

Control systems which drive regular tactical changes to keep the strategy on course are a positive boon to any organization.

On the other hand, if the control systems allow managers (through ignorance or panic) to make constant changes to strategy and direction, the organization will end up achieving nothing and going nowhere.

7.6.3   Using control systems to create change

We know from research and experience that people (staff) are frightened and threatened by the unknown. And the best thing to do with threats is to destroy them. This should alarm nobody; it is basic human nature and we should not be surprised by its manifestation in the business world. Rather than wishing for what might be, should we not concern ourselves with what is and determine what needs to be done in the 'real world' to achieve the aims we have set ourselves (see Section 6.6)? We know that:

(1) Performance targets are expected by both managers and staff:
  (a) Often, the achievement of targets becomes a macho/ego-driven issue.
  (b) Many people seem to thrive on targets and on achieving them.
  (c) People don't seem to worry too much about where the target or perform-ance measure comes from.
  (d) People don't seem to worry too much about why it is there.
  (e) People just worry about its achievement.

(2) Strategy, strategic issues and horizons seem to make many staff and managers uncomfortable:
  (a) The world for most people seems to be made up of what *I* can do 'now'.
  (b) Longer-term issues tend to be less clear cut and often outside an individ-ual's area of direct control.
  (c) Longer-term issues are best avoided.

So why worry about educating and convincing people that a particular strategic route is better than another? Why worry people talking about issues they do not wish to embrace and that fall outside the areas of 'comfort' that they wish to preserve? Radical thinking? Possibly; it certainly goes against many of the 'politically correct' trends in some of today's texts which are taken up with 'empowerment' and similar issues. Empowerment is fine and good, but do you have the time? How many staff want to be empowered anyway? My experience suggests that there are still large numbers of people who just want to be told what to do and then be left to get on with it.

If you really want to achieve change where it matters, with the customer, look at changing the control systems as a fast first step. Many existing control systems have been selected because they use variables which are easy to measure – sales revenue, defects, telesales contact time, calls per day, etc. If what matters to your strategy is customer satisfaction, find a way of measuring it (there are many ways) and substitute the new measure for, say, sales revenue targets. Stand back and watch the change take place.

Before you give me all the reasons why this can't be done, let me tell you that I am ready for this too. There is no doubt that it *can* be done, and quickly too. More to the point is how bad do you want to do it?

Conclusions – Part Three

Men who have changed the world never achieved their success by winning the chief citizens to their side, but always by stirring the masses.

Napoleon Bonaparte

This final section has focused on the important but often boring bits of market(ing). Knowing how to work within 'the system' that the organization calls 'home' can often make all the difference. The investment made in developing a market(ing) strategy is pointless unless the strategy is implemented. Too often, organizations can get in the way of a good strategy, not intentionally but just because *the system* has its own way of doing things.

As I said right at the beginning, in the preface to this third edition: Marketing was always intended to be the co-ordinating activity designed to identify, anticipate and focus the rest of the organization on customer needs. This is a far, far bigger job than producing the advertising and the brochures, but apparently one that some marketers feel hesitant to take on. Marketing is all about the *market*. If *marketing* is (still) confused with *marketing communications and services*, then you should remember that market(ing) in this book means so much more.

I hope that Part Three has shown you that you need to develop skills in the organizational arena if you want to become a good marketer. Yes, it was a shock to me when I worked that out too. In this part we have seen that:

- Market(ing) plans are not just a habitual process that an organization has to go through; they are a way of controlling the activities of the organization deliver the strategy that you have agreed. Use it as such.

- Market(ing) control systems are your primary tool at the implementation stage. Do not just accept the control systems that 'you have always used' or that 'everyone in the industry uses', choose ones that do the job.

- Your strategy will be evaluated, so accept it. But, make sure that you understand the measures that will be used to decide whether your strategy is deemed a 'success' or a 'failure' in the organization. There is absolutely no point in the strategy being seen a 'late success' two years after it had been deemed a 'failure' and the short-term spotlight aimed somewhere new.

- Identify barriers to implementation. There are always very good reasons *not* to do something. You know they are going to be raised, so work with it.

- Identifying drivers for change is key. Nobody wants change – but many people want the fruits of change. If what you get is attractive enough, then change won't be a problem.

- Use the system, don't fight it. You know you're right, even I know you're right, but being right just isn't enough if the system doesn't want it.

Epilogue

A great Nation should have a fixed Government, so that the death of one man should not overturn it.

Napoleon Bonaparte

It's time to sum up – what has, or should have, this book been about? The central 'takeaways' are:

Introduction

- *What is market(ing)?* A coordinating function that (ought to) helps the organization to focus all its resources on understanding, anticipating and satisfying customer needs so that your target customers 'prefer' your offer over the competition's.

- *What is strategy?* The longer-term (probably three-plus years) view of what the organization needs to do to achieve its business objective.

- *What is market(ing) strategy?* The longer-term (probably three-plus years) view of what the organization needs to do to position itself within its market so that it can align itself with the needs and wants of the customers it wants to serve.

Part One - Preparing for the Market(ing) Strategy

(1) *The internal business drivers*: The internal mechanisms that dictate much behaviour within the organization. Includes the needs of the key internal implementers as well as internal and external stakeholders – understand these needs and make sure that the strategy meets these needs, or all your work will be wasted.

(2) *The external environment*: The 'unavoidable' elements in the market that you have to deal with. Includes politics, economics, technology and competition and everything that just seems to get in the way of serving customers. We need to deal with these and, importantly, we need to anticipate environmental change so that we can build it into our plans. Surprise is a bad thing.

(3) *The business strategy*: The whole debate about the organization actually knowing where it is going, rather than just bobbing along on the water waiting for the wave to push it along or more likely knock it over. Identifying the

'financial hurdles', then putting them in their place is the first step, followed by setting a business objective and a business strategy that will achieve competitive advantage.

Part Two - Developing the Market Strategy (SCORPIO)

(4) *From business to market strategy*: Translating business objective and strategy into day-to-day organization-speak can be a challenge. The best route is to put things into customer terms; everybody deals with the customer and ought to know this.

(5) *The market(ing) objective*: The key stage and one that can make or break the market focus of the organization. Properly managed, the market(ing) objectives become the key performance indicators (KPIs) of the organization and drive all appraisals, rewards and behaviours. Make sure you take enough time to get these right.

(6) Developing the Market(ing) Strategy (SCORPIO):

   (6.1) *Industry and market (I)*: Decide what business you are in and what business you want to be in. There is no point just going along with traditional 'industry' definitions of your market that leave you exposed to substitute competition that you don't understand – this determines the external marketplace that you need to know, segment and master.

   (6.2) *The customer (C)*: The person or company that provides all your revenues and cash/profits – how well do you know them? Understanding what they want now and will want in the future is the biggest battle; providing it is almost easy in comparison.

   (6.3) *Segmentation and targeting (S)*: The mass market is dead and, apart from a very few organizations, we cannot serve customers on a one-to-one basis. You need to identify the segments in your market and agree which ones your objectives require that you 'own'.

   (6.4) *Positioning and branding (P)*: How are we going to be different? What are we going to stand for (market position)? What are the values and personality of our brand? How do we measure the financial value of the brand we have created?

   (6.5) *Customer retention (R)*: Customers who come back are the most profitable customers of all, how do we do that? Loyalty is a two-way street, so what are we doing to create loyalty in our customers?

   (6.6) *Organization – processes and culture (O)*: Making it all happen or blocking all progress? The organization cannot be ignored, so we have to manage the culture and the processes to create an environment within which customers receive real value.

   (6.7) *Offerings (O)*: The product or service that carries the identified customer value, but much more besides. The point at which we create the value proposition and the business design to drive the organization – to where the customers are waiting.

Part Three - From Market Strategy to Tactics

(7) *Making it happen*: Implementation is everything, although there is many a slip, and we have to work hard to make sure that what was planned gets done. Holding hard to the key implementation levers and managing the control systems are the key.

But none of this is obligatory – some organizations would prefer not to change, to go on making what they think they are good at making, even if their customers don't care. A death wish is a solemn undertaking and should be respected.

To end then on a familiar note, and the most relevant to market(ing) strategy:

It's not how good you are, it's how bad you want it.

Now, did Napoleon say that?

Appendix

Men of genius are meteors intended to burn to light their century.

Napoleon Bonaparte

A.1 The strategy checklist

	Strategic question	Strategic answers	
1	Who are our stakeholders?		
2	What do the stakeholders expect in the way of returns from the organization?	1	
		2	
		3	
3	What are the potential conflicts?		
4	What (therefore) are the financial objectives that the organization is dedicated to achieving? These are the *financial hurdles* you must jump	1	
		2	
		3	
		4	
5	Who are the key implementers in the organization and what are their personal values?		

6	What is the vision of the key implementers?			
7	How should we best describe their strategic intent?			
8	So, what then are the specific requirements of key implementers?	1		
		2		
		3		
		4		
9	Out of these various factors, do we have a clear statement or understanding of the corporate mission?			
10	What resources do we have and how are they being utilized?			
11	What are the strengths and weaknesses of the organization?			
12	What opportunities and threats exist in our broad macro environment?			
13	What business are we in? (See questions 23 and 24)			
14	How is our industry put together?			
15	What is the relative importance of the five forces in the industry?			
16	Who are our real competitors?			
17	Where are our competitors?			
18	What are our competitors able to do (competencies)?			
19	What are the opportunities for our organization in the competitive environment?			

20	What are the options for sustainable competitive advantage?				
21	What do we believe is the most appropriate sustainable competitive advantage we should be seeking?				
22	Managing the *handover* between corporate and market strategies				
23	What business are we currently in?				
24	What business do we want to be in?				
25	What is our business objective?				
26	What is the business strategy?				
27	What are the marketing objective(s)? [Note: these will become primary KPIs of the organization]	1 2 3 4			
28	What is the marketing strategy?				
28a	*Industry or market?*				
i	What business are we in?				
ii	What business do we want to be in or should we be in?				
iii	How does this define the market/customer needs we should be satisfying?				
iv	Where/how should we be growing the business?				

v	What are the strategic opportunities and threats?
vi	What competition are we facing?
vii	What are the boundaries for effort?
28b	*The customer*
i	Who are they?
ii	What do they currently buy from us/our competitors and why?
iii	What benefits are they seeking?
iv	What do they want from us now/will they want in the future?
v	What barriers are getting in the way?
vi	What will make them come to us?
vii	Where do customers interface (connect) with our organization?
28c	*Segmentation and targeting*
i	What is the current state of segmentation in the organization?
ii	What do we want segmentation to do for our organization?
iii	What segments exist in our target market?
iv	How durable are the segments identified?
v	How can we prioritize the segments for approach?

vi	Which segments should we target?
vii	How can we market to different segments?
28d	*Positioning and branding*
i	Differentiation or *commodity* marketing?
ii	What market positions exist?
iii	What market position do we own, or do we want to own?
iv	How are we going to be different from the competition?
v	What is a brand? What are its unique *values* and *personalities*?
vi	What are the costs and benefits of building a brand?
vii	How do we invest in the brand and a differentiated market position?
28e	*Retention*
i	How important is *retention* in our market?
ii	How big are the *problem* and the potential gains?
iii	Is retention just about customer satisfaction?
iv	Do accounting and reporting systems impede retention activities?
v	How good is our marketing information systems (MkIS)?
vi	What is the strategic role of customer relationships?
vii	How are we planning to invest in our primary asset?

28f	*Organization*
i	Is the organization focused on internal or external issues?
ii	What is the organization really good at – and does it matter?
iii	What is going on with culture?
iv	Is the organization joined up?
v	Is the organization driven by the right information?
vi	Which metrics are used to manage and drive the organization?
vii	Change management – what is that?
28g	*Offerings*
i	Do we (really) understand the target market?
ii	What is the value proposition?
iii	What is the most appropriate business design?
iv	Where are the new offerings?
v	How do we assess the risk?
vi	Are we managing the life cycle?
vii	How do we take the offerings to market?
29	How do we implement the strategy?
30	How do we retain control of the essentials?

Index